Scraps

RULES OF THE GAME

VOLUME 2

SCRAPS

MICHEL LEIRIS

TRANSLATED BY

Lydia Davis

The Johns Hopkins University Press

BALTIMORE AND LONDON

This book has been brought to publication with the generous
assistance of the French Ministry of Culture.

Originally published as *Fourbis: La règle du jeu, II,* © Editions
Gallimard, 1955
© 1997 The Johns Hopkins University Press
All rights reserved. Published 1997
Printed in the United States of America on acid-free paper

06   05   04   03   02   01   00   99   98   97   5   4   3   2   1

Published by arrangement with Editions Gallimard.

The Johns Hopkins University Press
2715 North Charles Street
Baltimore, Maryland 21218-4319

The Johns Hopkins Press Ltd., London

A catalog record for this book is available from the British Library.

Library of Congress Cataloging-in-Publication Data

Leiris, Michel, 1901–
[Fourbis. English]
Scraps / Michel Leiris ; translated by Lydia Davis.
p.   cm. — (Rules of the game ; 2)
ISBN 0-8018-5488-1 (alk. paper). —
ISBN 0-8018-5489-x (pbk. : alk. paper)
1. Leiris, Michel, 1901–   . 2. Poets, French—20th century—
Biography.   3. Anthropologists—France—Biography.   4. Surrealism
(Literature)—France.   I. Davis, Lydia.   II. Title.   III. Series: Leiris,
Michel, 1901–   Règle du jeu.   English (Baltimore, Md.) ; 2.
PQ2623.E424Z463513   1997
848'.91209—dc20
[B]   96-41035

Contents

MORS

"Curtain of clouds."

I always reacted strongly to these words—which evoked a theatrical space enlarged to the proportions of infinity—when I read them in a libretto, where they indicated the caesura between two scenes, of a work by Wagner or any other musician who chose, as did Nietzsche's illustrious friend, to put opera in the service of a mythology. As I resume—earlier, perhaps, than I would have thought—a piece of writing I had decided (for reasons having to do with pessimism, let us say roughly, so as not to come back to this again) to leave dormant for an unspecified length of time, it is this "curtain of clouds" I think of, the figure of a nebulousness drawn before one's view as though to signify twice over the interruption of duration: first of all as the curtain that it is, of print or almost transparent pieces of gauze superimposed like the panels of a tulle skirt; then, as a vague image suggesting the chaos that is the negation of the temporal and spatial world ruled by our coordinates.

Curtain of clouds. It is thus that the curtain of one's eyelids sometimes appears when, still sleeping, one is already about to wake up. Like a proscenium arch or some other stage hiding place with control pulleys so rusted, dusty, or plastered with cobwebs that to maneuver them a true *deus ex machina* would be required rather than ordinary stagehands, a shapeless veil continues to cover our consciousness and our sight and at that point, an authentic curtain of clouds—just as opaque and just as vague—is formed by the sometimes reddish and sometimes darker film with which our eyelids appear to us to be lined inside when we have our eyes closed. The immense force, it seems, that will have to be deployed to move us from the first rough attempt to recover ourselves to a complete mustering, when—after the three blows struck in some unknown place by the mysterious stage manager who oversees the daily recommencement of the action—the footlights of what we persisted in concealing of life are no less mysteriously turned on; the anguish, as soon as we are drawn from the dark by this signal, of feeling petrified, restored almost to consciousness but without any control over these inanimate limbs, these scattered bones awaiting some last judgment; the despair, without the attenuation of any outcry, of ever emerging from the mattress of sleep that has become confused with the physical mattress—itself thick and fleecy—on which the night has lain down with us; the brutal event, finally, wresting us from these pangs when (without our knowing how such a vapor, with its stifling billows, could have dissipated all at once) we find ourselves with our eyes unsealed. The threshold of awakening being, therefore, quite an unpleasant one to cross, each time this return requires that we stay thus lucidly suspended in limbo for an indefinite length of time. An incubation in halflight, an anxious awaiting before the dissipation of the mists or the sudden withdrawal of the curtain as when there comes, for instance, after a period of confusion and torpor, the clear space that causes us to begin writing, impelled also by something that remains foreign even though it is inside us, and required to take a leap which we are never sure will be taken because it depends only partially on our will.

I must, therefore, climb back up. Not only out of this metaphorical gulf— the sleep in which the desire and capacity to write can be buried for limitless duration—but from a much more actual hole: the hole that a book, the moment it has undergone its final transformation of being published, digs in the most intimate part of us, at least when the book in question is (as is the case for the volume that thus became fixed in place behind me early last summer) a work in which one has proposed, not so much to define oneself retrospectively, as to draw up one's inventory and take stock with a view to going beyond oneself. A feeling of emptiness, not only because we have quite precisely "emptied" ourselves of what was in our heart and mind but because we feel actually that, well or ill received by the many or few people who have employed in reading it a variable part of the leisure time society allocates to them according to the positions they owe to their respective opportunities and the nature of the works to which—by vocation or not—they are constrained to devote themselves, this book will have been, for us, a real gesture in empty space compared to what we had hoped for.

This accumulation of pages, which is today nothing more than the instrument of a disillusionment, had as its avowed aim to make us more vigorously alive (as though such an architecture, for which we had been both laborer and material, should, symmetrically, help in our own reconstruction); but now that this book has appeared, one sees that whether it is good or bad, and even if it should mark a stage in our progress toward a little more light, the only sure thing is that it does not exist or—if we make our evaluation without any romantic exaggeration—that its only existence is that of a book that has come to join thousands of other books, probably better than some of them but a "book" nevertheless and not the quasi-stellar projection of ourselves by which we might have believed that our fate would be—as though magically—transformed.

To have, for a start, attempted to take one's revenge on a life with which one was not satisfied, by seeking in the awareness of this failure an element of success, a basis for achieving in another domain something less insignificant and that this also, since one finds in it only inconsistency in the end, should have failed. To have next wanted—strengthened by this new fiasco as though by a liquidation—to try one's luck once more in this life of which, whatever delusion one had managed to entertain, one was certainly not entirely weary and that this new attempt should also end in failure, in the undeniable recognition that there was a decided *lack* in one's very life. Such is the all-too-real empty space—the actual hole between two chairs—from which I must now climb back up.

Now, the fact is, I am expressing these groping thoughts with my pen in my hand—and am therefore already more than half engaged in a relapse. As though after each disappointment, even if it be a literary one, there were no other solution, I long ago made the decision to go back to writing. Quite simply, I can't get started; my confidence being at its lowest, I mark time for months and months. Passing beyond that crisis of confidence, shouldn't I go on despite everything and—like a sleeper half awoken remembering his dreams before hurling himself into his daytime life—indicate before anything else what occurred behind that curtain of clouds I must supposedly either lift or tear apart?

Almost a year ago, I will say, therefore, I left on a trip to the Antilles and I came back last autumn. In many respects this trip certainly delighted me: sites at the end of the world and the beginning of time, palm trees, breadfruit trees, bamboos, tree-ferns, in short, all the enumerable features of a tropical setting that—without racking my brains any longer, and ceasing to stick at each idea and each word—I would perhaps not hesitate to describe as "enchanting" if, that is, this were really the sort of memory I wanted to talk about. I would like, of course, to string together a certain number of sentences—and, if possible, beautiful sentences—about the splendors of that voyage; become excited over the rich provision of images I brought back from it and, laying them out in a fan like (let's say) the palms of a traveler's tree spreading their half circles, try to revive my poetic vein a little. But that isn't what this is all about. I am, nevertheless, at the bottom of the hole and begin to know all too well that I will not climb back out of it either when I want to, or, above all, very soon. More inclined, in any case, than to any other exercise, to denounce the not very heartening things I saw there: the deplorable living conditions in which the majority of the people of color find themselves, the greater number of them miserably housed and undernourished (when there isn't famine, as there is for so many peasants of Haiti); the rich soil of the plain occupied by industrial cultures whereas the small peasants vegetate in the hills; the arrogance of the Creole whites—those whites so often the color of turnips, given that to most of them (especially the women) the sun is a scandalous thing from which they feel impelled to protect themselves as much for reasons of self-respect as health and given that the blood of almost all of them has been impoverished by an endogamous tendency stemming from caste pride—people who, on the whole, seem to think only about money and retain a slave-holding mentality; the nightmare introduced by that idiotic prejudice concerning the hierarchy of the races, a prejudice whose oldest and principal proponents have been the whites—who are as afraid of having an excessively swarthy complexion as of bearing the stigmata of the most ignominious of the so-called shameful diseases—but a prejudice that too many descendants of Africans display in their own spheres (as though every human being needed to feel that beneath him was another category of beings that he would not be able to enjoy despising if he did not recognize, in his heart of hearts, that they were like him); the generally stultifying ascendancy of the clergy and the tenacity of superstitions; the narrow outlook afflicting persons educated enough to regret that their island life keeps them away from the action; for the great majority, the insufficient number of schools; the difference in levels of wealth, one that is even more shocking than our own (for it exists over smaller spaces, where the contrasts are glaring); the horror of a society with such marked partitions that rich and poor do not even, in actual fact, speak the same language (since in Martinique and Guadeloupe, as in Haiti, French is spoken by educated people and Creole by the illiterate); the constant oppression of the small by the great, who regard the superiority of their standard of living as a mark of their belonging among the divine; the terrible rut of negligence or ill will from which no reform or change of regime has so far succeeded in wresting the administration of these countries, whose horrifying slave-holding past must perhaps be regarded— despite all the shreds of paradise one can encounter, here, in nature and among the darkest, at least, of their inhabitants—as the sign of a sinister vocation.

Curtain of clouds. *Brise-bise* [draft curtain].

If I look at myself, without seeking more than the immediate (and like one who, after too heavy or too agitated a sleep, first questions his mirror in order to be informed about the more or less altered look of his features), what do I see?

For some time—and this only worsened upon my return from the islands —I had felt I was growing deaf in my left ear; in order to catch what was said to me, I sometimes had to ask that it be repeated, whence the feeling of an interruption in addition to an imbalance (as though one of the two halves of my body were no longer supported in the same way as the other); this led me, when I overcame my inertia and decided to get rid of it, to an otorhino-laryngologist who removed from my ear a fat plug of cerumen—*"cire hu-*

maine" [*lit.*, human wax]—using a stream of warm water. Continuing to feel disabled even after I was relieved of my semideafness, I then consulted my doctor, who found that my liver was enlarged and who held the threat of cirrhosis over me. Because my eyesight was also deteriorating (especially at times when I was tired, after an evening, for example, during which, though I hadn't become intoxicated, I had drunk too much wine or liquor), this same doctor sent me to an oculist, and the latter to an optician, so that now I wear glasses for reading—even for writing—which gives me, when I am decked out in them, a feeling of pedantic heaviness that annoys me; as a result of that consultation I also use "blue eyewash" against conjunctivitus, which leaves a mark on my eyelids each time—or almost—that I allow myself to go wide of the mark. Suffering, lastly, from a discomfort in the back of the neck (an ache, a clicking sensation at certain times and when making certain motions), a discomfort that I had at first attributed to sitting in the wrong position during the crossing by air from France to Martinique, I was x-rayed about six weeks ago: the result was a series of three photographs—partial portraits of me as a macabre bust of "poor Yorick"—showing that I am afflicted with chronic inflammation (more simply, rheumatism?) of the first cervical vertebrae; and so now I am in the hands of a radiologist whose treatment I submit to even though he has not hidden from me the fact that, since my complaint results from the eroding of my bones, I must not expect a radical cure (because, as he warned me with touching care, one cannot put a thing back together once it has fallen apart). All this, coming in an avalanche of small troubles, not serious in themselves but signifying the approach of old age; along with that warning, just when I had decided to put myself back together, at least corporeally, after a love affair that represents a failure in my eyes even though I achieved the goal one ordinarily sets for oneself in this sort of thing or, rather, because of the very fact that attaining such a goal was tantamount, I may say, to breaking down a door that was wide open (something I realized very quickly but did not expressly admit to myself until after two months or so); because of the fact, also, that it's like having nothing at all in front of you to be face to face with a young woman so eager to seduce you that by wishing, on each occasion, to model herself after the image she believes most suited to serving her designs, she is no longer anything but a lie and even loses all existence, whatever may have been the illusions to which her color gave rise. An affair that was objectively reduced to a mere aftereffect of my trip to the Antilles and that now seems to me to have been so shabby and so disappointing that I almost laugh at using the word *love* in connection with it. Discomforts of a physical nature, a misapprehension of the heart, thus both descended upon me within a brief lapse of time, as though having to pay a serious bill were necessarily the direct consequence of that trip, the most distant kilometer-wise of all those I have taken so far, and as though, overnight, I discovered I had turned into the bull who is still capable of reacting but for whom the cowbells are already sounding, announcing the final third of the fight, in which the kill takes place.

Tumbled clouds. *Cirrus. Cumulus. Nimbus.*

If I look outside, what do I see? Am I the only one who has been dealt what is commonly called a *"coup de vieux"* [sudden old age]? Is it the fraction of humanity that I am (a fraction even more infinitesimal than an Antilles island and one whom I wanted to disguise as "the Ghost of the West Indies" and make the pivot of a whole long poem in the manner of *The Emigrant from Landor Road*), is it solely this archipelago—so very subject to the fluctuations of the sea!—of words and perceptions oscillating once again between his writer's table in a bourgeois apartment in central Paris and his office desk, who has entered—without knowing too well beforehand what it was all about—into this state marked rather paradoxically by a slowing down (combined with a sort of padding) of his whole being, correlative to a sense of an acceleration that is not yet quite dizzying, though that will no doubt come soon, of the exterior flow of time? Doesn't the world also—that great body never wholly asleep any more than it is wholly awake—turn out to be afflicted with aging, without one's being able to trust in the idea that nothing would ever, ever change for a sleepwalker of that species? Sticking, and marking time, whereas "events are moving fast" (as they say), weak sighted, hard of hearing, its mouth jabbering from having twisted its vocabulary in all directions, isn't this world, of which I have just visited a part not far from the coast of America where absolute marvels do not prevent life from remaining difficult—isn't this world traversed, these days, by nasty rumors running through it from top to bottom, from east to west, and against which stands out—issuing from some linguaphone with unimpeachable sentences even if their content is absurd—the moralizing voice of old Truman proffering, without a shadow of irony, the historic remark: *I shall not hesitate, should it become necessary, to use the atomic bomb to maintain peace?*

But if I am justified in speaking of a failure that goes beyond my own person and if it is, in truth, unnecessary to cross the Atlantic to find reasons for it, a wider survey of the situation forces me to specify that it cannot be a matter of the world as a whole growing old. The ruin is limited to the society within which I grew up, to a singular though already time-honored mode of organizing human relations. In the eyes of millions of individuals of all races, isn't China, for instance, which has been active for a long time now, presently a place where, day by day, *the red spot of hope grows larger,* as I heard it proclaimed one beautiful evening in Martinique by the mayor of Fort-de-France and communist deputy, Aimé Césaire, addressing all his people during a meeting held outdoors within the confines of the municipality? For a good hour, before the *Marseillaise,* then the *Internationale,* the loudspeakers—whose cones scarcely exceeded in diameter the corollas of certain flowers you could pick on the island—had joyfully broadcast beguines while on all sides the listeners poured in, one by one or in little groups of family or friends, among them many women wearing short dresses of a lightweight material, their heads covered with those vast straw hats people chose to wear after the sun had set or in the early morning for fear of the "serein" and flanked by a baby or a very young child which she would soon be holding up at the very end of her arms as though to offer it—signaling gratitude or ovation (oblation, I would almost say)—to the orator who draws support from the crowd, and the crowd from him, in an astonishing crescendo born of the extra heat sent back to the one speaking by the reaction of the people who have been struck to their very hearts by his speech and which he in turn sends back to them in the form of still more heated words that cause a new rise in pitch, a constant heightening back and forth until the apex of the acclamation.

Cottony sky. Walls of cork. Fine lace.

With this book—which neither exotic reveries nor concern for an improved social position prevents me from embarking on again, fully realizing that its purpose is more and more contained within itself and that, as it gradually eclipses my other preoccupations, it is becoming a reason for living when it was originally intended to be a means of enlightening me for a more coherent conduct of my way of living—isn't the mad race I'm running (a dream gallop that is galloped without moving) a "race to the death"? Even if this book, once it reached its end, culminated in a discovery, this would no doubt occur so late that I would no longer have the time to profit from it. And I don't even know how many more years I will be capable of pulling everything from my memory this way, as though by the strength of my arms! I must face this truth: more thankless than that of a scholar initiating an excavation or exhuming documents, my task will only be able to be pursued at the cost of increased difficulties—whether the memories already noted down which I am holding in reserve will have lost all their power when the moment comes to use them, or whether I will not have enough acuteness of mind at that point to relive them and, through my prose, make them come alive again, or even whether, like a swimmer that lets himself sink, I decide not to keep my notes up to date and neglect many facts that might have explained certain of those I recorded earlier, which, thus left in the condition of scattered materials, will remain—without even attaining the dignity of enigmas —mere *things* put down at random along my way, here and there, and denied, once I have set the final period to all this, the meaning that could have brought them to life.

A few mistakes I have made concerning the matters of detail; one or two assertions that—given the changes that have occurred during an intermission that was all too prolonged—I must reconsider if I don't wish to be unfair toward anyone; one point, lastly, that I can now be more precise about and show in another light. While awaiting the moment when I will emerge from my hole (and as an initial removal of debris that will make my emergence easier, since, if one is to believe the proverb Each thing has its own time, so that I will have helped time if I make a clean sweep of the place by discharging these minor but tiresome obligations)—this is the substance of the work of adjustment I cannot avoid getting through, despite my eagerness to arrive at something positive.

As I am preparing to leave for the Antilles islands, wanting to familiarize myself with the popular speech common to those among them which are the goal of my trip, I read a Haitian work called *La Philologie créole* by Jules Faine, published in Port-au-Prince in 1937. In it I discover that in Norman patois (from which the author believes Creole borrowed a good deal) one says *"s'éffants"* instead of *"ses enfants"* [one's children]. It was therefore a peasant expression, smelling of the farmer's smock, that, knowingly or not, my father used in the old days when he amused himself by calling my brothers and me *"les éfants."*

During a recent stopover in Paris, an English friend on her way to Sicily talks to me about the pubs in her part of town, pubs she considers to be the finest in London, and says that if I go into that area I will drink Guinness there; when I ask her if, where stouts are concerned, Guinness is truly better than Bass, she informs me that the Bass company makes ale and not stout. It was the severe aspect of the word *Bass,* no doubt, that always made me connect it, mistakenly—if I am to believe this friend—with a drink the color, almost, of black coffee; whence that awkward *"stout Bass"* [Bass stout] of which I was reminded by the expression *"boire un glass"* [have a drink; *lit.,* drink a glass] called to mind in connection with *verglas* [ice crust on snow or rock; glaze of ice on road; freezing rain] (a feature of winter and bad weather whose image would be less easily associated, anyway, with that of a more transparent and golden beer).

Also, *"Gaugé"* and not *"Gaucher"* [left-hander]—according to a piece of information my brother gave me a few weeks ago—was the name of the avenue where the villa stood which our parents rented at Viroflay two consecutive summers. *"Gaucher," "Gaugé":* though minimal, this discrepancy introduces a certain change of perspective and it is no longer so much the creak of a pump—hissing slightly—that I hear (an old noise I neglected to speak of but which is evoked by *"Gaucher,"* toward which this analogy had perhaps diverted my memory, deflecting it from *"Gaugé"*); ceasing to thrust antennae into the domain of hearing, the name corrected by my brother instead calls

forth—by reason of an actual proximity between the two roads in question
—that of a street which was connected, I believe, by a narrow passage we
called the *ruelle* [alley] to the avenue where we lived: the rue de la Saussaie
[*saussaie:* willow plantation], in which there was (if my memory is not once
again at fault here) a laundry and which contains in its very name—about
which for a very long time I did not know that it referred to a spot planted
with *saules* [willows], in other words a *saulaie* [willow plantation]—a sad,
musty-kitchen or wash-house smell, like the vapor of doubtful hue that rises
from a simmering sauce or from damp linen pressed by an iron.

Then, the song from the *Dragons de Villars,* whose authentic text I can
now restore, whereas I had altered it somewhat when quoting it:

> Blaise qui partait
> En guerre s'en allait . . .
>
> [Blaise who left
> Went off to war . . .]

was what I wrote; but actually, the song begins with the following lines:

> Blaise qui partait
> En mer s'en allait
> Servir un an la patrie . . .
>
> [Blaise who left
> Went off to sea
> To serve his country for a year . . .]

as I was able to read in one of the several opera and operetta scores that my
sister keeps in her house at Nemours, along with all sorts of old programs—
souvenirs from her evenings out as a young girl—and magazines devoted to
the art of singing.

In this country house whose roof has just been redone, for it threatened to
fall in, the room I had described as a chaos has been tidied, it seems, and the
player piano finally repaired. During one of my last visits, my niece insisted
on making me listen to it. Might I not, then, have entirely wasted my time
writing *Biffures* [*Scratches*]—since my sister and my niece, by clearing the

room and having the piano fixed (to the extent, at least, that such a thing was possible), had it in mind to contradict me affectionately on these two points —and might I not, without being too unreasonably demanding, hope to discover one fine day that I, too, without even noticing, have made some order in myself and put some dilapidated instrument in a condition to be heard, like that piano which I thought was forever silenced but which now manages, when one pushes on it with sufficient obstinacy, to exhale, at intervals, groups of jerky chords?

"Tu es rouge comme un coq" [you're as red as a rooster], *"Tu es en nage"* [you're bathed in sweat]: objurgations issuing from my mother, who feared I would catch a chill when I had run too much or moved around too much as I played.

Between Pointe Z'Oiseaux and Port-de-Paix, coming back by sailboat from Ile de la Tortue, my companions and I experienced, for hours, the sort of enchantment expressed more eloquently by the verb *être encalminé* [to be becalmed, in the doldrums] than the substantive *accalmie* [lull, calm], even though the former evokes in our minds the idea of an action undergone rather than that of flat calm or the absence, in fact, of any action. Torsos streaming, the boatmen had to go at it with their muscles, singing and sometimes rhythmically knocking the gunwale with their oars while a Haitian passenger and his wife—a Jamaican not at all pretty, but graceful, who spoke Creole and English—also beat in time on the planks of the boat to encourage them.

Martinique wooden horses worked by hand and turning to the sound of a clarinet or a flute, of a drum, of a nail box or *chacha,* plus a thick horizontal bamboo cane that amateurs in variable numbers strike with short sticks. *Lambi* conchs into which, in Haiti, I saw sailors blow in order to summon the wind. Voodoo drums from the *rada* ritual, incredibly percussive. Cracks of a whip and blasts of a whistle, which add to the percussion section in the ceremonies of the *petro* ritual and which I have never heard without being reminded—even though the baying of the hounds is missing from it—of the infernal hunt in the opera *Der Freischütz,* which was called by its first French adapters *Robin des Bois* [Robin Hood] even though this diabolical story of bullets melting on the stroke of midnight has nothing to do with the story of the English outlaw. Oratorical tremolos. Orchestral convulsions. Thunder. Fragments of that auricular world to which I have always been so sensitive, to my pleasure or displeasure.

On April 19 of last year—the day, therefore, before my forty-seventh birthday—finding myself in Nemours at my sister's house, sitting at a table in the garden and leafing through her collection of old periodicals and programs mixed in with menus from meals as well as invitation cards for dances or other festivities, I came upon an issue of *Musica* dated November 1906 and devoted to Jules Massenet, whom my father admired with such fervor (which was one of the reasons why, given the complete impossibility of their holding any views in common about poetry, he became friends with Raymond Roussel, whom he had known at the time when the latter was writing his first book, *La Doublure,* the hero of which is an actor who gets hooted off the stage). In this homage to the most popular, probably, of the French musicians, but unfortunately also one of the most, if not the most, vulgar, I noticed a portrait of the singer Lucy Arbell in the role of Persephone, from an *Ariane* composed from a libretto by Catulle Mendès by the master whose facile melodies, and the guaranteed pathos of whose subjects, are likely to satisfy an appreciable number of generations to come. In it she is shown standing, her hands loaded with flowers before her opulent hips, her head, with its long tumbling hair, crowned with a sort of helmet and her ears covered by two large metal ornaments, elaborate disks garnished with pendants. In the chapter, seven years old now, which I placed under the sign of the wife of the king of the underworld, the entire passage relating to the name of the subterranean goddess—a passage of which the larger part takes the form of a sort of poem—was certainly suggested to me by the lost memory of this photograph, as its recent rediscovery made me realize. The curved or spiraling elements that I enumerated in order to account for what *Perséphone* signified for me actually appear as a vague series of approximations by which I tried, proposing one after another without opting for any one, to replace these circular ear ornaments whose image had been obliterated (except for that barely perceptible vestige of their form) and which alone would explain why the divinity whose name I qualified with the word *floral*—as I could have been obscurely enticed to do by the sheaf that she holds in the photograph—seems to me so closely linked to the world of hearing. One of the two art nouveau busts that my father had in his house—and of which, on the very page where I reproached him for the dullness of taste that allowed him to delight in Massenet's drawing-room ballads, I spoke in my first attempt at a denuded explication of myself—wore, I believe, a helmet and ear ornaments of the same kind, made of real bronze (with openings caused by the interweaving of complicated patterns) whereas the bust was of terra cotta or colored plaster. I recall, furthermore, having heard it said of this same Lucy Arbell, when I was a child (though she was generous in build, to judge from her photo as Persephone), that one would have thought, listening to her, that she was singing *"dans un verre de lampe"* [into a lamp glass]; but as to this last detail, except for the ironic reference to the overdecorated aspect of the chandeliers and other lighting fixtures of the time of my youth, I don't see that it could be the source of any fragment whatsoever in any one of my writings.

Thus, under the conscious thread of my book—the one that is artifice to the extent that, necessarily preexisting each page that I write, it imprints upon it ipso facto the character of a fabricated object—runs a thread of which I am unaware, or of which I never glimpse more than trifling elements, by chance, through an image or a vague recollection. An underground path, no doubt more important than the official route where everything (except, as it happens, the timetable) is foreseen, even including the tip intended to reward the zeal (here unilingual) of the guide. A pilgrimage to familiar local spots rather than monuments, to places without any spectacular signs that might, to their advantage, attract attention, and whose names, known to a certain number but unappreciated by most, remain the only witness to the real or fabled events that occurred there. Places about which the question would be to know if, once honors have been paid to each one that I have chanced to notice, I will or will not comprehend the hieroglyph inscribed, perhaps—on God knows what soil!—by the itinerary they all mark out, like the wayside shrines on a sort of initiatory journey. A series, also, of points irradiating forces, a series whose hidden presence poses another problem that is not unimportant either: can someone other than me—even in the no doubt frequent instances where I do not succeed in drawing them from secrecy—at least perceive (beyond any possibility of distinct apprehension) their clandestine existence, so that, once the book is finished, the succession of sentences he will have read will appear to him as a panorama whose most distant backgrounds, though almost invisible, are indispensable because—whether mountains or clouds, plain or sea—however incomprehensible they remain they are what gives the whole its living depth?

Aside from these suppressed images onto which hidden connections are grafted, generating this sort of margin of the unknown, there are also—digging holes in me like the intimate, obsessive emptiness so often created, in the dreams I used to have, by the phonograph record that was so rich with a marvelous music but that I never managed to recover, or like the emptiness I tried in vain to fill by finding an object, any sort of external thing, to which I could have clung or applied myself entirely—positive gaps in my memories. Without mentioning (of course) the infinite mass of things I lived through that have been obliterated forever though I was clearly aware of them at the time, many experiences—a little reflection must assure me that this is so—have marked me forever even though as events they left no trace in me. My memory proceeding like the schoolbooks that teach history, the elements that have remained fixed there are the elements whose appearance is even slightly theatrical, those which—to the detriment of elements which are more discreet though perhaps highly important—commend themselves above all by their capacity to be made into illustrations. Battles won or lost, convenings of parliaments, coronations, abdications and assassinations of sovereigns, the raising of sieges, signatures of treaties, excommunications, famines, peasant uprisings, discoveries of continents, great premieres at Court, delivery of memorable speeches—such, then, if my history were History, would be the special kind of events that would fill its pages. Yet, in the growth and decline of nations as in the maturing and decadence of cultures it is not these spectacular star attractions that are the determining elements. Events much humbler in appearance, not on the same scale as the figures of the great conquerors or those, even more engaging, of the great vanquished (the Emir Abd el-Kader, immortalized by Horace Vernet whose immense panoramic picture, *La Prise de la Smalah,* was once shown to me; Toussaint-Louverture, or the "black Napoleon" popularized by certain Haitian postage stamps with his effigy on them) represent the true turning points, and to convince oneself of this truth it is not necessary to appeal to the philosophy of history or to sociology either, for it is enough to read, for instance, the work in which Commandant Lefebvre des Nouëttes—about whom I'm not sure if he served in the cavalry, the artillery, or some other harnessed, if not mounted branch of the army, dating from before mechanization—establishes that a technical modification in the manner of harnessing horses was, in the ancient world, one of the decisive factors in the disappearance of slavery (this invention having allowed the use of animal strength for works which, up to then, had required human labor). In my own life, which I could regard as belonging, at the very most, to the domain of "little" History if a wind of megalomania were to rise in me suddenly, observations of the same sort could be made and there is no doubt that thresholds such as the one I crossed when I learned to walk constitute much more notable stages than a certain discovery which, from a distance, assumes the guise of a revelation. The pleasure I take, like everyone else, in cartoon strip images, combined with the esthete side of me which makes me prefer to attach myself to what looks pretty and may furnish the material for a story, no doubt strengthens the natural tendency of my memory to retain, out of the prodigious sum of things that have happened to me, as to everyone, only those assuming a form such that they can serve as the basis for a mythology.

Cleopatra's nose. Cromwell's urethra. To say nothing of technical inventions like the cooking of foods, assuming the soup pot is indissolubly linked to family life as we understand it!

Of these obsessive lacunae—lesions that worry us and that must be repaired if we are to have the euphoric feeling of wholly possessing ourselves—there is one, perhaps, that makes me feel its emptiness in a slightly more troubling manner than the others and I would give a great deal to be able to fill it. Quite probably, however, what is in question here is not a lacuna or one of those cavities with whimsical trajectories such as one finds in pieces of old wood drilled by insects, but an absolute lack (an original deficiency, not a disappearance after the fact), so that, logically, one would be wasting one's time over a false problem to attempt, at any cost, to reconstitute the absent part the way one would mend a piece of moth-eaten clothing or an old sock. Yet it is not easy to resist the attraction exerted by this lacuna, just as when one finds oneself two steps from an abyss, one must force oneself to turn one's eyes away from it, even though one knows that by prolonging this useless contemplation one may expect to feel only nausea, not to mention a certain risk of falling should one's head begin to spin. However questionable, where good taste is concerned, may be the use of a word that drags behind it such a sulfurous wake, in the case described here, "abyss" does not seem to me excessive as a term of comparison. The paramount event that I have always been incapable of recapturing (for the simple reason that it must never have occurred, either because there isn't even the possibility of such a discovery, otherwise than in a purely formal manner, as long as one is not up against the wall, or because it acts only by degrees and in a surreptitious way as the end approaches) is in fact that which would have been constituted, for me, by my sudden awareness of death, or, more precisely, of the fact that my own life—that life which I cannot believe is subject to the same laws as the lives of others—would inevitably end, abruptly, in a complete collapse.

Difficult to imagine death as the three dots indicating suspension (a break, after which there is nothing more except, as it happens, the physical process of progressive disintegration) rather than as a fermata (indicating that not everything has been said after the emission of the note, which is followed by a pause of unlimited duration in which fioriture, a species of other life still traversed by a resonance, are possible). If the decisive break that is the fact of dying remains so inconceivable that the imagination furnishes only the poorest symbols of it (the idea of falling, leaping, or changing place, the last image being the basis of the word *trépas* [passage; *poet.*, death, decease]), death as a state—even though in truth just as hard to conceive since what is *nothing* cannot, by definition, be the substance of any representation unless it is an illusory one—the state of death, of which all religions, including Buddhism with its ambiguous nirvana, are the stubborn negation, seems to offer a field less unpromising for our minds' constructions. It is possible that on this matter (as on others, in fact, once I start generalizing) I'm sticking my neck out. Yet it is certain that where I personally am concerned, when I try to picture to myself what death is, I think, not at all of death seen as a razor's-edge limit separating a state from the absence of state, but of a sort of other mode of existence (the furious lust for survival coming into play here, natu-rally, and against all reason). Thus, what data I was able to glean when I searched again (with the naive hope of recalling some actual experience) for how what I called my "sudden awareness of death" could have come about, amounted essentially to situations in which it seems I had, not the sort of im-pression of slipping into nothingness given one by, for example, an indisposi-tion such as a fainting fit, but the impression either of finding myself situat-ed on the frontier of the *other world,* of receiving a message from it, even of having entered it without disintegrating there, or of embracing the course of life and death with eyes that looked out from beyond the grave. The attitude betrayed by such a statement is a religious attitude, an irrational one in any case, I won't deny it.

At Viroflay once again (and no doubt my age when I was taken there on vacation, four and then five, explains why that locality was the scene of so many of the experiences I am describing) I hear a high-pitched, apparently distant noise. A noise I am afraid of, because it is evening and dark on the road where we are walking. I don't think there were any of those trees there that were always so frightening when we turned at nightfall into an avenue or any sort of path bordered by them. No memory of foliage over my head or of one of those strange King of the Alder silhouettes so often traced by branch-es and trunks; rather, the open sky and perhaps even some stars. The noise that makes such a deep impression on me is a sort of rapid and continuous rattling, surely an insect's buzzing (but at that time I am incapable of such an identification). Do I look as though I am going to cry or do I seem *"tout chose"* [upset], my throat a little tight as I ask what sort of thing I'm hearing? My father says, to reassure me: "It's a carriage that is very far away, very far away," which makes me even more afraid.

Why not have said it was an insect? I think about it now and it awakens in me a little suspicion as to the veracity of the story. Perhaps I am distorting the quality of that noise when I describe a rasping comparable to the song of the cicada or the cricket, for it is doubtful that my father wouldn't have recognized this rasping, and the hypothesis of a misapprehension on his part being thus ruled out, what motive could have impelled him to talk to me about a carriage instead of quite simply ascribing to its real source a noise that, in order not to worry me, only had to be *explained* and would not have signified anything more alarming if caused by an insect's wing sheaths rather than a vehicle? Or have I taken this answer which my father is supposed to have given me and either changed it or coupled it with circumstances different from those in which he could actually have said something of that sort? Yet it seems to me that if my fear increased, it was in fact because of that explanatory phrase and its inadequacy, as though I had detected its falseness and thought it was only a white lie meant to *hide* from me something that I might have feared with good reason.

Whether or not this is a serious reason for rejecting my suspicion, it is still true that I have retained a very vivid memory of that fear. An imprecise, even fantastic memory of how my father might have been involved. A real memory of the fear provoked by that slight buzzing heard in the night, a noise the anguish of which resulted perhaps exclusively from the fact that it manifested the state of wakefulness of something infinitesimal or distant, the only sound present in the silence of a more or less country place where I imagined that at such an hour everything had to be asleep or beginning to fall asleep.

Fear of the night. Fear of the dark. But it is not only the impossibility of seeing or of seeing more than a compact mass of blackness that is involved. There is the idea of that opaque portion of time over which sleep reigns. A mysterious world, this, whose strangeness is felt when, awake oneself, one feels that others only live, now, with a reduced life, which in the adult can give rise to a certain euphoria but will be unpleasantly disturbing to the wakeful one if he is a child, ordinarily the first to bed and already unconscious while the grownups are still busy with their occupations. To take a walk on a summer evening, at the hour known as *entre chien et loup* [dusk; *lit.*, between dog and wolf] (the border of day and night and also the frontier zone be-

tween the world of waking and the world of sleep) in a suburb still fairly rur-
al some forty-five years ago was, of course, to a child as quick to feel uneasy
as I always was, not a very reassuring thing. First of all, the twilight, a time of
day that inclines one to dread (I noted this even when I was a grown man,
when I came back from my first trip to Africa and had a certain difficulty
reaccustoming myself to the Parisian twilights which, unlike the almost
nonexistant twilight of the tropical regions, were intolerable to me, so long
and sad did I find them). Then, the exoticism assumed, in the eyes of the
young city-dweller I was, by a landscape which, though only a suburban one,
was nevertheless more pastoral in appearance than the city setting I was used
to. Lastly, the fact that as night approached even the immediate vicinity of a
parish like Viroflay was deserted enough to create an impression of isolation
in a child used to a certain life in the streets, even in the neighborhood, ex-
tremely quiet at that time, where his parents lived. There was reason to suppose, consequently, that before hearing the noise that intrigued me so strongly, I felt ill at ease, already prey to a vague fear that only required the slightest
pretext to become concrete. What exactly, then, did that noise contribute?

I must answer this question if I want to reveal why such a story, more than
any other I could call upon to illustrate the uneasiness with which the night
inspired me, seems to me to sustain a particular relationship with the idea I
have of death. But as I answer, I cannot avoid some constructing, since I will
have to substitute reasoning and conjecture for what has been denied me by
a memory too often defective, in my opinion. If, then, I fill a lacuna with this
after-the-fact analysis and if, apparently reducing the excessively large portion
of unknown that yawns in me, it seems to me I am at the same time dimin-
ishing the lion's share that the emptiness has carved out for itself there in anticipation, the portion of myself thus recaptured from nothingness will have
been recaptured in a completely artificial and provisional way, without my
being able to flatter myself that I have successfully concluded an enterprise
that I would like to be able to compare to other filling operations like the
great drainage labors performed in the seventeenth century by the Dutch to
win habitable territories from the sea—labors I sometimes contemplate as

images illustrating what art is, in the case of the works one can regard as its most important manifestations: an attempt to organize or colonize parcels of land that it is vitally important to protect from the nameless thing in us whose flood threatens us.

There is no sea—or Zuider Zee—around us, but only the country, or rather, what is to me country. Definitely, the noise of our footsteps on the road. A few lights, perhaps, scattered as the houses are scattered. It is likely that we are talking, that, father to mother, brother to brother (or sister), and parents to children we are exchanging desultory remarks about certain events of the day or small details along our path. A short after-dinner walk to help us digest our food and "take the air," since temporarily removing ourselves from the miasmas of Paris is the great aim of this summer sojourn. We must be, at the very most, a quarter of an hour from our house. My father must have arrived, as usual, by an evening train which, his work finished, he took from Saint Lazare Station. Suddenly, the noise.

If I hear cicadas in a sunny landscape these days, it only carries to an extreme the pleasure I feel in finding myself bathed in light and heat: a festive din that would seem to have issued from a quantity of voices that are themselves only the expression, in another register, of an ardor and a luminosity too fierce to remain echoless. When, more than a year ago now, I heard the incredible racket produced in Martinique, as soon as darkness came, by the grasshoppers they call *cabrit bois* [wood goat] and the frogs—among other very diverse creatures customarily classified, all and sundry, as belonging to the animal kingdom—this too seemed comforting to me: no harmonic correspondence between this clamor and the moistness of a night in the rainy season in the tropics but, as in the case of the cicadas, a manifold jubilation and its musical result. In two different climates and at very different hours, a jumble of sounds, exuberance, a sonorous burgeoning signaling an incalculable number of presences, too infinitesimal to cause fear (as might an outburst from a human crowd) and, quite the contrary, reassuring since their number conjures up an intense life capable of proliferating to infinity.

Within the silence almost unbroken by our words and steps on the Viroflay road, what, then, did this noise—an insect's rasping or the thin rattle of a carriage whose axles and spokes might be no more than frail dry limbs— what did this noise, in its uniqueness, come murmuring to me?

After careful consideration, I think the noise said one single thing and the unique thing that it said was that it was *unique.*

World of waking, world of sleep: quite distinct entities which, like two parallels, are meant to go along side by side but without ever meeting. We chatted and we walked, a family awake, in a place relatively deserted and wrapped in darkness. Only a few lights affirmed that not everything was absolutely asleep in this sea where we were a little island of wakefulness. A timid affirmation, without strength against the silence that testified all around to our isolation in the middle of an empty space, where no image of any living body loomed up and where no creature seemed even to attain a sufficient degree of reality for that reality, involving at least one instance of active functions (breath, pulse, whatever?), to give birth to the least sound.

Because the motion of the day and the inertia of the night come together in him, a sleepwalker is always frightening. As was true of Jeannot, who, also in Viroflay, came one night to the foot of the bed of my cousin (the one who had such a marvelous railway in his garden) and said to him: "Come and play?" The noise I heard intruded, perhaps, into our little island in the manner of a sleepwalker slipping, all white in his nightshirt, through the shadows of a bedroom: an apparition proving that among all the things in sleep there is one—completely proximate to us though very distant from our world (for its gaze evokes nothing of what we find in the catalog of human sentiments) —there is one that persists in carrying on its life, all alone and all closed in on itself. Quite as strange as a diver, prisoner of a costume that turns him into an amphibian, or as a Martian severed from his planet, is the advent of this upright stature before us, who thought all the others were lying down, motionless between their sheets, and did not expect the coming of a specter as alone among us as he would be in a cemetery. The same is the case with the intrusion of the isolated, unexpected voice (which is not even a voice). A weak song flung forth only for itself alone and which one divines to be the accompaniment or the direct product of some occupation that will not let itself be divined: a fragile sound that will not have carried any message through the labyrinth formed by the internal parts of the organ of hearing except to designate itself, too, an ambassador from the world of sleep (so neighbor to the world of death) since its high-pitched clinking introduced itself into our sphere of wakeful creatures as the unique sign of a unique obstinacy too solitary to be situated otherwise than *beyond*.

I am performing a series of shifts: from darkness to sleep, from suburb to desert, from oblivion to the Zuider Zee, from insect to sleepwalker, from solitude to death. With truly close associations of images or notions there mingles, here, a certain enthusiasm of the pen, always so quick to skip from one subject to another as soon as a severe censorship (a weighing of all the words) ceases to be exercised; and I hardly see why, at the pace I am going, I would restrain myself from calling upon *mandibules* [mandibles], for instance, to justify, with the help of the new link that arrives by the tortuous way of rhyme, my passage from the insect to the *somnambule* [sleepwalker]—himself associated with that deep-sea worker, the diver, and then with the monster fallen from another planet—and thus strengthen the connection, a little too slack, that has already been established between the tardily susurrating little beast and the waking sleeper based on the idea of a *solitary from a strange world* (or *peculiar isolate* [*isolé insolite*]) *in nocturnal intrusion*. Doesn't *mandibules* [mandibles], more than *gueule* [mouth of an animal] or *mâchoire* [jaw of a person or animal] (so firmly situated in everyday life), harbor a singular danger, like the anthrax-carrying fly I thought I recognized in each of the fat buzzing flies whose brilliant, bluish black bodies were the color of anthracite?

If I return to the very banal anecdote I have been mining this way, shaking it a bit to make it cough up and not resigning myself to setting it aside despite all that is dubious about it, I notice an omission: following the trail of the insect heard in the night, I ignored the carriage. Even if I am off the track when I attribute to my father the explanation of the noise by the distant presence of a vehicle (a vehicle drawn by an animal, and not an automobile, for *voiture* rolls along in me outfitted with that meaning, in this real memory or memory already in part mendacious and warped once again by the point of view of the here and now, which is that of a memory of a memory—a surprising false bottom! somewhat as there exists a theater of theater: the pantomime staged by Hamlet to unmask a guilty man who is himself only a king with a tinsel crown, or the silent scene unfolding in the background, watched by a few of the actors placed on the proscenium and themselves watched by the public, so that those in the silent scene, second-degree actors set in a distance accentuated by their muteness, pass almost to the rank of apparitions, as is the case for my memory, elevated to the second power by the written recollection I make of it quite aside from the fact that in itself it is already an unwarrantable interference of a noise faint enough and little enough localized so that one may believe it has risen from the background of memory), even if such an attribution is only an error that thrusts me into the unreality of fiction, it remains true that at a certain moment of the time according to which my life is made and unmade—a moment no doubt remote since it was most likely earlier than the period when, in common language, *voiture* began to be used to mean *automobile* (which, if the moment in question had been later, would inevitably have produced in my thinking at least a little uncertainty about exactly how the vehicle was moving along)—this carriage which could only be pulled by a horse advanced toward me like one of those stage props contributing to produce an effect of fear, whether it may have been physically part of the real scenario, or whether through some indiscernible affinity it may have added itself, one day, to the vague recollection that was the more or less distorted reflection of that scenario.

The passage of a hackney carriage in the street, in the very depth of a Paris night, when one has already been in bed for a certain length of time. Nothing like the insect (for the shock of the hooves against the pavement looses too thick a noise) and nothing even, really, like anything at all definite that one could pose as a parallel and that any sort of analogy would allow to be introduced as a term of comparison. Unless one were to summon up the diver at this point, with lead soles heavy enough to be likened to horseshoes; but one hardly imagines a diver capable of moving, once he has emerged from the depths, with such agility that his step would have the merry aspect of a trot. The passage of a hackney carriage, then, being neither insect nor diver; only a hackney carriage pulled by a long-headed quadruped whose mouth, by way of the bit, to which the reins are attached, is connected to the hands of a cab-man and whose flanks are caught between two shafts, the sorts of shafts that break so often when the quadruped falls and thrashes convulsively on the pavement, a sudden scandal because it is a public explosion of tragedy, like the collapse of a person struck by epilepsy or a person whose blood, all shame obliterated in the wake of some accident, spreads out at once in a horrible ex-cretion.

No notion, however, of violent death. The hackney cab, passing thus, is peaceful. Nice and rhythmical, it jogs quietly along. But what is it doing? And where is it going? Here things begin to go wrong, because one can't imagine an outing in a hackney cab at such an hour. No doubt it's going back to the stable? But that would be even more sinister. One pictures the straw, the hayrack, the weak light of the stable lamp, all this in a hovel in a poor neighborhood, within walls spotted with damp and on a floor choked with refuse. Too wretched a neighborhood for those who inhabit it to be true liv-ing beings. Creatures of another species, a species one doesn't know, that one only sees. The fear the middle-class child has of the drunk is really a fear of the *poor* drunk—of the poor man, quite simply, when he lets himself go at all, rejects the seemliness imposed on him by the order of well-to-do folk, and zigzags along the sidewalk or roadway bellowing like a true savage, thus show-ing that in fact he belongs to another species whose reactions, when they are no longer policed and he is on the loose, can only be formidable.

The passage of a hackney cab, at a meek trot, however, neither drunk nor revolutionary, a cab that could very well be, not a cab, but a barouche, if it weren't for that heavy step, which is not the step of a luxury horse (lighter and, as they say, more *fringant* [spirited]) but of a proletarian horse, a horse who has finished his day and whom his cabby, perhaps half asleep, drives without a lash of the whip and without saying a word, to or from an un-known job which, having thus by definition become a mystery, worries us.

What is it doing? Where is it going? Insect, vehicle, or anything else at all, this is the question posed by the *isolé insolitement éveillé quand tout le reste est (ou paraît) endormi* [isolate oddly awake when all the others are (or seem) asleep]. We know nothing about what it really is and it exists for us only through the intrusion of its noise. Indifferent to everything, totally external to us (except that it insinuates itself through our ears), its activity is pursued. Perhaps its capacity, in the right circumstances, to provoke dread depends, even more than on the fact that its nature is so mysterious, on this simple, separate persistence, formal proof that—in the same way that we can be awake when others are asleep—something can be alive *without* us?

Something that, because of this fact, can only be heard by us as the sound of a knell: without anything in common with our own life (since this thing, whether we call it an insect or a horse-drawn carriage, remains fundamentally impenetrable given our ignorance of what it is occupied in doing), independent of us as it is independent of the others (of all those creatures who are, in appearance, asleep while it is awake), doesn't it express in a tangible way an imperturbable permanence which is the very permanence of the course of things, that is, one of the aspects of death the least easy to consider without trembling, namely, that our end will in all likelihood not be the end of the world but only an end limited—unjustly, it will always seem—to us?

Mors cars, once ranking among the fastest, their name evoking the soft and regular sound of the old electric automobiles (no engine in front, but a simple casing behind which one sees the liveried driver sitting straight up at his vertical wheel). The *alphabet Morse* [Morse code], which caused one to ask oneself if it hadn't some collusion with the signals from the planet Mars. The *morse* [walrus], an aquatic mammal of the same order as the seal (the juggling seal shown in circuses or the seal that dives with such a great splash into the zoo pool), very closely related, but perhaps fatter? and furnished with, besides the beautiful mustache of long stiff hairs planted in his muzzle, two great teeth jutting upward in the manner of tusks. *Mors,* death, as one will learn it when one studies Latin, when one will have forgotten the fear caused by the *"chauffeurs de la Drôme"* [Drôme scorchers], who are not *chauffeurs d'automobiles* [automobile drivers] masked in their goggles but brigands *chauffant* [scorching] the feet of peasants to make them reveal where their money is hidden.

On the Picardy road, near Viroflay, there was also the Père l'Auto outdoor tavern: gardens and groves of trees, a gym set with rings, knotted rope, trapeze and swing, a game of *tonneau* [toad-in-the-hole], perhaps, but no game of *loto* [lotto]. At least once, I think, we drank lemonade there, unless it was a syrup of grenadine for me (a drink for which I substituted, several years later, *grenadine au kirsch,* a first step toward the frankly alcoholic beverages consumed by those for whom such slogans as *"La phtisie se prend sur le zinc"* [what you imbibe at the bar may be a case of consumption] and other prudent aphorisms have no validity). It seems to me, however, that associated with the imprecise and almost disembodied image that has remained with me of the Père l'Auto Tavern is not the unctuousness of a syrupy drink, but the fizzing of lemonade—due to the bubbles visible in the glasses and even on the wood of the table, across the meniscus of each of the little pools formed by the small amount of liquid scattered almost inevitably at the moment of uncorking—so that, if it is clearly understood that not to mention grenadine (so plausible in such a place, in such a period, and at the age I was then) would indicate a lack of circumspection and, consequently, an error with respect to the scientific spirit from which I am absolutely determined not to depart, I am, at least, justified in mentioning it only secondarily.

I don't know if we went by way of that Picardy road, with its smell of tar, the day we visited Les Jardies, Gambetta's mortuary house, and returned home passing, it seems to me, by way of Jouy-en-Josas. What exactly is in that Jardies house? I've lost all memory of it. But there is definitely, at least, a bust and perhaps also some roses (unless here I am transforming a withering of immortelles or box into living flowers). Les Jardies—with rosery or without rosery, with the great man or without the great man in effigy—is, in any case, a curious name: it resembles *jardin* [garden] but does not have its freshness; it is damp, flat, emaciated, a little like the Picardy road.

In fact, what it designates is an oddity: a country house changed into a museum, immobilized—it and its outdoor setting—at a given point in time as though by a fairy's wand (so that, if there are roses in the garden, they are not present-day and natural roses but roses from the past which some artifice has endowed with perenniality); a place of habitation where a man lived and concerning which one no longer knows which of the many souvenirs one sees gathered there were things *of his* that surrounded him when he was alive, and which of them were only put there later, impersonal souvenirs of History and not repositories of a human memory. Gambetta roses, roses of the time of the visit to Les Jardies (which one is inclined to believe are the same and everlasting roses rather than roses seasonally renewed); and then the roses I am speaking of here, which are a memory of roses or roses I invent. The uncertainty in which I presume I was plunged as a child as to these roses blooming at the suture of two moments of duration, the prejudicial uncertainty that causes me here to use the term *presume* to *cover myself* (as they say in the language of the bureaucratized) in case of a possible accusation of frivolousness or even falsehood, leads me to approach obliquely one of the main cruxes of the question: the vertigo I feel as soon as I lose the thread of duration, as soon as I hesitate, too, between recollection and invention—like the vertigo I am yielding to at present and which is reaching its highest pitch, as though the motion by which one tries to contract time and resuscitate what was once experienced (a motion that, by its very nature, arouses suspicion, since to remember is, after all, only a more down-to-earth way of imagining), as though this motion, already suspect in its essence and which I cannot envisage without vertigo, turns out to be more disturbing when I try my skill at giving an account of old vertigoes and even more disturbing in the case of a story like this one which, centering upon a doubt about time, also contains the piquancy of being doubtful in itself.

Consommé, which is merely the more distinguished verbal envelope in which, in a restaurant, bouillon is served. *"Consommation"* [drink in a café], which for me designated, at first, certain metal tokens won in mechanical games in bistros and which one could exchange for a drink (I knew nothing about these penny machines and I was also unaware that *consommations* were things one drank, but occasionally I would receive a little coin like that from the pocket of one of my uncles, who had no doubt won it in the café but hadn't wanted to use it—the uncle I had hardly ever seen order anything else, if he had to have an aperitif, but innocent *madère-citrons* [Madeira-lemonades]). *"Tout est consommé"* [all is consumed] coming after the wine mixed with gall and the sponge soaked in vinegar, *"consommation des siècles"* [drink of the centuries] in bell bronze like the *"confusion des langues"* [confusion of tongues] and like the *"fruit de nos entrailles"* [fruit of our womb]: expressions learned at the time of my catechism and differentiated absolutely, by their too serious sound, from *consommé* and *consommation,* which are liquids that one drinks; expressions assuredly too heavy, one with the death-agony, the other with the end of the world, for me to be able, even now, to make this comparison without feeling I am yielding to a low cabaret wit by indulging in the most pernicious sort of play on words.

Yeux du bouillon [specks of fat on soup; *lit.,* eyes of the bouillon]. *Yeux qu'on roule en boules de loto* [eyes that one rolls like lotto chips]. In contrast to these eyes in the plural are the eagle's eye, the sparrow-hawk's eye, the lynx's eye, the viper's eye. In sum, what you see are *eyes* but it is *an eye* that looks at you (or it is with that singular eye that you look). Inside, the two black chambers that we supposedly have in our heads (but it is only true viewing the thing this way from outside, because inside, we don't experience any of it) with those two skin-thin lenses; outside, the beyond-the-grave air assumed by what is diorama, scene artificially lit and inserted in space, as by everything that seems arranged so that we may recognize in it the external projection of the true chamber within—that well-sealed cavity which is the imaginary realization of what is called the *for intérieur* [conscience; *lit.,* inner tribunal]— suddenly illuminated and changed to a sort of wax museum mortuary fixedness. Mortuary chapels, then, are many of the spectacles offered to the undivided gaze in which our two eyes spring into action—this being the case when these visions are marked, either by their very nature or by circumstances, by a certain theatrical air that half disengages us from life and when their content fulfills the supremely important condition of lending itself to our becoming, when confronted with them, King Claudiuses witnessing the reconstruction of our crimes, petitioners to whom a symbolic staging reveals the arcana of the initiation, prisoners condemned to death dreaming of our punishment as we see in certain pictures (with the guillotine or gallows in one of the upper corners in the middle of a little cloud), even a person whose eye —necessarily only one—is glued to a keyhole to spy on the unfolding of an erotic act in a closed room whose walls, floor, ceiling imitate the blinkers of his mind which is almost entirely obnubilated by the view of the salacious scene.

No doubt it is in the nature of underground caves, chasms, and everything that on the earth imitates, on a gigantic scale, the concavity of a mouth to engender an apprehension that one will always have to overcome, even if this recovery of oneself takes place instantaneously and practically without effort. As is perhaps the case with the uneasiness experienced in darkness (that other sort of cavern in which we already feel swallowed up, quite apart from the many other dangers that threaten us), it is possible that such an apprehension must be associated with the childish fear we have of being eaten, the most rudimentary form of aggression among all those to which we may imagine our presence in the midst of the world exposes us, during that phase of mental life in which we are still so close to the state of the baby who scarcely emerges from his sleep except to suck on his mother's breast or ingest food in some other way. Isn't it possible that death, which Christian allegories represent as a skeleton with empty sockets and very conspicuous teeth, might be —with the two black holes that it uses as eyes, and its sadistic ogre's rictus— the dark, gazeless thing that will eat us some day? It is the memory of a veritable incursion into the bowels of death (as though I had been devoured quite raw by the monster just as the initiates of many ancient cults were supposed to have been), the memory of coming into contact with the abyss or of a descent into the underworld that I have preserved from certain touristic excursions or various other circumstances that led me to visit underground caves, quarries, or, at least, to find myself confronted with what passed, in my eyes, for such.

The famous well of Padirac (where I went just once, in 1934) has at first something comical about it, outfitted as it is with a building on the facade of which one reads: *"Entrée du Gouffre"* [entrance to the abyss] written in big letters as though this were an attraction like some *Train fantôme* [ghost train] or *Rivière mysterieuse* [river of mystery]. Having passed through the entrance gate, one gets on an elevator and descends into a vast natural cylinder (or sort of upside-down gasometer) which, just a few meters down, includes a ledge on which a *"Restaurant de la Terrasse"* [terrace restaurant] has been constructed; after the elevator, a number of stairways, and a gallery that one walks along, one arrives at a dock on the bank of the underground river. Up to that point, nothing really sensational: a geological curiosity such as one might imagine, arranged very much à la Jules Verne. The amazement will come with the excursion by boat on the wrinkle-less river: lofty vaults, of course, with stalactites and, at every moment, rocks of fantastic shapes whose names the boatman unfailingly gives you, all indicative of creatures or objects that they evoke; but—and this is the surprising thing—the vault is sometimes reflected in the water, in appearance completely motionless, so perfectly that one forgets the existence of that water and can believe that the skiff is moving without support over a plane strictly median to a double vault of which one does not know, in many spots, which appears the more vertiginous, its zenith, situated at a height to which it would seem that neither ceiling nor cupola of any human construction could attain or its nadir, which is the exact replica and toward which the same walls, inverted, lead. No outdoor spectacle, I think, could impress me to the same extent as did this immensity in an airtight chamber, where earth and sky were repudiated and where infinite space, engulfed at the bottom of an enormous pocket, appeared as a content and not as an envelope.

"Ici chambres à coucher pour géants" [rooms to let for giants] was the graffito I read three years later in one of the quarries of Les Baux-de-Provence, those extraordinarily elevated and spacious recesses, half caves, half architectures, which resemble Egyptian sanctuaries carved right into the rock and remind one of the cave in which, in the last act of *Aïda,* the young officer of the pharoah and the Ethiopian captive who became his lover were walled up, dying. In the quarry which some practical joker had imagined transformed into a caravansary for titans, a large skeleton equipped with a scythe had also been drawn and it was also at Les Baux that—one of the times we went there on foot from Saint Rémy, where we had settled for the duration of the summer —my wife and I visited a *Grotte aux Fées* [fairy grotto], a quite ordinary cave, in truth, but from which departs, so it is said, a subterranean gallery so long that it goes all the way to Arles, where it emerges under the amphitheater. Isn't it the case that a place like the amphitheater of Arles—where Spanish-

style and Provençal-style bullfights are held nowadays—adds to its glory as monument a prestige current enough for it to be one of the most important spots in a region? And furthermore, should one be surprised that in this same region, where quarries have been worked since the time of the Romans, the popular imagination should have worked on the idea of an almost magical communication between one of these ancient constructions of which Arles, Nîmes, and their environs still bear the ruins and a spot like Les Baux, so spectral with its old abandoned palaces, their gaping casements scarcely distinguishable from the elements of some necropole or dormitory for workers from Babel hollowed out of the rock by the quarrymen? It is probably difficult to escape the summons of fable as soon as there is a grotto, quarry, any sort of hole giving the impression of a vestibule—if not a domanial parcel—of the subterranean world, confused with the world of death in countries like ours where people are buried.

In the immediate outskirts of Saint Rémy, not far from the place called the Plateau des Antiques [plateau of the antiquities], there are quarries; and we discovered it by chance, without knowing at the time what we were seeing: old Roman mines abandoned today. Having been determined, the very evening we arrived, to take a look at the little triumphal arch and the mausoleum that constitute the "antiquities," we saw nearby the beginnings of a path and, wanting to prolong our before-dinner walk a little, also curious to know where this path led, we started off on it, even though by that time, at the end of the day, and on such a path, bordered on both sides by shrubbery and underbrush, it was already very dark. After a few bends and a brief descent, I found myself all at once face to face with an immense screen of blackness: total darkness looming up all of a piece and perfectly impenetrable; in all probability the opening of a vast cave, but appearing in such a sudden manner and so closed to one's gaze that it was much more like a portal leading to nothingness. If I was frightened by it, the feeling was much less like the fear caused by a wall, a precipice, or any other obstacle that had abruptly revealed itself and forced us to stop in our tracks with the sensation of avoiding a collision or a fall than it was as though really I were a few yards away from the threshold one crosses when—to use the hallowed expression—one passes *"de vie à trépas"* [from life to death]. A fear less sharp than the fear that may be aroused by the imminence of an actual danger; a fear that, nonetheless, was perhaps the more profound, for its object occurred in a pure state, as it were, removed from any atmosphere of violence and without there being present, to obliterate in me the quite naked dread of death, the idea of a specific possibility of catastrophe toward which my entire being would strain, actually forgetting what would be the unavoidable consequence of such a brutal accident. When—the very next day—I saw the place again in the full light of day, I realized that in fact what the path led to was not a cave. Not a cave, but a sort of hall, obviously carved by human hands in the rocky wall from which it opened out, and the first of a long series, of which I walked through the less dark ones, somewhat disgusted by the large, reddish bats that fluttered about in them. In one of these excavations, I found several two-wheeled carts, their shafts resting on the ground, which had been stored there as though part of an encampment abandoned for a longer or shorter time by creatures belonging to one of those epochs independent of all chronology evoked by certain rustic implements related to thatched roofs and flocks of sheep; so that I liked to believe that here—two steps away from the Alpilles, that strange chain of miniature mountains, scarcely higher than the Russian mountains in an amusement park and arranged, sometimes, like a public garden where simulacra of ascents have been planned for the strollers—there had once been an old lair of smugglers or brigands like the cave spoken of in *Mémoires d'un âne* [the memoirs of a donkey] in the chapter where one sees the astute Cadichon alert the guards with his braying and thus bring about the capture of the band of highwaymen who had kidnapped him and taken him to their hovel. Once back in town, I learned that I had been walking in ancient quarries long since abandoned. The idea came to me of exploring them in depth; but when I went to the town hall to obtain the necessary authorization, the official I saw kept trying to dissuade me from it: the passageways went very far in; to explore their labyrinth, I would need to equip myself seriously where light was concerned because of the holes and shafts I would perhaps encounter; in short, it would be a real expedition. I therefore gave up on it, in the end; but I returned several times to those quarries, and each time

with the same emotion. It was no longer the anguish of my first visit at nightfall facing the curtain of absolute black beyond which I would have been
blinded; it was a much more mixed feeling: that of a child who, playing at
certain games, confronts dangers he knows very well are merely semblances of
real dangers; that of a child, too, who finds himself in church, not necessarily in front of a crèche with rocks of papier-mâché but, at least, within that
other world reduced to proportions still imposing but habitable and purged
of all mystery too poisonous by the ABC of its emblems and its imagery; the
emotion, too, that one may feel in the wings of a theater where ropes, frame-
works of flats, practicable doors together with what one divines of the trap-
doors and the below-stages give the impression of a voyage into the infernal
regions or of a masonic trial one must undergo without flinching, braving the
risk of getting lost, coming up against an unexpected obstacle, committing a
blunder that would lead one to fall suddenly in the visual field of mirthful
spectators or suffer an ignominious exclusion after the collapse or puncture of
a stage set. Much more than when touring the ruins of Eleusis, for example,
I was able to imagine—as I visited the old Roman quarries of Saint Rémy after having stumbled upon their shadows—that I had penetrated into the *cavern of mysteries* and had emerged from it quite alive.

The isolate oddly awake when all the rest are (or seem) asleep. The vertigo of
one who believes he has managed to contract (or deny) time. The gaze directed toward something immense in an airtight chamber, deep inside that re-
versed world which is the world of the underground. The joy of having
played Daniel descending into the pit and returning without a wound from
his dealings with the lions.

   To counter the fear of the solitary waker which one will not be, one seeks
various illusions. Isn't it true that the illusion that, in its brief duration, has a
chance of procuring the greatest contentment is the one through which one
can amuse oneself for a moment by thinking, not only that one has symbolically passed to the other side or held at bay, if only just a little, the hostility
of time, but that one has become that very same solitary being who remains

in the light when all the others have been obliterated? I had, almost, the physical sensation of such a metamorphosis, one of the rare times I happened to appear on a stage; it goes without saying, however, that this transfiguration existed only for me and I am not in the least proposing that it was obvious enough to impress any one of the spectators who had gathered in the darkness of the hall.

A short time after the Liberation, a poetry matinee was presented at the Théâtre des Mathurins in memory of someone whose birth had branded him with ignominy, according to the views of certain people, and who had been one of the countless victims of a delirium bearing on the nature and destiny of a race: Max Jacob, whom the Nazis arrested as a Jew in his retreat at Saint-Benoît-sur-Loire and who died interned at Drancy. One of the theater's directors—a great admirer as well as a great friend of Max, as were many of the writers and artists in the generation we all belonged to—asked me to introduce this matinee. Despite the repugnance I had always felt at the role of public speaker, I had no intention of refusing, because what was operating here, besides the very simple reasons having to do with my affection, was the fact that I considered it the most positive honor to pay the first public respects to the memory of such a poet, and that it also seemed to me an obligation I could not decently shirk, since it involved the person who had actually initiated me into the literary world.

What I had to do was deliver a short speech, typed text in hand, then do my share in the reading of poems and prose pieces that made up the major part of the program. I was moved—no need to stress that—and I was triply so, since in addition to what the situation contained that might give one a lump in the throat, there was also the fear that I would not be equal to my subject or would fall into what is so likely to be odious about the funeral oration as a genre, and, on top of that, the very egotistical terror of anyone stepping up onto a stage, a terror to which a novice like me laid himself open—one might well believe—more than another. The staging, as planned, was actually as reassuring as possible: I not only did not have to speak extempore or even from notes, but was quite simply supposed to read my few pages; as for Max's works (of which the featured piece was a burlesque written in dialogue for several characters: *Ne coupez pas Mademoiselle ou les Erreurs des P. T. T.* [hold the line, Mademoiselle, or the telephone company's mistakes]), they were to be read, too, not recited. I was therefore protected from the risk of getting tripped up in my speech and also from that of being stopped by a failure—always possible—of memory.

To hold sheets of paper in your two hands, when you speak in public, moreover, confers a certain bodily security in the sense that the paper to which, at least intermittently, you must turn your eyes is not merely a memory aid but a known object that you are touching and that gives you a certain poise while at the same time representing a screen that separates you from the people and, by occupying your gaze, prevents you from feeling you are face-to-face with them. To avoid that direct confrontation, I also had another barrier to rely on: the table behind which my companions and I were supposed to sit as we presented ourselves, rising only in turn when the moment came for each of us to take part, a protocol which, in short, required of the reader that he stand at various times (instead of sit) behind his wall but would not require him for an instant to be exposed on stage entirely unprotected. In the same way, the man who prepares to conjure up the demons must ask himself many questions about the efficacy of the talismans available to him and of the magic circle he will not fail to draw, a limit calculated to isolate him from the maleficent creatures from whom he has so much to fear if he does not succeed in subjugating them.

And so I trusted in the idea that the table, on the one hand, and my sheets of paper, on the other, would intervene between the spectators and me and that this twofold defense, though not enough to do away with a fear that was more than simply a performer's stage fright, would at least be a screen shielding from public view, to a certain extent, the all-too-obvious signs of it that my body might betray. I was fairly calm when, the curtain down, we took our places behind the table, but—since I was the one upon whom it devolved to stand up and speak first—I nevertheless dreaded the moment when, the three blows having been struck and the curtain raised, I would find myself, about to suffer the initial shock of it, in front of all those faces of people sitting watching me. What would I feel then? And would I be in a condition to read my text in any other way than in a neutral voice, without any inflection that could establish between those people and me a communication certainly made more difficult by the very appurtenances that reassured me: my sheets of paper like the pages of a balance sheet, the table like a desk around which company directors or politicians hold discussions?

In the hall, as I was aware, were a number of friends and relations scattered through an audience that had to be favorably disposed, on the whole, since it had come to join spiritually with us in remembering a great poet. Yet I cannot say that this was entirely satisfactory to me. If it is already annoying to appear less than brilliant before an audience of indifferent strangers, it is all the more unpleasant when they are people who know you, because then their disappointment risks being equal to the very confidence their friendship caused them to place in you; and clearly the ordeal is even worse if there are, among your examiners—as there were among mine—individuals who have a sort of family claim to the subject of which you are speaking and are in a position to reproach you with having committed a positive impropriety in handling it as you have. My fear, on this point, rose almost to the level of a moral scruple: Wasn't I going to pay to a deceased friend a tribute so clumsy that those who had known him for longer and had fought alongside him for a revival of art and poetry would feel I was betraying him? No doubt every single spectator —if endowed with any perspicacity at all and intent upon observing how I bore myself—could see how much I, behind my table, resembled an accused in the dock at the moment when the curtain went up.

What (for more than five years now, since the thing took place) I keep experiencing, when I think of it, as the strangest sensation is that, once the critical moment came and the stage on which we had positioned ourselves was suddenly opened to the gaze of the public, I saw nothing in front of me but the footlights. Dazzled as I was by that row of electric lightbulbs whose luminosity rose toward us, all I had in front of me was a black hole, beyond the limit thus drawn as the strict separation of two worlds: a few square meters of floor, the base of what was our own space, well defined and illuminated; then the hall, so dark that it seemed not to exist. Incapable, during the first minutes, of distinguishing even the palest spot of a face, I spoke as though at the edge of a vast cave in which I saw nothing and in which I only knew there were those who were watching me. In this world where I was blind, in no way *seeing*, I knew I was entirely *seen*—alone in the light, alone perceptible and (contradictorily) delivered from the intrusion of gazes since, of all those eyes that had to be fixed on me, I myself saw nothing. Will I invite laughter if I say that during those few minutes, speaking for a dead poet and feeling invested with a little of the radiance of his fame (as I stood on that stage, like a statue on a pedestal displayed to everyone but closed in on itself by its absence of sight), I almost thought I had taken a step beyond and—like the one who "victorious twice crossed the Acheron"—no longer had to fear the assault of death?

If I were imbued more than I am with the Christian ideas that were Max's, I would not fail, today, to accuse myself of having sinned through heartlessness and pride. Instead of thinking of that friend, victim of the frightful persecution we all know about, I was thinking, from beginning to end of the performance, of the effect I was producing, prey first to a sort of drunkenness, in the face of that black gulf where I divined the breathing of the people listening to me—then to an anxiety that, in a cooler form, reproduced my original stage fright: as by degrees, my eyes becoming accustomed to the darkness of the hall and seeing into it more clearly, the charm broke, I studied the few faces I could discern, in order to read in them whether people were approving or disapproving of me; having finished the reading of a poem, I was—I confess—chagrined not to receive as much applause as I had hoped. In short, after those minutes of glorious euphoria, having descended from my plinth, I returned to this world and fretted over the very immediate judgment that, in a narrowly limited and not very important sphere, might be passed on me by a few samples of the creatures of this world. Although I had raised myself, through an unexpected play of the light and with a dead man for support, to an illusory immortality, my blind illumination had only to come to an end and the public appear to me in its living multiplicity for me to find myself instantly engaged once again in the most futile of egotistic preoccupations. Following the ecstasy, so deceptive and so quickly dissipated, was—stripped of all disguise—the very simple fear of not having made an impression, a fear that had tormented me from the beginning and had changed into a proud exaltation when I found myself in that sort of grandiose isolation where, at the edge of a mass of indistinct beings whom I sensed only by their confused rustling, I could almost believe there no longer existed anything but me. Thus, I did not recover my limits and did not return to real life until those watching me appeared before my eyes, as though, so long as I had been watched without being able to watch anyone myself, that lack of reciprocity had extracted me from the human world and as though, placed in a position such that I could think I was refracting toward invisible eyes (eyes that were not yet judging me) a light that I absorbed entirely, I felt I was suffused with the intangibility of an idol. A mirage soon dissipated, as is necessarily the case with a mirage and, all the more so, with a mirage that occurs in that most artificial of places, on a theater stage. But even though the theater may be only a laboratory of mirages, isn't it precisely because of the fact that here, actors and spectators (the former in the glare of the electricity, the latter in the darkness of the photographer's camera, in which they have allowed themselves to be locked up) make such imaginary voyages to the borders between life and death that the theater fascinates us?

The theater: that place of feigned death, of death à la Charles the Fifth, and that classroom where, without chalk or blackboard, a number of lessons about this subject will have been taught to me.

When I was still a child, what I anticipated the most in an opera or play was the death of the hero (or heroes): of Romeo and Juliet, of Cyrano. To know how to die was the criterion of the great actor. Today, I am quite prepared to believe that for him this is the "hour of truth": something reminiscent, allowing for the differences, of the *estocada* for the bullfighter. No way of getting out of it: if the actor does not know how to die the play loses its dignity just as the corrida is no more than a grotesque butchery if, in order to bring it to an end, too many cautious or ill-timed blows of the sword are needed. In both cases—the badly acted death or the unsuccessful killing—it seems that one has been cheated out of the most important part and it hardly matters then whether the rest was brilliant: all that stage business, those inflections, those passes of the cape or other motions that had filled one with enthusiasm fall back into the nullity of profane things; like a Mass in which the fact that the transubstantiation has not taken place becomes glaringly noticeable to the congregation. That few contemporary actors can confront the great Elizabethan slaughters without looking ridiculous may be the most obvious mark of the decadence of the theater: it no longer answers its primary purpose—to throw a bridge from our world to the other world—when the art of dying is lost.

Of course I am simplifying here (an inclination into which it is easy to let oneself slip). Many genres of theater exist that are not dramas; and there are even tragedies without death, such as *Bérénice,* in which nothing happens except a moral laceration. Can one say, for all that, that the pinnacles are not reached in it? I don't think one can seriously maintain this, but it is not carrying things to extremes to affirm that death is never altogether absent when true theater is involved, whatever the appearances may be.

It is all too easy to show that a broadly comical play in which one sees men and women reduced to the state of mere puppets (whether their identity becomes uncertain because of misunderstandings, or their caricature appearance turns them into ambiguous characters, half masqueraders and half demons, like homosexuals leading their sabbaths dressed in evening gowns, or whether they become the unfortunate playthings of the intermeshing machinery of chance or of another character's malice), a vaudeville or a farce, even a revue of naked women (with stupid gestures, plastery makeup, and tawdry finery) or simply a spectacle whose banality and poverty appear degrading—it is all too easy to show that, being in some way the negatives of tragedy—ludicrous equivalents of what is, on a serious level, the implementation of a destiny operating on human beings with moral depredation or ravages profound enough to signify a moral death—they contain that death which I consider essential to theater. One can also say that death is no stranger to classical plays constructed according to the rule of the three unities, whatever may be their subject, since their action, governed by the rhythm of the sun, develops as the day progresses and finishes in the night, like a human life shown foreshortened. Most difficult will be to include, for instance, the comedy of manners in this system, or any sort of modern comedy, unless one excludes them without qualms and denies them, on principle, the attribute of "true theater." I would be tempted to solve the problem this way if there were not also the comedies of Shakespeare, among other examples of plays that ignore the three unities and are not light comedies or farces but could nevertheless not, without crude philistinism, be ignored.

Here it is necessary to shift the question a little and bring in poetry, magic, and, more generally, everything else that causes theater to disengage itself from reality and—as we see it prominent on the parallelepiped of the stage under day or night illumination—present itself like a dream that unfolds before our eyes without our being inserted into it. And it is this guise of objectified dream that will perhaps allow us to rediscover here, too, waiting patiently for us, death.

A dream objectified, a dream that we look at, that touches us though we are not in it—What can this be, then, if not a set of actions that are proposed to us and that we consider with a passionate interest, as we would if, extracted from our lives but remaining lucid, we could be detached from our own history and see it played out before us, transformed by the perspective inherent in our new status? Or as though others, whose lives have already passed or who are simply withdrawn from time, were enacting for us, still completely in this world, a condensed version of what has happened to them, their gestures also coming to us modified by an effect of refraction, given the difference between the states in which, respectively, we find ourselves?

It therefore seems, when all is said and done, that death—even though it is assuredly the most theatrical of events—does not need to be shown on stage or put into words in a narrative in order to haunt theater: the mere presentation of individuals in makeup and costumes moving about in the falsified reality of a stage set and inserted into a time that is not ordinary time makes the stage—providing the truth is wrenched with enough clarity, there, as often as it should be—an antechamber to that other world that one cannot help constructing when one tries to imagine death. Death, to which we are brought close by everything to do with masquerade (old clothing within which one does not find a body but the emptiness of a ghost); everything—in the realm of luxuries—reminiscent of makeup, violet, black velvet masks with lace edges, frills and furbelows like mincing additions to a kind of nudity; all simpering and grimacing, stuccos, wainscotings, daubings, embellishments, and various sorts of added-on things by means of which man removes himself from the state of nature, disguises himself or masks the implements that are his witnesses, as though to deny himself as living and perishable creature or step out of himself, become acclimatized beyond the grave and in the end dupe it, this thing called death . . .

Funeral hangings. Screens of cloud or darkness. The drapery behind which Polonius is hidden. More than beautiful settings, which flatter the eyes or create too great an illusion, a certain poverty, a certain lack (through which one merely reaches a sort of grim allusion, very much within reality)—this is what is needed, in the last analysis, if death is to bear down with all its weight on a spectacle: a destitution that is only the residue of an effort toward festivity and perhaps evokes, by its derisiveness, the final destitution one will enter at the hour of death; a fair-booth shabbiness, creating, in contrast to the fairy play, which is fantasy by excess, a fantasy by default, which is necessarily endowed by its negative nature with a sinister coloration.

The Musée de Saint-Pierre de la Martinique, devoted to vulcanology and including, among other documents relating to the eruption of Mont Pelée, a poster of *Les Cloches de Corneville* [the bells of Corneville], which the municipal theater presented in May 1902, when the incandescent cloud of ash was about to destroy the town. The fake red nose I thought was being worn, in the avenue Mozart more than thirty years ago, by a man dressed (I believe) in a correct black suit and who, riding on a bicycle, had injured himself by colliding with the tramway in which I happened to be. The macabre jest of those musical comedy bells elevated to the dignity of a tocsin and of that bottle-nose of blood similar to the false nose of that sort of clown whose machinations are unclear, equivocal, like those one attributes to the "king's fool," not knowing if he is a true madman or someone "making believe." And the terrible—though infinitesimal in its actual dimensions—make-believe of those dolls which, in 1913, on the main promenade of the Ramsgate beach, mimed an execution by hanging (the two wings of the double doors of the prison opening wide to make way for the cortege, then the trapdoor vanishing under the feet of the condemned man, a rope around his neck over the piece of black cloth covering him), this, in return for a penny, in a hall filled with penny games, the sign Admission Free posted above its entrance.

At Saint-Pierre de la Martinique—where everything has grown up again, houses as well as vegetation, on top of the ashes and lava—one can see, near the museum, the ruins of the theater, a section of wall against which has been placed, since the catastrophe, a Roman-style bust forming the support for a sort of terrace reached by several steps. Terrace or, more correctly, patch of waste ground, a garden that has returned, almost, to a state of wilderness and which one would not even think of calling a "garden" if there weren't a statue here as is customary in public gardens.

Carved from a blackish stone that is obviously a product of the volcano, the statue rests on a wooden pedestal as though it had been put up on a packing case in a completely temporary way, to get it out of reach of the proliferating vegetation. It represents a woman of African type lying flat on her front and leaning on her two arms, her face lifted toward the sky and her naked body half upright, in the pose of a drunken bacchante catching her breath after rolling around in shameful debauchery or in a harvest of grapes. The subject is *Saint-Pierre being reborn from its ruins.* But another interpretation—an unofficial one—seems more valid to me: according to an old woman I questioned when I walked into this garden the second time, the statue portrays a young girl who, struck by the incandescent cloud of ash, threw herself into a body of water and thus "died twice," because for her the pure and simple burning was followed by a scalding—an explanation which I at first thought derived from mythology but which I afterwards learned was not so very fantastic since it was in this way, apparently, that many people of Saint-Pierre perished, seeking to take refuge in pools from the insane temperature of the ash cloud and not foreseeing how burning hot their contents would become. The old woman's account was evidently quite far from agreeing either with the declared intention of the sculptor or with the definite eroticism with which the sculpture was marked; yet shouldn't one view this as a supreme indication of the very equivocal nature of the expression of carnal pleasure and, more generally, ecstasy—which also partakes of death—so close to the expression of sorrow insofar, perhaps, as, being disturbed things themselves, they can only be presented with ambiguous features?

The humid heat of Saint-Pierre, where one feels as though each noon the earth opened and allowed the dead to walk through the streets, one in her flowered dressing gown, another in his large hat of basketwork. The statue, of an iron gray color rather like the gray of a stone for sharpening scythes; the daughter of fire and water whom I am tempted to compare to Empusa, to Norn, or, more simply, to the *she-devil*, a beautiful dark-skinned creature one encounters on roads at the hour of the strongest heat and who is the Creole form of the demon of midday, leading the imprudent follower astray or hurling him into the abyss after enticing him far away from the cultivated fields, behind her capricious faun's steps.

At Luna Park—where I was taken shortly after the installation, in the vicinity of the Jardin d'Acclimatation (with its famous little tramway), of that specimen of variety show which is to the fun fair what the Cirque d'Hiver or Médrano, permanent circuses, are to their traveling colleagues—the barker of the Labyrinth shouted out, among other proclamations intended to rally his customers: "Come and see the devil jump into his silver bathtub!" This labyrinth, which I was not allowed to visit (and I preferred that, because what I was told about it scared me very much) had no relation except the name with the sort of Tower of Babel—specifically: the truncated cone girdled with a single spiral gallery, unless it was several circular galleries in tiers—which I had seen depicted in one of the squares of a Game of Goose in which other traditional obstacles were also represented, the *inn*, the *well* and (this last being an obstacle without remission) *death* symbolized by a skull close to the very end of the long spiraling ribbon of a path.

I don't know what form the path of the Luna Park labyrinth would have taken, reproduced on a map. I only know that this path—which I always, against all likelihood, imagined to be subterranean—was punctuated by surprises: in the darkness, or at least in the half darkness, sometimes it was the ground that disappeared from under your feet, sometimes an electric shock for your groping hands; people swore that at various hours of the day an employee of the establishment made the rounds and brought back into the light of day anyone who hadn't managed to find his way out; people even said that the authorities had had to intervene and prohibit a certain trick in rather questionable taste: a mechanism devised to make one fall down, which, in the beginning, resulted in not a few broken legs. Perhaps all that was nothing but talk or the fruit of my brain, tormented by the idea of this "labyrinth." Nevertheless, Luna Park, despite what might have been indisputably exciting about its open-air attractions, such as the *water-chute** (with its great splash-landing) or the *scenic-railway** (with descents that took one's breath away), was a place as unreassuring in spots as one might expect, given its name, which evoked trips to the moon and stupendous adventures of the sort related in the novels of Jules Verne, the comic books of the cartoonist Robida, and the filmed fantasies of Georges Méliès.

In truth, it was neither the devil jumping into his silver bathtub (handsome Mephisto in red tights on the point of diving, at the risk of breaking his horns, into a receptacle with sparkling sides and not made of zinc or covered with white canvas as at the baths to which I was taken at that time, when we lived in an old apartment without conveniences), nor the prospect of being precipitated by some trapdoor into a windowless room in the depths of which, until I was delivered by the proper authority, I could meditate on the fate of those whom our Renaissance kings caused to be thrown into secret dungeons such as I had been shown at Blois during an Easter vacation spent visiting the châteaux of the Loire valley, it wasn't the anticipation of seeing any of those fantastic apparitions or consequences of bad practical jokes that disturbed me when, at night, in bed and about to go to sleep, I saw parading through my head everything that the light and the games or other occupations of the day had allowed me to conjure up. Rather, what came back to me from my visit to Luna Park and plunged me into an agony was, for a certain time—a time which probably did not exceed a few days but which in retrospect I am inclined to turn into weeks or months—an actual memory, the memory of a sideshow that was neither diabolical nor in the least adventurous, a mere documentary, and on the order of a diorama, consequently very

Translator's note: An asterisk is used to indicate text that appeared in English in the original work when this would not otherwise be clear from the context.

different from the labyrinth, and that remained a pure spectacle whose capacity to haunt had no other basis than this: smaller than natural size but, apparently, strictly accurate, it illustrated a public calamity that had occurred in the United States at a time that was probably recent but that had receded, for me, because of the particular perspective of the stage setting, into a legendary remoteness in which time could no longer be reckoned and in which the immemorial and the immediate, imperative presence of an event were in some sense welded together and merged.

A small town in the Allegheny Mountains, with scaled-down models of houses, among which—very likely—was a church topped with its steeple and furnished with a clock. Perhaps also a sort of town hall or other municipal building. An announcer gave the public the necessary explanations. The day has ended peacefully; night has now fallen completely and one hears (as it seems to me) something like the muffled fanfare of a torchlight procession followed, after a very short interval, by the ringing of a bell marking the hour or ordering a curfew; these noises, tiny and distant, on the scale of the village itself, where everything subsides little by little. What happens next? Nothing, I think, for a time. Only the speaker, with a quite professorial gravity, holds forth. Up there, in the Alleghany Mountains, there is a mass of water held back by a dam and, while the village calmly reposes, the dam breaks. Projections undulating over the stage where the group of artificial constructions stands show the water that gradually spreads and quickly turns into a gigantic flood in which everything is submerged. While the waters came, perhaps the alarm was heard? I don't know what happens after and whether one sees —the sun having come up again—an immense expanse of slack water, without anything there, or almost nothing, reminiscent of the village, or whether —even later—the ruined houses are revealed, their roofs and walls caved in, reduced to the state of wreckage that, after having drifted for a long time, finally takes root once the waters recede. Of this spectacle, I can't recapture any definite detail, and I can barely, if at all, regard as such the image of the invading flood, first oozing out quite high up and almost innocently in the mountain, then descending the length of the slopes or the cleft of a valley and overrunning everything little by little. I no longer recall anything with precision, except for the inexpressible anguish aroused by this catastrophe without collision or crash unfolding as though in slow motion and muted—the tone, finally, and the rhythm too, having been established once and for all by those brasses and that bronze bell, themselves half extinguished, announcing the imminent extinction of the fires and the peace of a sleep that nothing, at that moment, gave reason to think would not be of the most ordinary kind.

An execution by slip knot, reproduced at Ramsgate in the glass box of a penny machine not larger than a dollhouse. The engulfment of a town, shown at Luna Park on the scale of a theater stage very much smaller in its dimensions than an ordinary stage. Although what is involved, here, is still a spectacle, one could not, in the case of either of these reconstructions, speak of dramatic art. No actors, no dialogue; with no setting other than a documentary one, drama in a naked state, displayed with the poorest means, the most literally *reduced.* Whence, perhaps, in addition to the explicit horror of the content of each of the two tableaux, that other, more insidious horror: the impression of a destiny, of a scenario staged since time out of mind and whose dry unfolding takes place mechanically, without any of the blunders— or the beauties—that human operation could introduce into it, and this within a format such that, for lack of any common measure between the thing seen and the spectator, the latter may imagine that a supernatural pedagogue is causing him to follow a lesson in pictures, from very high up and very far away.

A real hanging would have, without any doubt, horrified me even more and I would have been prey to an absolutely panic-stricken terror if I had found myself in the situation of perishing by submersion. But would either one of these conjunctures have made me experience the sort of uneasiness that, when I conjure it today, changes into such a particular anguish? Having no distance from it, and unable even to look at it, wouldn't I simply have been horror-struck, crushed, by the intolerable violence of the event? What can the value be, in such conditions, of the experiences I am talking about if it is obvious that in order to speak of them, and even to remember them with enough lucidity, they must have been sufficiently harmless in the first place so that, living through them, I did not lose all lucidity? No doubt I am, therefore, condemned to labor away at trifles since everything of a more imposing form would, for that very reason, escape my gaze and remain confounded with the enormous, opaque mass that I must confess I will never never be capable of penetrating.

The idea of a mesh of circumstances from which one cannot escape, of a disaster preparing in the wings while one is soundly sleeping: particles of truth relating to death, which at first sight I believe I can extract from the two descriptions I have just given. One must, however, refrain from forcing events, and not take for original givens the reflections they suggest as soon as one bends over them to examine them closely. For if the distance that exists between an experience and the memory one has of it is increased not only by the distance separating such a memory from its being put down on paper but also (another type of deviation) by the separation between the memory thus described and the same memory when reflection is applied to it, once these distances have been telescoped there is no way of restoring the situation: the memory is altered forever and no furious line deleting the passage in which one has gone astray can repair the damage thus done. No other way out, then —ceasing to slave away over minute corrections which cause no storm to rise from the streaked sky of the page but my own irritation, redoubled at each stroke of the pen—no other way out than to push my reflection further, to the point where, having at last run up against something solid (something that is no longer an idea but a compact body), I will at least have the certainty that I have not allowed what was my own possession to be diluted in abstractions.

An apparatus set in motion by the insertion of a coin; a diorama subjected to various changes, without perceptible outside intervention. In my memory, therefore, two mechanisms exist side by side, theatrical illustrations of death but both divested of human protagonists and the second, even, bringing into confrontation only some water and some houses, in the absence of any character. Two pieces of machinery, systems endowed, apparently, with a sort of personal life and consequently belonging to the disquieting world of automatons, that world which extends from the locomotive one sometimes hears whistling in the night and emitting loud sighs when it arrives in the stations, or the motorcycle (which I used to call a *"pétrolette"* [moped]) whose noise is the most obvious confirmation of the correctness of the term *moteur à explosion* [internal combustion engine; *lit.,* explosion engine], to the diver with his spherical metal head, passing by way of the ventriloquist, a living phonograph inhabited by innumerable human voices, and the somnambulist, an automaton of flesh and blood, very closely related to the cadaver, in which, until the moment it achieves the final immobility of the skeleton, certain internal movements and unconscious transformations occur. Effects—these, too—of machinery, the relaxation that causes the dead person to "void," the swelling of the abdomen, the intestinal gurgling, not to mention the beard and the nails that continue to grow for a certain time, are signs of that species of miserable survival by which the dead person, before being promoted to a specter who haunts, is himself haunted. If cadaverous cold and rigidity are merely deceptive appearances disguising as mannequin or statue the creature now caught up in a series of unnameable tribulations, the horror that this creature arouses must come from his ambiguous position, the quality he shares with bat, batrachian, land crab, or any other animal that one can describe as *from a border region,* just as the automaton, in his own way, is a hybrid of living creature and machine.

Also situated in a border region was the female figure—not reduced to the proportions of a doll but of natural size—representing *Saint-Pierre reborn from its ruins:* on the edge between fire and water, between pleasure and pain. A mediocre study from the nude, she had hardly any charm except in her wild expression, the curve of her body, more sensual than sculptural, and the realism of her lines—a true nymph of the volcano, lying all black and naked as though in a sweating-room or a Turkish bath, in a rather secluded corner of this town which remains so sleepy and so provincial, against its background of tropical luxuriance, that it is hard to imagine it was the site of a great disaster. Enveloped by the ash cloud which clothed her, perhaps, in a flame-colored bathing suit, the young girl (if one is to believe the woman to whom I had spoken) had hurled herself, already scorched, into a pool but— less fortunate than the devil who (according to the barker at Luna Park) executed, apparently without any resultant harm to himself, a spectacular leap into his luxurious bathtub—she only encountered, as she became the water sprite of that pool, a second death. After which, more provincial than ever, the town had been rebuilt on the old stones of its enclosure walls, on which are carved here and there, indicating lots, old marks of ownership: the names of great white local families, followed by numbers referring to the land register; and bearing witness to the original catastrophe or to this renewal was the solitary presence of the lava sculpture, in that spot so strangely secluded, to which led the double theater staircase as to a sort of aerial aquarium.

Following for a moment the path opened to me by a scrap of legend concerning a statue in truth not very defensible despite the quality of savagery and voluptuousness it emitted, I thought of the she-devil, seductive incarnation of the snares laid by desire and of certain of the malign forces that man in the tropics senses oppressing him all day long. But now this same path has just forked, swerved, leading to an image that is more concrete and darker.

In all climates—warm skies or cold, smiling or gloomy—there exists, in contrast to a greater or smaller number of people whom one can describe as "strong souls" a mass capable, in any waking or sleeping hour, of being assaulted by a fear of ghosts. And in Antillean folklore, this fear takes the form of a belief in zombies, who, whereas they are simple phantoms or other infernal emanations for most of the peasants (and even a number of the townspeople) of Guadeloupe as well as Martinique, become, in Haiti, mechanized dead people or living people who have been deprived by magic of consciousness and will; a sorceror can thus, supposedly, procure cheap labor for himself by employing as slaves either cadavers taken from the cemetery and artificially reanimated or individuals whose personalities have been reduced to nothing by his evil spells. Automatons, in short—those bodily frames without intelligence but capable of moving and, dead or living, being used. Automatons, also, are the madmen, the somnambulists, those who dream out loud—even who merely snore—in sum, all varieties of men reduced to being no more than a carcass dispossessed of the lucid and universal reason without which one ceases to exist except for oneself. It would seem that in these creatures— who have all, in some fashion, come to assume the posture of the *aliénés* [deranged; *lit.*, alienated]—ravings, mechanical motions, incoherent words, or noisy emissions of breath show that the human being from whom they emanate is a human being radically removed. This is the case for the cadaver, who is also locked away and still inhabited by a special life expressed in a way that is merely more hideous, by the biochemical activity of decomposition. Given this, and without paying more attention to it than some old wives' tale, how should one regard the Haitian zombie, which can just as well be an incompletely resuscitated dead person as a living person degraded to the rank of a machine?

No zombie, it should be understood, did I ever see during my visit of barely a month in Haiti. It is true that in a voodoo meeting place in Port-au-Prince's Saline quarter (a house that one reached by taking a left off the Grande Rue just opposite the *Tête boeuf rouge* [red bull's head] which used to be the shop sign of a butcher) I had the opportunity of greeting, with my two little fingers bent and hooking onto two other little fingers similarly bent, and even of kissing on both cheeks, *Baron Samedi,* one of the principal spirits of death, whose *"reposoir"* [altar, usu. in procession or for consecrated host in church; *lit.,* resting place] is generally a cross similar to those in cemeteries and who ordinarily presents himself as a man correctly dressed in black and wearing a top hat. When I, in some sense a tourist, was invited by the masters of the house to pay my respects to the god, he had incarnated himself in a fat woman at that moment lying on her back dressed all in white like the chorus of her officiating colleagues, many of whom were vendors in the market during the day and trafficked in fritters, fried fish, or other minor foodstuffs. Soaked in sweat from the agitation of her earlier dances and trances, she was miming, when I greeted and kissed her as I had been bidden to do, the immobility of a cadaver. Had I remained on the island a large enough number of months, would I perhaps have encountered some zombies or individuals reputed to be such? Having visited too briefly, I can speak of them only from what I have read or heard and therefore it would be better if I did not continue. Yet, haven't I found myself, in other circumstances, in the presence of a type of zombie, having the impression, without analyzing it, of being alone with a dead person who continued to live, whose life was limited, certainly, but nevertheless sufficient to save him from that end of everything which, de-

spite the sort of immortality (very relative anyway) to which I alluded, is in-
contestably the lot of every cadaver? It was in a dream, already old by now,
that I had this experience, which is marked by certain crucial events, the
death of my father and, about two years later, a separation that—though not
necessary—was admittedly in the natural course of events too, which does
not in any way diminish the pain of it.

In the municipal museum of a foreign town I am visiting briefly, I discover a room in which many human bodies are sitting, their backs against the
wall. Some sudden rupture of their organisms has no doubt immobilized
these bodies here, stuck to the floor by a sort of glue emanating from their
flesh and preserved intact by a natural mummification. Having reached a
small chamber situated under the eaves, I see a woman, probably a widow,
with an air of poverty about her, who has taken refuge here with her little boy.
Bread crumbs are scattered about on the floor. She is heating her coffee not
far from a cadaver in a blue smock spotted with plaster, most likely an old
peasant who has died next to his treasure. I go down into the garden adjoin-
ing the museum and here I find other cadavers sitting in tall chairs; nurses are
helping them drink and eat, slipping stone basins under them to collect their
excrements. A break, and it is night, in the same garden, now lit by Chinese
lanterns, which give it the look of an outdoor cafe with arbors where idlers
come to kill time or as members of a pleasure party. Here I encounter several
of my friends, with veins that appear phosphorescent, visible through their
clothes, then the woman from whom I had parted and from whom—when I
had this dream—I was definitively separated after having been tied to her in
the way you often are to the person who has first revealed to you the sort of
love that burns your flesh. With a gesture of her hand, she showed me her
heart, bared as though in an anatomy plate.

The worm-eaten and probably creaking floor, the glue that had flowed
from the bodies (like a kind of Seccotine, in hard protuberances from the
rolled and fissured pale blue tube), the garret or attic with its probable dust
and its cobwebs, the smock of coarse faded linen, all powdery, the crumbs,
no doubt stale, the widow's black dress, the coffee being made in a wretched

manner, and, mingling with these accessories, the naturally mummified people, and then the miser, the mother, and her little boy, characters all human
to the same degree, whether dead or alive.

Long ago, I was shown, in the display case of the old Musée Guimet—the
only thing I have retained from that visit, made perhaps on a Thursday (a day
better loved than Sunday, when you are a schoolchild, because it is your own)
—a mummy called *"momie de Thaïs"* [mummy of Thaïs]; I looked for a long
time at the little that remained of the repentant courtesan behind her thin
wall of glass, but she was so dead, so dried up, that I had no more fear of her
than of a yellowed branch of boxwood. On another afternoon, I was taken to
a small theater, the Trianon-Lyrique, which has since disappeared, to see a
performance of *Les Cloches de Corneville* and of this show I have preserved
two memories: the charming peasant girl Serpolette pinching her petticoat
with her fingertips and boldly lifting her hem to reveal her calves while
singing: *"Voyez par-ci, voyez par-là . . . "* [look over here, look over there]; old
Gaspard locked up alone in a hall where suits of armor stand, terrified when
he sees them move, not knowing that hidden inside are practical jokers who
are trying to get him to cough up what he has; perhaps also—a third fragment from that matinée operetta—the tenor's song: *"J'ai fait trois fois le tour
du monde . . . "* [I have been thrice around the world]. At the peasant in his
blue smock, frightened by pseudoghosts within the simulated walls of a castle, I laughed, like all the other spectators.

It is often by quite indirect routes that the fear of death creeps up on us:
the rasping of an insect heard in the night, the clacking of hooves on the surface of the street when one is in bed, the creaking of furniture (manifesting a
life foreign to us), the click announcing the start of a mechanism or—like a
death rattle—the snore of a sleeper, to mention only noises. Unlike the
creaking of one's bones (undeniable proof that one is rusting), they contain
nothing that is of a nature to worry us especially: a stammer emanating from
an indeterminate spot, or a clue to a life separate from ours—only upon reflection might we detect anything that could turn either one or the other of
these traits into signs reminiscent of death.

As for the dream I described, it is completely silent. From beginning to end, I am only someone strolling through and no one talks to me, neither those friends who are in the garden nor even that woman, who expresses herself only through a gesture. It is also in silence that care and attention are bestowed on the cadavers. The muffled bedrooms, perhaps, of the dying? People stopped talking—or only whispered—when my father was dying from the aftereffects of an operation on his prostate that hardly did anything but add more pain to the pain he was already suffering, when he could no longer urinate except through a tube (which, if I proceeded to a rational exegesis of the dream, would perhaps explain the needs that continued to torment the dead people and required the use of basins, of stone and not of enameled metal, as though to emphasize their importance and give them more solemnity). But, really, I think that if my dream was soundless—a series of tableaux not animated by any dialogue and in which I was not involved until the final gesture showing me that heart, hardly more dismaying than the piece of meat decorated with lace paper you see from the street in the chiaroscuro of a butcher shop—it is because, from the outset, it was a dream about death.

Automatons and robots. The fake humanity in shop windows, some imitative, others purely allusive or produced in fragments (such as a bust with an alluring décolleté, a leg or a hand). Museum mannequins, sometimes alone, sometimes in couples or gathered in groups, to show the martial gear of the Gaul with his long mustaches and his breeches, the feathered headdress and the skin coat of an old Indian sachem, the male and female costumes of the Basque country toward the middle of the last century or perhaps a certain scene from the daily life of the primitive peoples of Africa or Oceania. If a cadaver—and especially that of someone we know—arouses such anguished questions, isn't it because, in addition to the rigidity, there is this very same silence, and because, without any apparent great change, it finds itself, even while in its own way continuing to exist, in a state from which it can no longer answer us? And if, sometimes, an almost equal disturbance is caused in us by a noise that for us becomes a voice from beyond the grave, isn't it because what lies concealed behind it is also silence, a silence from which it seems to have returned like a survivor from the abyss, when it comes to tap at the door of our ear and ask us its question?

> Ou-vrez-moi
> cet-te-porte
> où-je-frappe
> en-pleu-rant
> La-vie
> est-va-ri-able
> aus-si-bien
> que-l'Eu-ripe . . .
>
> [Op-en-this
> door-to-me
> Weep-ing
> I-knock
> Life
> is-change-able
> as-the-Strait
> of-Ev-ri-pos . . .]

Thus spoke, some twenty years after it was made at the Archives de la Parole, a recording of the late Guillaume Apollinaire, restoring a voice that is already gloomy (because of the very tone of the recitation) but also deadened by the poor quality of the impression and as though streaked with rain like a very old film. The idea of this deeply sad, dead man whose soliloquy comes from so far away and is uttered in such a tired voice, as though by someone who is being pestered when he should be allowed to rest. Cervantes's tragedy about the capture of Numantia by Scipio Aemilianus (in other words, the Scipio of *Songe* . . . [Dream . . .]) has a cadaver speaking too, a cadaver questioned by a necromancer: the dead man, first objurgated verbally, then whipped as hard as possible, is forced to leave his tomb and tell what will become of the town beset by Romans. And when I was studying chemistry a very long time ago, didn't I learn that one can cook bones (of animal origin, of course, but why not human? It would work just as well) in a pressure cooker in order to extract gelatin from them? Similarly, toward the end of the war before the last one, the rumor went around France that the Germans were processing the cadavers of the soldiers who had been killed in order to extract fat from them—which (in 1938, when the threat of a worldwide catastrophe became clear) provided me with the subject of a dream: a sort of premortuary medical review or lottery required of those who, like me, were eligible for mobilization, the point of the procedure being to discriminate, among the future dead, between those who would be left in peace and those who would be chemically salvaged for the needs of the war.

As though, therefore, certain dead people will not be at rest even in eternity—and could this even, perhaps, be the fate of all dead people? But the little we know conspires to assure us that the dead person, once dead, is quite dead and that, therefore, only a childish apprehension can cause us to fear posthumous adventures which, in truth, involve only the body. However free we may be of all superstition, our imaginations will nevertheless always work to fill in a certain gap: the hiatus that makes us pass irremediably from the presence of a being to that of a figure occupying a determined portion of space but from whom consciousness is forever absent; the lack of common measure, despite the formal identity, between the person whose life has stopped and the remains that survive. This, consequently, might be the opening into which pious illusions and spectral effluvia might take the opportunity of insinuating themselves.

A curtain that can be lowered or a hanging that can be drawn. Eyelids that with a single gesture of the hand one can slip down over the eyeballs, as though to put the eyes in harmony with the muteness of the mouth. Even before a dead person is buried, don't we have to cut off all communication between ourselves and that terrible world where he is but about which—even as his wide-open eyes reveal to us all its horror—he can't speak to us; cut short also the thing that is his scandal, the wordless discourse carried on by not only his glassy eye but also (if it weren't for the chin bandage) his dropping jaw and (supposing one should delay too long in stealing him away) the metaphors difficult to accept that are being worked by the liquefaction of his features? It is easy for a taciturn person to seem profound, and in the same way, the silence of a cadaver leads one to believe that he has much to tell; as with regard to the taciturn person, our attitude toward him is marked by ambiguity: that he says nothing gives rise to uneasiness, but we are also afraid that, if his tongue loosens, it will only be for the most incongruous of revelations; better, then, that he persist in saying nothing and that, without danger of being disappointed, we remain free to reckon what sublimities hide behind this profound mask. What is important to safeguard, when all is said and done, is the imposing muteness of the cadaver, because it would be too crushing to discover through his drooling-idiot grimaces that if he says nothing, the reason for this is simply that he has nothing to say to us.

To offer the most disarming enigma because one is absolutely silent (and, furthermore, reduced to a state about which there is nothing to reveal); to be an eye all the less tolerable because, deprived of vision, it is nothing but an eye seen. A potential phantom or zombie, an apparition in any case (since, without thought or gaze, he is a human form who merely appears), the dead person, by his very inertia, occupies the center of the stage. In order to play his character suitably, he has only to maintain a certain style, which is the reason for those more and less complicated measures that may extend to embalming, as though we were afraid that any slovenliness in his grooming would force us to see death in all its obscene nakedness, something of which the majority of mankind has not shown itself capable in any known civilization up to the present. Yet, is it inconceivable to imagine a type of education that would accustom one to regard death as too natural a thing to clothe in such alarming colors as these? And shouldn't one—for the very reason that death is regarded as tragic by them and represents, in sum, the crucial experience—judge deficient societies in which the norm is to be deceitful about it and to try, as much for oneself as for another, to elude it by means of a lie: belief in immortality or something resembling it, fallacious speeches designed to be employed on ill people for whom there is no hope when one wishes to hide from them the fact that, if they have some declaration *in extremis* to make, it is high time to prepare themselves to utter their last words?

I myself believe that my persistent incapacity to control my obsession with death prevents me from being altogether a man and even, in some way, from existing: nothing, in my eyes, can be worth my dying since everything, for me, is devalued by the fact that at the end of everything is my death; now, if nothing can make me forget that I must die and if there exists nothing for love—or liking—of which I feel prepared to confront death, I am dealing only with nothingness and all is reduced to zero at the same moment, myself not excepted. Free of all true passion, all vice, and even all ambition, I am, while I am still alive, subject to a torpor similar to that of the museum figures who once intruded into my sleep, and the acts that I perform are scarcely more than the gestures of an automaton or the mechanical works of a zombie, as though fear, by obliterating everything in me, had transformed me here and now into that bodily frame without consciousness that I am so afraid of becoming. The prescience of the sickening moment when everything will vanish—as the ground disappears from under the feet of a person tumbling into the darkness of a secret dungeon—is enough to make me, reduced as I am to the abstraction of a geometric point, the center of a cottony sort of world inhabited now only by vague forms, except for those, all too distinct for my taste, in which I believe I read a threat. In my ears, nothing sings any longer and, for a number of years now, even my nights have very rarely been animated by dreams: it is as though everything not confined within the limits of the serious frightens me, like a sin with fatal repercussions whose aftereffects could only hasten my ruin. Couldn't it have been the result of too much frivolity that the volcano reduced the inhabitants of Saint-Pierre to ashes after *Les Cloches de Corneville* and their noisy harmonies echoing the multitudes of laughter rising from one spot or another through the carnivals?

Whether my failure has caused me to acquire, on the other hand—since it is an ill wind that blows no good—a certain ability to see things in an unemotional and positive way, or whether for me, nowadays, everything tends to center upon the pivotal point of what continues to terrify me, or whether the dream to which her silent reproach apposed a paraph is now too distant to move me, the vision that I had of that woman who for some time already had no longer been central to my life and who showed me her bloody heart as the sign of the torture I had supposedly inflicted on her unappreciated love, that anatomical vision of the organ charged with the highest power of signification of all the viscera no longer appeared to me as absolutely as it had at the time to be an image of some sort of remorse (with very shaky foundations, anyway) or some sort of regret, a result of the state of disarray and emotional destitution in which I was then floundering (and about which, let me say in passing, I see no evidence that would allow me to think that at that time it was not mine alone); in that figure—of the same type as those strictly didactic figures that reproduce our internal structure in its most naked reality—I also find a glimmer of one of my old superstitions: the dangerous and always more or less criminal nature of carnal passion, here represented by that organ exposed to view as it would have been by a surgical operation and situated on the plane, less of an emblem of warmth than of a symbol of the macabre, like the glue secreted by the dead people stuck to the dusty floor or the basins that reminded me of what my father had endured in the region of the body where the functions of excretion and reproduction are located.

More than twenty-five years ago, when magic was more accessible to me than science, and hermeticism than plain philosophy, I noted the following reflection in a notebook with beige paper-board binding and a red percale spine in which I kept my journal at that time and which is punctuated, throughout the pages I wrote during that period, with accounts of dreams and observations relating (more naively, perhaps, than I would have intended) to pataphysics.

Our death is bound up with the duality of the sexes. If a man were male and female at the same time and capable of reproducing alone, he would not die, his soul being transmitted unadulterated to his posterity.

The instinctive hatred of the sexes for each other comes, perhaps, from an obscure knowledge that their mortality is due to the differentiation between them. A violent resentment, counterbalanced by the attraction toward oneness—life's only number—which they try to satisfy through coitus.

Of these lines—whose gravity was not without a hint of humor intended to spare me from looking too ridiculous to myself—I retain, despite the element of confusion within their intentionally dogmatic tone, the idea of death experienced as being tied to the division of the human species into two sexes. Making love amounts, in short, to reverting to a state of indistinctness in order to attempt to remedy the original lesion and would thus explain why the desire a man feels for a woman is necessarily ambiguous: the instruments of that plunge into chaos are the organs of procreation, in other words the very same ones whose existence manifests the duality according to which we are incomplete and transitory beings, who cannot endure but are merely capable of reproducing; nothing surprising, then, about the fact that sexual commerce—an exchange between two bodies more alive than ever whereas the machinery of the lower parts gropes along its course—should be regarded in all latitudes as being of a certain seriousness, as is borne out by the obstacles opposed to absolute license, even among peoples whose mores seem to us the most relaxed; nothing astonishing, either, in the fact that within societies quite distant from ours but where men occupy, as they do everywhere else, a preponderant position, woman—who bleeds every month, and, at irregular intervals, opens painfully to give birth—represents, more than her partner, a sinister element, as though it were clear that by such signs one recognized implicitly in her the one term out of the duality that existed *in addition* to the first and had consequently—since it was radically *other,* occurring as an intrusion—to be held responsible for the pernicious dichotomy.

Undecided as to how I should suitably dispose of this note dated October 13, 1924—a Monday (as I see in my journal), and it was at 2 rue Mignet, at the corner of the rue George-Sand at Auteuil, my father having died, my military service ended, as I was endeavoring to write, living without women since my affair had ended, and staying with my mother, relieved of all immediate worry about earning a living, all this at a time when we did not see another war looming on the horizon, when we were not fighting as we are today in Korea while awaiting a carnage closer to home, when I was young, romantic, theoretically in despair and able quite at my ease (without any sort of threat) to speculate on the great theme of death—undecided as to the heading under which I should classify the lines in question: as a thought that no doubt ultimately deserved to be explored, corrected, and brought out of its fog but could nevertheless be taken as a point of departure; or simply as a document relating to my state of mind at about the time poetry was revealed to me?— I opted, spontaneously, for the first of the two choices and, with the necessary reservations, called these lines a "thought"; I followed them with a rough gloss intended to extract something worthwhile from them, but I know only too well to what extent purely personal reaction is involved in a construction of this kind, of which the least one can say is that it offers only a castle in the clouds, if it does not include a vast, difficult, and tedious examination of real human events to support it! Having derived a representation of reality essentially from my own experience or from my own feelings and having formulated it as a primary truth that was not only my own truth but also everyone's truth, I had certainly done something rather ill considered. Yet isn't it one of the most natural aims of literary activity (and that by which writing is differentiated from the other modes of thinking) thus to forge from one's own experience, using language as one's tool, certain approximate truths which some people will accept as their own and which, by the very fact of this sharing, will cease to be the idle dreams of a single mind or mere vain appearances? It therefore seems to me that, even granted that I was guilty of an abuse, I can, without deleting or denying anything, correct it adequately if I indicate in passing that I am at least clearly aware of the dubiousness and, in any case, the relativity of what I have just proposed. From the portrait of myself I am painting and from the shreds of more distant truths I endeavor to catch hold of in order to transform them into some species of illumination for this portrait, and at the same time its radiance too, can I not, at least, hope there will arise, someday—and if necessary without my knowledge—some general truth?

What shows me clearly that an old residue of *Credo* makes me put the act of love in the same category as defilement and perdition whereas I would like to see it only as the most tender of human gestures (and quite simply the last element in a series: talking, holding hands, kissing, embracing) is that I tend not to make love—or, to use a verb with a rather entomological appearance from the literature of the Church, not to "fornicate"—during periods when I am afraid. Not only do I have a tendency, when I am uneasy, to withdraw into myself, to go to ground (to be nothing, so that death will forget me, and perhaps it is also for this reason that the alarms of our epoch tend to distance me from poetry rather than open its sources for me, already so ungenerous, usually, toward me), not only do I feel a need to withdraw that conflicts with any impulse toward effusion, but sexual pleasure, in itself, appears too illicit for me, if I yield to it, not to risk my being chastised, something that does not make much sense in calm times but becomes more clearly meaningful when one knows that a storm threatens to descend on the world and that soon one may be put in the situation of the child who hears himself told: "It's the Good Lord who has punished you!" if he has misbehaved and is, shortly afterward, the victim of some small misfortune. Far from seeing carnal relations as the most naked expression of human fatalism, at such times I would, on the contrary, be dismayed by the challenge to destiny that they represent and it would be, consequently, not so much their symbolic link with death (death being a disappearance without return whereas the other is only a "little death") that would paralyze me as what is still scandalously incompatible about them, in my eyes, with serious situations, even quite apart from any libertinage and as though pleasure alone, without any need to imitate the rakes or the Don Juans with more than a thousand and three women, would be enough to make one feel the weight of the Commandant's fist.

If—as though through a sort of stinginess complementing the prudence that has almost consistently kept me from debauchery—I have never had anything but disgust for what is the natural outcome of—and, if the religious bigots are to be believed, the only justification for—the intimacy between the sexes (to the point of having for a long time made sterility a moral position: the refusal to propagate life, because life is too great an evil), isn't this rejection due to the fact that procreation, the only means of perpetuating ourselves, illustrates our mortal condition most distinctly? To move to the rank of father means, in effect, that we officially descend one step toward the grave, since we are taking an active part in the mechanism of the continuous renewal of the human stock, a mechanism that requires each generation to be succeeded by another, installment after installment, and that engendering amounts to creating a being whose growth, progressively signifying to us our dismissal, pushes us back toward death as though, through an inexorable play of exchanges, its rise could take place only on condition of our own descent. To move to the rank of father—not of the imprudent procreator scattering children here and there, but of the *father of the family* who keeps them with him and raises them—also means carrying to its extreme the, by definition,

incestuous nature that invests marriage, whose function is to change love relations into family relations and which is fully realized when the husband, do-
mestic variety of the lover, becomes the person who can be described as "the
father of my child," which is equivalent to classifying him as kin (a relation
obviously more subject to criticism, where passionate love is concerned, than,
at least, that form of incest which is the love of brother and sister, because it
is preferable, from this point of view, to forget the blood tie in the flame of
pleasure than to let passion—or what would claim to be such—cool down,
with the passing of time, into familial affection). To move to the rank of father—either because of the aging that it openly marks or because of that
comfy-domestic-incest color it eventually spreads over the shared life of the
man and woman, or because of the burden and the responsibility it represents
—it is this which has always repulsed me and I don't think I am such a moral
individual that I could grant priority over all these reasons to the idea that it
is not charitable to give life, the saddest gift of all those we are entitled to give.
It may be yet another hypocrisy if I allege, in support of my horror of pater-
nity, a refusal to assist in the perseverance of a species launched on the most
absurd sort of venture; I maintained this point of view until I noticed the following contradiction in myself: I am against procreation but I am in favor of
posterity since, without expecting too much from its opinion, I envisage with
displeasure the prospect that any destruction—or any form of oblivion—
might prevent those writings of mine which certain of my contemporaries
have been willing to print from having at least a few readers among future
generations (so that I refuse, in sum, to give birth whereas my activity of
choice, the one from which I hope for a semblance of survival, is not fully
meaningful unless others work at what I condemn and prolong a venture
that, moreover, I can't view as absurd without writing becoming one of the
thousands of absurd human endeavors and this would be the case even if I
wrote only in order to denounce the absurdity of the world, for to speak of
the absurd to an absurd world is necessarily absurd).

So marked a propensity to regard love—whether it bears its fruits or not
—as a culpable activity probably testifies to some infantilism with respect to
it. Much more than a confusedly metaphysical idea that would make death

dependent upon the dichotomy of the sexes, what keeps me in check here is my lifelong terror at the prospect of *being a man,* a creature free in himself and no longer under the aegis of parents whose role has been to help him and, sometimes, punish him (which is another way of being attentive). Thus, the fears that cause me to surround love with certain taboos are probably accompanied by some nostalgia and express, not so much direct apprehension, as a need, always apt to show itself, to return to the period when I was afraid of being punished and when "forbidden fruit" could scarcely apply to anything but food that had been locked away and perhaps to *another's goods* whereas on the other hand the word *covet* appeared to make of the object of covetousness something more than a simple *friandise* [tidbit] (such as *bêtises de Cambrai* [mint humbugs] or other *gourmandises* [sweetmeats]) and to join the ranks, instead, of the shifty character curiously known as a *prevaricator* (or one who *betrays the interests he is obliged to uphold* if I am to believe my *Littré* dictionary, which I've just consulted).

As sparing of myself as any peasant may be of his pennies; inhibited by fear; reticent in love (perhaps because of that dread of having to pay with my body that also leads me to make myself very small at the idea of pain); liking to play at being a torero but without ever having a real bull in front of me, and at being a Don Juan, without any conquests nor challenge to the Commandant; no longer existing except through writing and, at each instant, attempting to formulate sententious phrases with the distant tone of last words, as though my fingers were already squeezed by the stone gauntlet of death, am I not a proxy unfaithful to the destiny I have dreamed of, in other words am I not that prevaricator? The examination I have made of what is hidden behind my refusal to engender and more particularly the bad faith detectable in one of the explanations for it I proposed (my recourse to rather specious notions about incest) commits me to think so. I would be lying and, therefore, in any case a traitor with respect to my own person were I to posit—as I so often do—as a moral attitude my rebellion against the yoke that is always imposed (in various forms) by belonging to a family when I know that, if I tend to break my ties with my people while everything makes me incline to return to infantile states and to resurrect old memories which I did

not experience alone and certain of which are not even my exclusive possessions, it is not simply for the proud joy of putting myself outside the flock;
even more, by this deliberate segregation I seek to reassure myself by insinuating that as for me, I am from a *different* species (a species not subject, like
theirs, to ills such as senility, painful diseases, death) and by thus taking
refuge in the vague hope of being beyond reach, since, through the negation
of my roots and my rejection of a progeniture that would make me the link
between what was before and what will come after, I can imagine to myself
that I, in my uniqueness, preserved from any succession, remain outside the
flow of time.

Ouvrez le ciel, fermez l'enfer!

[Open heaven, close hell!]

sang—black under their white robes and backed up by the choir of everyone
else present—the *ounsis* at the home of Lorgina Eloge the mambo of Port-au-
Prince, the evening of the *"coucher des ignames"* [laying down of the yams].

Ici comme devant la mort
Le plus lâche fait des efforts

[Here, as when faced with death,
The worst coward tries his best]

had been scrawled firmly and without a mistake by the hand of a stranger on
the wall of the latrines of the Centre Semi-Permanent de Revoil Beni-Ounif
(South Oran) at the time of that *"drôle de guerre"* ["phony war"; name given
to the Second World War during its first phase] during which all servicemen
—or almost all—explained their sexual inertia by referring to the myth of
bromide.

Rien ne se perd, rien ne se crée,

[Nothing is created or destroyed]

an axiom that the older of my two brothers quoted with the profound air of
a philosopher and that I myself—without at that time knowing Ronsard,

who tells us that *Matter remains and form is lost*—savored as rich with meaning, unlike other dicta such as: *Take not back what you give, He who leaves his place loses it,* or *He who sees a mote in his neighbor's eye sees not the beam that is in his own.*

> Faux témoignagne ne diras
> Ni mentiras aucunement . . .
>
> [Thou shalt not bear false witnesses
> Nor lie in any way . . .]

in which ". . . gnagne" [. . . nesses] instead of ". . . gnage" [. . . ness] could prove my mediocre skill as reader if not the excessive stammering of an *enfant grognon* [peevish child], the lazybones repetition, the dunce exaggeration of the *gnangnan* [spineless, flabby] tone in which the Ten Commandments are recited in earlier days when *"holocauste"* [holocaust] with its burnt taste evoked the fires of *Pentecôte* [Pentecost] which *rôtissent les côtes* [roast the ribs].

> Bien d'autrui ne convoiteras
>
> [Thou shalt not covet another's goods]

nor his wife, nor his ox, nor his ass, nor anything considered by the gleaming, concupiscent eye, since according to the *Rédempteur* [Redeemer] (glimpsed behind his bars like *Daniel le Dompteur* [Daniel the Lion Tamer] in his pit) a camel would pass through the hole—or the eye—*of a needle sooner than a rich man would enter heaven by thought, by word, by deed, or by omission.*

> L'entendez-vous, il blasphème!
>
> [Do you hear him, he blasphemes!]

shouts Caiaphas, tearing his clothes and abandoning the Son of God to insults and spitting.

"When an electric lightbulb bursts," my older brother also explained, "one really should call it an *implosion* rather than an explosion." The small death signified by any abrupt irregular motion—an arrest of consciousness, an interruption in the uniform flow of time—and as well illustrated by dreams of falling or startled wakings as by electric shocks, sudden jolts reverberating in the soundbox of a phonograph, magnesium lights (like those I used to have to suffer when they took me to have my portrait done by the photographer Otto), or those detonations which I detest, even more perhaps when one waits for them and they only occur after some time (as in the old days on the boulevards, at the Kinéma Gabka, an old movie theater with "imitations of noises," in that film in which a clown, clearly an adult, played the role of a beret-clad boy whose balloon suddenly begins to inflate—unless it is the boy himself who inflates it with a bicycle pump—and succeeds in filling the entire volume of the room just before the final burst which one predicted would be noisier and noisier as the seconds went by).

The fire and overflowing river in the *Götterdämmerung*. The collapse of the temple of Dagon when its two main columns were toppled by Samson, a slave with blinded eyes who had until then been turning a millstone. The Sardanapalian end of the prophet Jean de Leyde footing the bill for an orgy in the course of which his stores of gunpowder were set on fire (which is what the curtain falls on in the last act of Meyerbeer's opera). In Guadeloupe's Basse-Terre, the rue Delgres, which slopes steeply down in the direction of the seacoast and whose name commemorates a man of color who, defeated by Bonaparte's soldiers, blew himself up along with the rebels under his command. In Martinique's Saint-Pierre, a black form: allegedly that of the girl killed by fire and water, caught in a trap when she tried to flee what one can never more than temporarily foil. The last firework launched by a *toro de fuego*, the whirling "crown" sent high in the air and representing the soul which has supposedly been exhaled—in a final, tumultuous sigh—by the wooden and cardboard *toro*.

Whether it comes to me in the form of a catastrophe or whether, bourgeois style, I feel it slipping between my sheets one day, death, whether violent or not, is not, for me, "natural," and I cannot conceive of it as anything else but an accident, which can only happen unexpectedly, even if it is unavoidable. The end of the world, if I admit the existence of nothing beyond my own person, or an end that I will furiously impute to my "bad star" if I sense that others stay on while I leave, this accident is not only an absurdity in itself (the unexpected descent of a *deus ex machina* with the preposterous behavior of a spider which abruptly unwinds its thread and plunges into the soup) but makes my whole life absurd, degrading it—as it would any possible life—to the rank of the bad scenario that will not really be resolved but will end because, in one way or another, the performance must end. I am less afraid in the country than I am in the city, because there the prospect of the changes that will be undergone by my body (future shrub, tree, or other sample of the botanical world like the wheat in the form of which Persephone returned to life) appears to me less frightful than when I am surrounded by town life; but whether I am here or there thinking of death, the little drop of absurdity that thus fell into me at a time I no longer remember ceaselessly extends its ravages, and isn't my truth as a man reduced to nothing here and now if fear will not allow me to recognize death as one of the essential components of an intrigue that constantly presupposes it and each episode of which can have only a fallacious signification if I have to blind myself in order to be able to carry on with my business? Since this death from which I try to turn away—but which I know, nonetheless, is there—breaks my life down even before the latter has come to an end, will I be taking absurdity to its highest degree if I hope to be able to make something of that life, having fulfilled one initial condition: that I stifle my horror and watch it come, my eyes wide open, my mind clear, so as to play my part without wandering away nor attempting to be devious toward the destiny awaiting me? The conversion that I ought to bring about therefore has the amplitude of a total revolution, one such that instead of hating the family—in a sort of childish rejection—because the fact of my belonging to that ancestral formation is, for me, a guarantee of death, it would be, on the contrary, by endeavoring to scorn death that I would seek to place myself outside the normal framework of families and would attempt, without rebelling against genealogies, to turn myself into a creature from another planet through his nonconformism with respect to the common horror.

Tattoos on the sky. The zodiac. The delicately chiseled ear disks worn by the opera singer playing the role of the goddess of the underworld. With my eyes, I follow in a dream the rotation of naked bodies in a half-dark space while the ray of a projector, continually moving about, carves in their skins—which it illuminates only in successive portions—scars assembled into complicated figures, numbers, or the coats of arms of these acrobats. As long as death does not seize me, it is, finally, an idea that must not be thrust aside but tamed instead. Such is the meaning, perhaps, of my recalling a few meager experiences, trifling fragments in which something resembling death seemed to occur and which, I persuaded myself, would upon examination yield to me a few features with the help of which its face would become a little less mercilessly alien to me. But to pass away is, by definition, to fall into a formless hole which no cartography, real or imaginary, permits one to delimit, and I know perfectly well that I elucidate nothing if I say that I am supporting, resting on the palm of my right hand, a heavy column of marble (decorated as the columns in certain frescoes in Pompeii appear), a majestic weight the burden of which oppresses me to the point that I would have cried out if, at that precise instant, someone hadn't woken me; and that it clarifies nothing, either, to tell how, being slightly drunk, I went into my kitchen one night to eat some bit of food and swallow a little water before going to bed, then remained standing there stock-still, smoking a cigarette, my back against the wall, and thought how I was inevitably going to have to die, while my gaze alighted now on the gas meter, now on the Roberval balance with its two copper plates. I could just as well summon up certain elements of the Antillean landscape: the old chimney of the distillery, for instance, that juts up sometimes in the middle of a bouquet of palm trees and is the symbol of the "factory" (as the dungeon is that of the feudal market town), or those great hemispheres of rusted pig iron—true sorcerers' cauldrons or cooking pots of grandmammas all black and wrinkled—which were originally boilers for processing sugarcane juice but are used nowadays as firepots for heating the plates on which cassava flour is cooked; these are seen most particularly in the vicinity of Basse-Terre, near the remains of the "habitations" dating from "antiquity" (as it is described to us, my walking companion and I, by a peasant who designates thus the whole of the time prior to the abolition of slavery).

From the moment—now thrust back, as well, into a sort of prehistory—when, deciding to shake off my torpor, I rid myself of my bands of silence, I have done nothing else, therefore, though without discovering anything positive, than try, one after another, various different paths and passageways. Lacking experiences capable of enlightening me, might I not have some resting places that—whether bastions or oases—might function as wayside altars for my anguish?

At Nîmes, during the international crisis that preceded the Munich Agreement, everything on which I had based my life up to then seemed to me to collapse like a house of cards and I could observe then that the only external objects the sight of which procured me some repose (because I had the impression that those things were marked by grandeur, even on the scale of the war) were the Roman monuments: the Maison Carré [square house], the temple of Diana, the arena. On a more modest level, I am clearly less unwilling to accept the certainty that I must die when I look back upon various pastimes that delighted me as a child: for instance, fishing for tadpoles which we would keep in an aquarium with the hope of seeing them turn into frogs, an expectation that always disappointed us, my brothers and me, in our keenness as experimenters watching over the unfolding of a natural process and determined to observe it *de visu,* for, of the three stages of the metamorphosis (two feet, four feet with tail, and, lastly, loss of the tail), I'm quite sure we never got beyond the first.

Fishing for tadpoles, a sport for the summer months, was practiced without any other implement than one's hand, very close to the fortifications and the Bois de Boulogne in the shady streams leading to the "Auteuil pond" (the former, like the latter, now gone, because the racecourse, quite some years ago, swallowed up the spot where they were). The "pond"—which I knew long after a certain little English boy was taken for walks there, later recalling it when he imagined the story of *Peter Ibbetson* and his life, more than half dreamed—the "pond" was this pool, invisible before one emerged from the path that forced its way through the greenery, and its banks were girdled by a regularly traced walk, a beautiful, almost circular track that inspired footraces, just as the neighboring copse lent itself to games of hide-and-seek. At the end of the pool closest to the mouth of the path, there was (it seems to me) a bridge with parapets of imitation wood, with fake branches of cement above the tracery from which one leaned down to contemplate the sudden zigzags of the "water spiders" moving by almost horizontal leaps, with an automaton-like precision, on the surface of one of the streams. It was at the same end, probably, that a certain hillock stood, leveled, for me, in oblivion until just recently when, at Nemours, my sister and I, urging each other on, talked about it, but concerning which, since it reappeared thus, not without some relief (like a theater's practicable door that one sees again in a new light after its eclipse behind a curtain or a screen of clouds), I remember that we climbed it following a spiral path and that, like one of the most disturbing attractions in Luna Park and one of the figures in the Game of Goose—which, they say, was handed down to us from earliest Greek antiquity—it was called the Labyrinth.

Sports Notebook

Les Tablettes sportives [sports tablets] (not bars of chocolate but tablets one writes on)—this was the name of an annual that, for three or four years, the daily paper *L'Auto* published before the war of 1914–18.

Experts who no doubt had realized—or calculated—that one of the main characteristics of the true sportsman was that he hated any sort of encumbrance, the editors of this notebook had chosen for their publication the form of a small pocket book in which were recorded, along with the various official records up to that day, the results of the championships or other important events that had taken place during the year and also all the performances worthy of being remembered through "statistics." On the cover—cream for one of the installments, gray for another, pale green for a third—a series of medallions contained the portraits of some celebrities: an aviator in a helmet, a jockey in a silk cap, a cyclist in a round-collared jersey, a boxer wearing his gloves, or any other figure already popularized by the illustrated magazines. The printed content, reduced to the most succinct pieces of information, was nevertheless rich in expressions the perusal of which left one daydreaming: *"Omnium"* [open race, handicap, or championship], *"Critérium"* [eliminating heat in boxing, racing, etc.], *"Biennal"* [biennial], *"Triennal"* [triennial] sparkled with Roman nobility alongside "challenge"* (which was pronounced *chalange*), evoking long strides over an expanse of green or flights of oars, powerful but nonetheless silent, between the banks of a river; *"huit rameurs de pointe et barreur"* [eight rowers (as opposed to scullers) and coxswain] referred to those freshwater coursers, whereas "racers"* [racing yachts] and its matching "cruisers"* [cruising yachts] (pronounced as they should be, the one *réceurs,* the other *crouzeurs*) created a great noise of engines and splashing on the surface of the sea; the names of pugilists of color—Joe Jeannette, Sam Mac Vea, Jack Johnson—glittered in the boxing column and those of Anglo-Saxon jockeys such as Fred Archer, Tom Lane, Percy Woodland, appeared elsewhere alongside those of the filly Sauge Pourprée [purple sage] and the colts Endymion [bluebell], Negofol, or Faucheur [daddy-longlegs] (the crack horse who broke a leg and about whom the racing press published health bulletins for a long time); on the inside of the cover—or on some other page given over to advertising—one learned that "The Sport* (pronounced *thé sport*) dresses well."

At the gates of Paris, and very close to the neighborhood I still consider somewhat mine because I was born there and lived there almost continuously until the beginning of the last war, there are two open-air spots—the Auteuil racecourse and the Parc des Princes cycle-racing track—which represented, in my younger days, a little what the arenas represent in a bullfighting country and which hung a curtain of crowds and shouting in the background of some of our walks.

My brother Pierre and I only rarely went to the Parc des Princes: here under our very own eyes, Daragon ran a race of eighty kilometers, here before us, the pacer Lawson in his leather helmet abandoned (quickly and without harm to himself) his motorcycle, which burst into flames, and here we also saw several rugby matches, including one between France and Wales; it was within the trough of this track that the *"Bol d'Or"* [golden bowl] took place, an annual twenty-four-hour race the posters for which I recall admiring (long-distance runners behind their pacers in cars) but which—for the simple reason, perhaps, that the refusal was a guaranteed thing because it would have meant our staying up late and because our instructors, in any case, would not have been so indulgent as to accompany us to spectacles they judged to be stupid and, for that reason, pernicious—we never urged our parents to allow us to attend.

Much more attractive to us, and within reach, was the Auteuil racecourse, whether, on the day of the Grand Steeple* [grand steeplechase] or some other major event, the sum of one franc paid out for each of us gave us the right to enter the *"pelouse"* [public enclosures], or whether—and this was most often the case—it was enough for us to be, at the right moment, at a certain point on a road outside the racecourse bordered by a riding track that went partway around the racecourse.

From this observation post, my brother and I could watch the jockeys—in multicolored caps on their horses, whose coats gleamed—jump a hedge, then climb a grass-covered knoll behind which they would disappear. "Chestnut, white scarf, chestnut cap": the colors of the Lieux stable; "cherry, sleeves and cap corn": the colors of the Veil-Picard stable; "sea green, belt and cap orange": the colors of the Hennessy stable. We knew that it was in this enclosure and for these riders with their sparkling finery that people (those whom we sensed were crowded in the bleachers and whose clamor we could hear at the moment of the finish) placed bets and sometimes ruined themselves, like that former colleague of my father's who, after having had his own "carriage and team," had lost through gambling the entire fortune he owed to speculation and now touched him modestly for a hundred sous when he met him at the Bourse. A marvelous place, this vast grassy terrain, because of the epic struggles that took place here, the considerable sums that were won or lost here; a place that was fascinating but rather shady, against which our father fulminated, worried by the idea that later we might become "gamblers"; an almost supernatural place, in a word, where everything seemed to be weighed in terms of grace or disgrace, fortune or misfortune.

One of our greatest joys was when the start of the race was close to the "Oak Hedge," that is, near where we were standing. The starter, in a frock coat, on a horse muscled like a wrestler, a great strapping fellow next to the thoroughbreds taking part in the event; the group of competitors gathering for the start, stamping like cocks, weaving like swans; then, after the formation of the line, always laborious, the sudden gallop and the noise of hoofs on the ground, from which it seemed to us we could perceive the tiniest vibrations. From this moment on, the din of the public following the moving phases of the race began to reach us, sometimes weaker, sometimes stronger, according to the point where the competitors were, according to whether one of them was gaining little by little on the bunch after remaining in the back or, inversely, had been overtaken after being the one in the lead, and finally according to whether an accident—a jib before an obstacle or a fall coming out of a jump—irretrievably deprived one of the competitors of his chance and, at the same time, caused for a section of the bettors a loss of money.

Even though I have always (despite some slight inclinations) been the opposite of a sportsman, I have retained from that period an impression of amazement that may play a part, now, in making me see every sporting event as a sort of ritual ostentation. The jockeys' saddlery gear, the white ropes of the rings, and all the preparations: the parading of the competitors, the introduction of the adversaries, the duties of those who—like the referee, the starter, or the judge at the finish—are known as "officials"; behind the apparently unbroken facade of a detailed regulation, everything, too, that one senses having to do with applications of liniment, massages, administrations of drugs, special diets (as for fighting cocks, over which spells are cast). It is as though the protagonists of such events move through a world apart, at once more isolated and closer to the public than actors, for example. For here nothing is false: however important the stage production may be, here, and however strong the element of illusion, the sporting event, whose outcome is theoretically unpredictable except within the limits of a bet, is a real act and not a make-believe, all of whose vicissitudes, down to the least important, take place in conformity with what has been arranged in advance. Whence, along with a sharp consciousness of being less than these supermen, there is a most intense participation, since the creatures from whom we are thus separated and who hurl themselves recklessly toward victory or defeat are not conventional mannequins—vague reflections of ourselves or effigies reduced to a substanceless geometry—but creatures like us, of at least equal density, who could be us.

Besides the Auteuil racecourse and the one at Longchamp, scarcely farther away from where we lived since it, too, was within the area of the Bois de Boulogne, and besides Enghien (which we were not familiar with but knew to be close to a casino where we were taken one evening for a performance by a professional singer, a relative of ours) there existed—and there still exist—other racetracks scattered through the environs of Paris: Le Tremblay (which I believe was not long ago known for its "heavy ground" and whose name recalls the noise of the field galloping on wet earth), Maisons-Laffitte (with the same name as a great vineyard, like Château-Margaux), Chantilly (the most aristocratic of all, even though its name made one think much sooner of lentils [*lentilles*] than of lace mantillas [*mantilles de dentelle*] or of whipped cream [*crème Chantilly*]), Vincennes (which was nothing to us, for we felt only disdain for trotting races, whether in harness or mounted). The race-courses to which race-goers went by railroad and not by piling into horse-drawn charabancs as one did for Auteuil or Longchamp were, for us, lost in an almost unreal distance; we had of them a knowledge that was only, so to speak, secondhand, through the newspapers that we examined, in the manner of true bettors, to establish our selections.

Reading fairly regularly *L'Echo des Courses, Auteuil-Longchamp,* and (sometimes) *La Veine,* we derived from them a documentation that became the basis of laborious calculations involving multiple factors, often difficult to evaluate, both in themselves and as to their relative importance: the weight—or rather, load—of the horses (the top-weight,* in other words the most heavily loaded, posing a delicate problem since his present disadvantage resulted precisely from the fact that his past record had demonstrated his superiority); earlier performances by each, from which one deduced that a certain horse would "strike out" a certain other horse (by means of a long series of operations allowing one to evaluate the merits of the competitors by taking, if one could, other horses against whom they had already run as standards of measure which were themselves subjected to a similar system of evaluations); the state of the ground (considered to be better or more poorly adapted to the abilities of a certain horse); pedigrees; the reputation of the owners and trainers; the quality of the jockeys, their spot in the "general ratings" and with respect to the "percentage" of winning mounts in the total number of mounts (a criterion we preferred because it was less crudely quantitative than the rating according to the gross number of victories), the good or bad form of said jockeys added to the risky notion of "deviation" (that is, the number of consecutive defeats one of them might have just suffered, a greater deviation, in the case of a good jockey, allowing one to think that his period of bad luck would soon end); the predictions of certain newspapers that had shown themselves to be particularly shrewd on this subject, even though they were not exclusively devoted to it.

For my brother and me, there was no question of confirming, by even a fictional bet, the predictions resulting from this work we did together, with a disinterest and a seriousness close to those of chess players or researchers seeking in their laboratories the solution to difficult scientific problems. If we were ambitious for success (touchstone of our abilities as bettors) it was simply for the honor of it, and it seems to me, at this distance, that, because of our very innocence, we were perhaps apt to choose winners more often than other people. We ignored, it is true, the trifling small fry, the handicaps and the "selling races," competitions of rank outsiders that their owners want to get rid of, and we only concerned ourselves with the important races, in which the contest was more or less circumscribed, between known horses, and, because of this, measurable with a smaller margin of uncertainty despite the inevitability of the unforeseen. It is also true that, given the fact that our game cost nothing, we did not have to ignore a favorite and support an outsider in the hope of cashing in on long odds and did not make use of any system, such as the "martingale," relying almost exclusively, in deciding which of the various competitors would triumph, on the research we had carried out with such patience and methodical rigor.

During this whole period in which we were so passionate about racing, my brother and I easily imagined that when we were older, we would become jockeys—just as so many boys from the poorer sections of town may dream of becoming racing cyclists or boxers. Like the founder of a religion, like a great revolutionary or a great conqueror, a champion seems to have a destiny, and this vertiginous rise of someone who is, often, a product of a most underprivileged sector of the population, is the sign of an exceptional fortune— or magic force—that allows him to pass all stages in a single bound and attain a social rank that is, of course, somewhat marginal, but out of proportion to anything an ordinary man can reasonably expect, as assured as he may be of the advantages of his birth. In certain respects, the champion is reminiscent of the magician and, very specifically, the shaman of societies conventionally described as primitive, a figure who also quite often starts out as no more than an underprivileged person but takes a brilliant revenge on destiny in the fact that he alone, to the exclusion of everyone else, is in league with the spirits.

No doubt my brother and I sensed this confusedly when we imagined ourselves clothed in those jackets that were like some sort of armorial bearing or liturgical vestment, distinguishing us from everyone else but at the same time uniting us with everyone else, since we would become the target, the vehicle for a certain collective effervescence, the convergence point and the receptacle for those gazes fixed on our persons as so many pins to which to attach prestige. More effectively that the top hat, the cylinder revolver, the purse full of gold, or any other symbol of the father's authority, these thin silk tunics would have signaled our power, our *mana,* as people who caused all obstacles to pass under the bellies of their horses and exposed themselves triumphantly to the dangers of falling. Time passing and my ambitions becoming less lofty, perhaps it is a distant glimmer of those jackets that still attracts me in the names of certain cloths for suits or overcoats: *shetland,** *worsted,** *covercoat** [covert coating], *tweed** (whose first name is "Harris" and not necessarily "Irish," as I thought for a long time), *chalk striped** (or *rayé de craie*), *sharkskin** (or *peau de requin*)?

Next to the *Tablettes sportives*—more modest in their presentation—there were, in the cupboard where we put our books, a number of those volumes with gilt edges and percale binding which, though children don't always find them very entertaining, are at least an ornament to their libraries (in this respect not at all different from the libraries of many adults, who see books as a form of window dressing rather than instruments for reading). Among these works for children was one that fermented my imagination to the point that I began writing a theater adaptation of it. As I knew scarcely any other aspect of the theater, this quite naturally took the form of an opera libretto: *"Violà Partner, Ce n'est Fend-l'Air"* [here's partner, he's not air-cleaver] was more or less the text of a song that, in the epic mode, brought face-to-face two thoroughbred rivals. In a Louis XV frame, *Le petit jockey du duc de Lauzun* presented my brother and me with the example of a boy from across the Channel who displayed both the greatest sporting spirit and the most moving devotion to his French master. After the latter made a bet with one Count or Marquis de Conflans, the jockey had to foil the maneuvers of a wicked lackey named Laurent (devoted servant of the opposing party) in order to bring back from England the famous crack horse Partner, which, after a series of adventures, he would ride to victory somewhere in the neighborhood of Chaillot or Passy. Like Chérubin [adolescent character in Beaumarchais's *Marriage of Figaro*], little Bob wore a powdered wig tied in back with a ribbon; but no tricornered hat on top of it: a hemispherical black skull-cap like a jockey's or huntsman's cap, and his calves barded with riding boots instead of the rakish silk stockings of high-heeled fancy dress. Did the story continue with something about imprisonment or some scenes depicting a revolution? Upon reflection, I don't think so; but it seems to me that one saw that great rogue Laurent roughed up, even copiously thrashed, by the members of another set of servants, as punishment for his misdeeds.

The substitution of an old nag for the marvelous horse Partner. Was it Laurent who, on the boat sailing toward France or (more likely) on a stagecoach overland, disguised some hack as the precious animal so as to leave the abduction of the latter undiscovered for a time? Or was it Bob who made use of this subterfuge to deflect the machinations of his sworn enemy onto some other beast which the scoundrel would kidnap—or drug—in place of the amazing quadruped? Whatever the reasons were and in the secrecy of whatever night this took place, one horse was disguised as another by having the color of his coat changed with a few strokes of paint, a comedy of errors the uncertain episodes of which ended with the hero scoring a point and the traitor abashed, his contemptible wiliness ineffectual against the intelligent honesty of his young adversary. Loyal like Mme de Pompadour's little Negro or the mameluke Roustan so dear to Napoleon, brave and noble Bob will have gotten his master, that hothead, out of a truly awkward situation when the author of the book feels the time has come to put an end to his tribulations.

The probity, the acumen, the seriousness displayed by the duc de Lauzun's little jockey were the same qualities that we attributed to the jockeys we admired. Not only is the greatest jockey the best horseman (which one can judge by the easy manner in which he sits his horse), but he is the one who "doesn't live it up," the one who submits best to the strict diet dictated by the necessity of making weight, the one who never violates the harsh discipline of training; and these ascetic qualities go hand in hand with qualities as moral as intellectual: the great jockey doesn't cheat, doesn't fraudulently "haul in" his horse instead of giving him every chance; he is a good tactician also, preferring the "waiting race" to the "leading race" and knowing how to husband the strength of his mount in order to send it forward at the right moment in an irresistible burst of speed.

That a horse sets the pace from start to finish doesn't happen often and is, in any case, not at all desirable for the interest of the race: the great pleasure is not to see one of the competitors relentlessly dominate the rest of the bunch but to see him improve his position and overtake the others one by one, sometimes easily, sometimes with difficulty, one's joy reaching its height if he has stayed at the back for a long time and, fully urged on by his rider, who brings spurs and whip into action, comes up to beat, almost at the post, an adversary who seemed already to have won the race; a neck, a head, even a short head will be all the latecomer will win by, as though his jockey had calculated down to a fraction of a second and a few centimeters the effectiveness of his move.

The horse who leaps out ahead, or the *comingman** (as fans of cycling like to call him) preparing to outclass his elders and already causing them some uneasiness. Like the challenger* with respect to the champion, the comingman is a younger son who burns to take the place of his older brothers. Of a man like this, not yet established and young enough not to have to spare himself, one knows that he plays a straight game and (like the *novillero* who, in order to attract attention, takes risks he will not take when he is a recognized matador) always gives all he has; also, mingled with the impassioned attention attracted by his meteoric rise, there is a kind of love: wonder at the spectacle of such a promising youth, sympathy toward someone whose ways of behaving are still without cunning, a feeling of complicity with the person whom one expects to see topple some firmly founded reputations from their pedestals.

Though he had gone far beyond the stage where one is merely a hopeful prospect and was numbered, as a steeplechasing jockey, among the finest whips, for a long time René Sauval—son of a butcher from la Villette—was the object of a veritable devotion on the part of my brother and me. During an entire year we expected him, who was second (and very precisely because he was second), to replace Georges Parfrement at the top of the general rating and thus take the lead from an individual we detested, resenting him for the fact that he was the only one in their area of expertise to have won more races than Sauval, also that he was older and occupied the top place unfairly since Sauval, claiming a lesser number of victories but riding less often, had a percentage that we judged to be more creditable than his. The fact of seeing him comfortably installed in his fame was at the root of our animosity toward Georges Parfrement: if we sympathized to such a degree with René Sauval, it was because he represented a threat to that successful man. I don't think I'm responding to a very different impulse nowadays when I sympathize with the oppressed classes, who are in the position of challenger with respect to the dominant classes, and when I prefer, to the great, long since recognized talent, the writer or artist rejected by his society who—having died too early to know a victory he did not even necessarily aspire to—runs, on the scale of the centuries, a waiting race.

In addition to the jackets, sometimes of a single color (only the cap being different), sometimes of two colors (juxtaposed in stripes, circles, squares, or one being belt, scarf, sleeves, or spots standing out against the other color) there were, not only the white of the breeches and the black boots with yellow tops, but the horses' coats. No spectacle of greater sumptuousness than the passing of these fields of horses, compact or strung out, on tracks of a green, it would seem, no meadow ever attained. And I truly believe that no court costume or soldier's uniform (with aiguillettes, frogs and loops, kalpak, dolman, epaulettes, stars, braid, gorget, facings, pipings, sabretache, shako, shapska) could compare, in our eyes, to these thin uniforms, so dazzling and with such a very modern appearance.

A certain taste for the epic—nourished by reading Géneral Marbot's *Mémoires*—induced us, certainly, to regard the jockeys' exploits as feats of arms, of a sort; in the stories we told each other, it often happened that our animal heroes, before winning renown as warriors or heads of state, were eminent jockeys or aviators during a preliminary period in which they proved themselves, not unlike what we read, in accounts of their "childhoods," of the characters of chivalric romances. When, after having been unable to do more than sketch out a few crude drawings (such as *"Drogant, roi des lapins, en tenue de campagne et de revue"* [Drogant, king of the rabbits, in country dress and review dress], an amply decorated animal, named thus because of the page Drogan, female role in the operetta *Geneviève de Brabant,* which my sister had told to me), I began scribbling in notebooks, where I set down the life stories of Bob Singecop, Chienchien, Moutonnet, and other amazing mammals, I drew them in ink and colored pencil, sometimes depicting them as they accomplished a brilliant action (capturing a flag or carrying a message across enemy lines) and sometimes as they ran in a great race.

It seemed natural to me that a champion should be equipped with all the military and civic virtues, and it was also part of his function to be—after the fashion of men like Ader (with his bat airplane on view at the Conservatoire des Arts et Métiers) or Santos-Dumont (with his "Demoiselle" or "Libellule," tried out, I believe, at Bagatelle)—an inventor capable of constructing machines like the *tricycle-bird-engine* and the *sliding lightning-conductor* just as we ourselves were also capable of having our little inventions: *automobile-chairs* in the rue Michel-Ange consisting of dining-room chairs which we laid flat on the floor and climbed upon, sending them forward by means of jolts imparted by the action of our feet resting on the uprights of the chair back and of our hands clutching the two horizontal bars which were the forward legs of the chair thus lying on its back; Viroflay automobiles made of old packing cases painted with Ripolin enamel paint (and one in yellow and red, like the Spanish flag), the whole thing carried by two old pairs of wheels; an ironing board which, in the same house, we slid noisily down the steps of the inside staircase, when we wanted to play shipwreck. Unlike the superman of today's American *comics,** the heroes of the childish mythology with which I covered the pages of several notebooks were not demigods and even less all-around athletes: neither the greatest, nor the most vigorous, they were simply courageous, loyal, intelligent, skillful, and by virtue of these advantages, not so much of body as of heart and mind, they managed to triumph in every-thing they undertook. Their primary quality, however, the one that for me had almost the meaning of a test, was a love and a knowledge of the sport of racing, as though their ardor and mastery in this privileged domain were the surest sign of their merit.

To accord so much importance to the masterly exercise of a certain form of horsemanship is not in itself apt to be surprising: experts in physical edu-cation and military preparation are forever expatiating about the benefits of bodily training, a promise of good health and asceticism indispensable to the formation of character; furthermore, an abundant literature presents athleti-cism as a schooling of energy and the practice of team games as developing a sense of solidarity, a sense of self-effacement before a common interest, in other words: a spirit of sacrifice. It is nonetheless true that my choice of the jockey as prototype of the individual whom sports turns into an accom-plished man may seem amusing: there is no question of self-forgetfulness with horse races, where the competition is essentially of an individual order, and it is, in addition, imprudent to expect of someone whose profession con-sists of riding thoroughbreds that he remain alien to all schemes involving money, since the pari-mutuel is the very basis of horse racing. There was cer-tainly a good deal of childishness in my devout attitude toward the jockeys, as well as the need to find a moral justification for what captivated me, un-less, much more simply, I immediately regarded as a representation of the Good whatever I found captivating.

"Celebration of courage," "celebration of the stout-hearted": it is thus that the toreador in *Carmen*—the one who, we are told, will soon achieve "the glory of men like Montès and Pepe Hillo"—sings the corrida, in his famous great aria. Even though horse races are not fights but "races" in the ordinary sense of the term and one can't speak of "struggles" in connection with them except in a metaphorical sense, it was with expressions of this sort that I my-self could have sung of feats of horse riding, particularly those that occurred in the steeplechases, trials that seemed to demand of the horsemen more vir-ile ability than was required by the flat races. In the latter, there were no hard obstacles such as the one represented, at Auteuil, for example, by the water jump next to the stands near which, when we chanced to go to the "public enclosure," we liked to position ourselves in order to delight in the spectacle of the horses clearing the tall, thick hedge and then the very broad stream beyond which it was uncertain, for each of the jumpers, whether he would land on terra firma again. Experience, however, showed us that despite the risks inherent in these thrilling circuits our predictions were more likely to be confirmed when they bore on obstacle races and we deduced from this that unlike those run, as at Longchamp, on a level track, they were more or less free from the perfidies that so often render the wisdom of the bettors ineffectual.

The slender, closely shaved gnomes leaning over their horses' necks did not all, therefore, impress us to the same degree: our preference was for the steeplechasing jockeys because the steeplechases seemed to us not only more moving and more spectacular, but characterized by a greater morality; certainly, also, because it was easier to construct a heroic myth about men who jumped streams, gates, and hedges, whose collarbones were often broken, or who even suffered the same fate as the jockey Boon, who died of a skull fracture after he fell at the last hedge during the last race of the day (and perhaps of the season) as he was riding for the last time, being about to retire. However, this preference was not entirely undiscriminating: I have mentioned the detestation we felt for Georges Parfrement (a detestation similar to that which one feels, in school, for the class grind, and so wholehearted that we booed him one day as we watched him return to the weighing-in after a fall, bareheaded and hobbling); as for most of his colleagues, we were definitely indifferent to them, the existence of these supernumeraries confined to names we had read—unconnected with any anecdote—the only ones conferring any substance on their bearers being those which, possessing a strong British flavor, struck us as exotic; on the other hand, certain experts in flat racing were endowed, in our eyes, for obscure reasons I will not even try to fathom, with considerable prestige (Maurice Barat, for example, who raced in the colors of the Baron de Rothschild and whom, later, during the 1914–18 war, I was proud to rub elbows with in a small bar in the rue d'Antin also frequented by the former boxing champion Marcel Moreau and the great ace Navarre shortly before the latter's career ended suddenly with his famous automobile run through the streets of Paris, going full speed and trying to crush policemen even on the sidewalks). Finally, those of the steeplechasing jockeys whom we held to be the greatest scarcely appeared to us otherwise than embellished with a halo of saintliness: boldness, self-control joined with a perfect simplicity of manners, a sporting spirit implying a hatred of fraud and a good camaraderie, these were the exemplary qualities we recognized in them. I tend nowadays to attribute similar virtues—moral in the highest sense—to everyone I admire, particularly to men I regard as "authentic" poets or artists. But I definitely think that, now as in earlier times, it is not to a Good such as that preached in catechism and other edifying books that I attach these virtues; esteeming them to the degree that they are associated with activities that captivate me and are the product of persons in themselves fascinating—either in boots and jackets or without any special attributes—I don't treat them as moral virtues properly speaking but, much more, as proof that the true summits have been attained and that one can allow oneself to be dazzled without compunction, as guarantee that this is in fact the most accomplished art (since it is not sophisticated), as the signature, in sum, apposed to a work of very great style. If, in place of the "great jockey"—at once the most conscientious, the most intelligent, and the one able to win his races in the most beautiful manner—I have come to revere the "genius," creator of enchantments and complete man, of whom it is difficult to admit that he is not the best and the most perspicacious, whatever his faults and his mistakes may really be, the distance I have gone in passing from one to the other of these personages is not very great: of course there is little relation between their activities, but in my eyes they cut the same figure, the second differing from the first only because he presents himself in a more nuanced form and not with the summary distinctness habitual to epic heroes.

Having formed for ourselves a pantheon of jockeys—Sauval, Alec Carter (of whom, once the war came, we learned with interest that he was mobilized in an artillery regiment), W. Head, Lancaster, Barat, and perhaps two or three others, a sort of central system around which gravitated less important stars —we were quite naturally led, my brother and I, to identify ourselves in our games, even in our daily life, with certain of these horsemen, who seemed to us to represent such a brilliant segment of humanity. It fell to my brother and the boys older than I who shared our pastimes to play the roles of the stars of the first magnitude; I, younger than they, had to be more modest and played the part, most often, of characters less conspicuous or almost beginners, without its even occurring to me to dispute my elders' monopoly. Nash Turner, a jockey already on his way downhill who generally rode in flat races but sometimes also in steeplechases (a fact which made him, despite his small number of rides and, consequently, victories, a sort of all-around jockey), had a surprising first name—that "Nash," so close to "Nat" of *Nat Pinkerton,* the famous American detective, but as though crushed, finally, like a curse which one secretly champs down on without letting it spring from one's mouth; these were the two reasons why, during a certain period, it was Nash Turner's cast-off clothing I liked to put on. As for George Mitchell, who was then beginning to become known as a steeplechasing jockey, he was distinguished by a patronymic more or less identical to my own first name; he was a young jockey and this, joined to the resemblance between the names, created the conditions favorable for an identification whose reasonableness seemed to us beyond question and which, in fact, was more consistent and more enduring than the preceding one.

Thus abandoning the great leading parts to the older boys and lending myself to this abandonment with good grace, for want of assertive spirit or, perhaps, because it confirmed my status as the younger boy, which was satisfying for me because the more a child one is the fewer responsibilities one has and the wider margin one feels between oneself and the man one will certainly have to become someday—an enviable position, however avid one may be to see oneself taken seriously and however impatient to enjoy certain of the prerogatives that belong to adults—I very early became accustomed, not to contenting myself with playing a walk-on part (too humiliating a situation), but to striving for no more than the role of *second.*

An emperor is "more" than a king (and this is why, for a time, I was an imperialist), a major general "more" than a brigadier, a count "more" than a viscount. Like most children—and like too many grownups—I attached an extreme importance to hierarchy, whether of a military, political, or social order.

Well before I played at entering the skin of one of the jockeys I ranked immediately below the greatest, I amused myself—like all boys—with games of mock battles, and it was agreed that I had the rank of commander in chief, one of my brothers or other partners occupying the more elevated position of President of the Republic or Minister of War. For nothing in the world would I have wished to be a simple soldier, and one of the forms of teasing that I resented most keenly, of all those of which I was a victim on the part of the older boys, consisted in "reducing me to the ranks": to imagine myself in the posture of a man whose stripes are torn off, then his buttons, previously unstitched and now holding only by a thread, to find myself stripped of my dignity as commander of armies by those whose complicity was indispensable if I was to believe myself invested with such a function, made me cry and dance with rage. Apart from these instances of bullying, it was understood, once and for all, that I was neither a president nor a minister, but that the rank of commander in chief was the one that fell to me by all rights; entirely satisfied by this rank, I regarded as normal the fact that the highest positions remained inaccessible to me.

The challenger rather than the champion, the unacknowledged talent rather than the well-established fame, the pupil of great ability rather than the head of the class, the right-hand man without whom the leader would be lost rather than that leader himself: a preference, in sum, for the individual who (whether still a beginner or too little concerned with honors, even too nonchalant) does not occupy the place he deserves or for the distinguished figure situated in a high rank but some distance from the top. It is tempting to see this preference as a sign—or a prefiguration—of a romantic scorn for what the bourgeois regard as a crowning achievement; doesn't it seem, in fact, to be the logical counterpart of a repugnance for what is finished, perfect, as closed as an egg or as closed as a life to which death has come and apposed its initials (a thing now given, forever defined, and to which nothing can be added, from which nothing can be taken away)? But such an interpretation of oneself by oneself, which urges romanticism, has some likelihood of being tainted by it: no one can flatter himself (even in his innermost being) that he is a romantic without his assertion—containing the avowal of a tendency to idealize—becoming suspect to him as long as he is willing to reflect on it in good faith. If I am to explain this repugnance I believed I detected in myself, wouldn't it be better, therefore—dismissing at least temporarily any idea of implicit revolt against common ambitions and admitting the possibility of a more prosaic interpretation—to try to discover what part might have been played (here as in many other areas) by weakness pure and simple?

To prefer the person who is not yet, or is not altogether, to the person who is, may signify that—where oneself is concerned—one would rather not take a certain step so as to keep a reserve in front of one, for after the finishing line one would thus have crossed, life would be played out and death would become the only place one could henceforth come to rest; it may signify, on the level of a child's life, that one resists entering the category already occupied by one's elders because it contains greater perils of all sorts and because once there, one will no longer be able to count on the same indulgence nor employ, as a shield, the right of the smallest to be protected or, at the very least, spared; it may signify, lastly, that, without seeking to struggle, one resigns oneself to being a mere underling and that if one admires the challenger—far from seeing him as someone who resembles one—it is much less because he is a man still in a subordinate position than because of the courage he has (but which one does not have oneself) to attack the strongest.

A certain need to feel protected, to put myself under some wing is probably one of my most consistent traits. If I have so often aspired, in various forms, to be *second*—in the sense of the one who comes immediately after the first and in the sense of the one who seconds—the reason for this can't be merely that I have too wretched an idea of myself to bid for first place in any area whatsoever, the second therefore becoming the most brilliant that I can, if really necessary, apply for; if I show a moderation on this subject that may certainly be relative but is hardly in keeping with the very high value I set upon prestige, it also seems to me that (until further investigation) there is no need to question a lack of energy so complete that I would limit my ambitions in advance—with a sort of wisdom or, rather, tepidity—to the pursuit of goals felt to be not absolutely beyond my reach with some help from chance and capable of being attained without my confronting any insurmountable danger or imposing on myself a quantity of difficulties that would make my undertaking, if not the quest for a chimera, at least a heroic labor. Without proof to the contrary, it seems to me inconceivable to explain solely by these negative reasons my lack of excess in aspirations which belong to the domain of childish dreams and ought as a consequence to testify to a smaller concern for their capacity to be realized practically; I am convinced that my dream would, quite properly, have known no boundaries if proper limits had not been assigned to it from the beginning by a positive factor.

The desire that a margin be retained and the comfort I feel if someone whom I situate above me is willing to trust me are illustrated by two facts which I noted long ago on the slips of paper that are like official records of the observations or experiences I'm comparing here in order to derive from them laws from which there will in the end emerge—unless I pack it all in, exasperated by so many procedures, counterprocedures, detours, returns, and standstills—the golden rule I should choose (or should have chosen) to preside over my game. The hatred that I have now for the very finest hotels, those that in the language of tourist guides and printed advertisements are known as "luxury hotels"; the pleasure I took, after hearing Offenbach's comic opera when I was twelve or so, in identifying with Nicklausse, Hoffmann's faithful friend and confidant, instead of with Jules Barbier's actual hero (Barbier being the librettist responsible, in whole or in part, for the texts of many of those lyric operas that were as instructive for me as the Bible stories were for others)—these are the two facts that seemed to me, on a certain day in the past which I can't remember now, worthy of being captured and which today I must examine in order to find, in them, both a usable meaning and a shared characteristic.

The luxury hotel is what is called a *palace,* reserved in principle for a rich clientele. Even if it is in good taste and nothing in its decor strives exaggeratedly after an effect, it exudes money and security. To live there means that one represents monetarily le *"dessus du panier"* [the pick of the basket, the cream of the crop], that one ranks oneself in a class of pretentious people whose code one must clearly adopt (if only in appearance) and its argot too, if necessary, during the time, at least, of this residence. I am, it goes without saying, nowhere near being an ascetic disdainful of his comforts, but the fact is that I've never felt really easy in any of these arrogant structures, so vast that one is lost in them and with amenities so perfected that the very absence of defects is a defect, because it provokes a feeling of disturbance, as do the overly groomed appearance, the overly polished language, and the too meticulously refined manners in an individual with whom circumstance would make it desirable to have a little human contact. In these hotels, where the staff and the packaging are equally terribly impeccable, I confess also that I am prey to an anguish stemming from my timidity: it seems to me—a worry well known to those whose skin is never washed of the bad opinion they have of themselves—that I am being watched from all sides and that not only the living eyes but even the walls are prepared to register each of my possible blunders. I am at once unhappy about publicly classifying myself among the privileged (something I am ashamed of vis-à-vis the plebs outside) and (with respect to the patricians inside) unhappy to expose myself to the possible scorn of these same privileged people or to the scorn of their henchmen, the overly well schooled servants. If I prefer good hotels to those of too grandiose a category—except when the latter are completely outmoded and derive from that a charm comparable to the charm of a beach or resort out of season —it is, therefore, not so much in order to reserve a margin for myself with respect to the future (to be able to say to myself that perhaps some day I will be in a position to stay at a princely establishment, a possibility of later promotion thus being open to me) but is, rather, if indeed there is any opening at all, because I need to have available to me a margin of another kind: the kind that allows one some elbow room and which is very precisely the margin of imperfection thanks to which things, both living and livable, have a healthier flavor and can be tasted without any constraint with relation to anyone at all. Naturally I have a lively desire to accede to the enjoyment of what seems to me perfect, but I am afraid of it too: perfect spells finished, which means without hope, and it is true, especially, that in the midst of perfection—in dealings with "perfect" people—what nonetheless separates us from them in such diverse ways (as we scorn them for a self-importance that is proof of stupidity and they reciprocate this scorn on a different level) can only be experienced with an irony of which—discovering that we are sensitive to the scorn of people we scorn and, because of this, scorning ourselves—we are the first object.

In the same class as these luxury hotels there are yet other things that too clearly constitute outer signs of wealth not to be undesirable: the great restaurant where one goes quite expressly to have a good dinner (such as the one with the sign of a seaman, La Pérouse, situated almost directly underneath where I live, a restaurant in which I have never set foot except once twenty years ago, at the time of the marriage of the daughter of my pseudosister, today retired to Nemours); any sort of gala (whether employing the pretext of charity or without any clearly determined aim); first class in a railway train (whereas one of the reasons I appreciate the airplane, besides its speed and the fact that one doesn't get filthy on it, is its nature as means of transport with a single class); luggage too numerous, too elegant, and too heavy (which, as you get onto a train as well as off one, turns you into a sort of invalid who can't manage without porters); excessively new apartments arranged by an interior decorator or excessively beautiful dwellings provided with collectors' furniture and piles of artwork; evening dress (which people now say is "recommended" or sometimes, still, "required" and which, at least in France, has assumed the absurd appearance of ceremonial dress rather than being something taken for granted when going out for the evening); sumptuously bound books or editions on "large paper" (which I leave to the bibliophiles, for though I am maniacal about my books, I prize them only as a function of their printed content and place very little importance on their published form, as container); women as well as men who are too rinsed, pumiced, and ascepticized (for an excessively meticulous cleanliness gives me an unhealthy impression of a pharmacy). In the opposite direction, however: theater seats (which I always want to be the best); seats for corridas (which I would like to be in the first row); spirits (unacceptable, in my opinion, if they are not choice brands or of "genuine" provenance, even though in practice I am not so particular and have, moreover, never been a connoisseur on that subject, even during the period when hard liquor and aperitifs were not forbidden to me); trifling, serviceable objects such as fountain pens and cigarette lighters (which I feel must be made by the best-known companies). Here, then—and without much searching—is an appreciable number of illustrations, but also exceptions, to the rule that I had already gone more than halfway to laying down! Quite a capricious rule, and one that no doubt expresses, more than any other truth, the fact that it is the rule with me to try to justify caprice by turning certain of its chance products into the paradigm of a rule.

Now, just what is this Nicklausse, whom the librettist and the composer of *Tales of Hoffmann* made an indispensable element of their work even though he is a character of only secondary importance?

It must be pointed out first of all that the role of Nicklausse—vocally, a mezzo-soprano—is sung by a female singer in male clothing portraying a very young man: a figure who belongs entirely to neither of the two sexes, and whose youth is accentuated by its femininity. Ten or twelve years old when I saw this performance at the Opéra Comique, I probably felt closer to a crea-ture of indeterminate age and sex than to the other protagonists, who are completely defined men or women (despite the fantastic nature of some of them) and who would not be induced by any charming condescension to lower themselves to our level, as does that female singer, who even wears knee breeches so as to look more like us and separate herself from the other actors by this particular disguise, just as children everywhere are different from grownups. A woman belonging to the theater, and consequently to the realm of fiction, who is not—like so many of her kind—a mother or a magician but rather a big sister, quite within our reach, and who has put on a boy's cos-tume expressly to join with us in forming a separate group and become a comrade.

Was my age at that time (quite close to what they call the critical period) the essential cause of the attraction I felt to this equivocal character, who was in no way differentiated—if one thinks only of the fact that she is a woman playing the part of a man—from many other characters in the operas or comic operas I had already seen performed: Romeo's page in *Romeo and Juli-et*, a role sung by a woman with legs sheathed in tights, and also, in *Faust*, the role of Siebel, Marguerite's young lover? It is possible, no doubt, that at the time when I discovered *Tales of Hoffmann,* I was more sensitive than at the time of Siebel and Romeo's page to what is exhilarating about a woman dressed as a man. In particular, I recall that at about the same time I was half in love with a Jewish girl who had played the part of the young vagabond in Coppée's *Le Passant* for an audition with my piano teacher; I was delighted to see disguised as a Renaissance page this rather pretty girl with her somewhat Chinese look whom I had always seen in a dress and who was the very active older sister of a sickly boy with whom I went to school and had good relations. But it is equally possible that because of its very nature the Hoffmannesque transvestite offered something more stimulating than other transvestites: the narrator's companions are young German students of the romantic era and could easily be our contemporaries; isn't it the case that a woman wearing a suit and elegant boots—which was how the woman portraying Nicklausse appeared, as far as I can remember—imposes her singularity more vigorously than the woman relegated by her archaic disguise as page or scholar to a rather colorless distance?

Going beyond his physical appearance, all the way to his soul, I find traits in Nicklausse that seem to me to explain why I attached myself to him much more than to the other theatrical figures portrayed by women in men's dress: Nicklausse is not only the hero's lieutenant and vigilant guardian but the one who solves the riddle that three apparently unrelated tales have posed. This double, who follows Hoffmann in all his adventures and declares himself his "mentor" (because he seeks—in vain, what is more, and without any great faith—to conceal with his own good sense the vagaries of an imagination too quick to go astray), is the one, in effect, to provide the key phrase by which the action is explained and reveals its unity—that reply which I had forgotten was put in Nicklausse's mouth but which I have rediscovered, in its exact wording, in a score of *Tales of Hoffmann* in the possession of my sister at Saint-Pierre-lez-Nemours where I am currently convalescing (after an attack of jaundice which for a while changed me into a Mongol, into a yogi emaciated by his visceral gymnastics or an inveterate smoker of opium, to my amusement and that of a few friends attentive to a metamorphosis whose progress, stagnation, or recession they confirmed at each of their visits):

> Je comprends! . . . Trois drames dans un drame:
> Olympia, Antonia, Giulietta
> ne sont qu'une même femme:
> La Stella!

> [I understand! . . . Three dramas in one:
> Olympia, Antonia, Giulietta
> are but a single woman:
> Stella!]

To the students who, drinking and smoking, have listened to the poet narrate the three love stories which, between prologue and epilogue, furnished the substance of the three acts—those of Olympia the tailor's dummy, Giulietta the courtesan, and Antonia the musician—Nicklausse, as the good disciple able to penetrate the master's most secret thoughts, hands over the key to the mystery: the three stories are actually one, and simply illustrate the various different seductions of the singer Stella.

The tavern setting on which *Tales of Hoffmann* opens and closes has only a faint relation, of course, to that of my "luxury hotels"; the central part of the action does indeed take place in Venice, in it we see gondolas, and a barcarolle is sung, but there is nothing touristic about it and I don't think it would be over that Venetian canal that I would be able—except in self-mockery—to cast a bridge. What must be examined in order to establish the connection is still the character Nicklausse and the exact manner in which he fulfills his duties as favorite companion and adjunct.

Nicklausse, realist though he may be, has no similarity to a thickset Sancho Panza and even less to a groveling Leporello. He is a levelheaded but lively and generous boy, quite capable of taking risks with no thought of danger. He lacks neither a sense of humor nor a sense of poetry and is certainly the most devoted to Hoffmann of all the members of the group at the same time as the one who best appreciates the extent of his genius. If in many instances he argues the part of reason and attempts to bring his friend back to a more accurate view of things, it is in order to prevent him from landing in a bad situation and not at all out of concern for his own safety. In richness of feeling and intellect he is scarcely inferior to Hoffman, when all is said and done, but he is more perspicacious and represents, in relation to him, the sage who endeavors to protect the madman from himself. Far from being a lukewarm sort of person, impervious to any enthusiasm, or a regular killjoy, he benefits from a wisdom that includes not only moderation but a faculty of understanding through which he can grasp the truth hidden behind the poet's divagation and reveal to the assembled uninitiated the bitter signification clothed in the seductive guises of the beautiful tales invented, with the help of the heat and flame of the punch, by the amazing drunkard.

The power of Nicklausse, golden-mouthed censor, confidant for good and bad days alike, initiate who hasn't tried to avoid any of the trials (not even God's rebuffs) and of whom one can believe that *nothing human is alien to him*. The power of the actress who portrays him, whose male dress charmed us and who—impulsively, like a good child, without arrogance or affectation—has made herself the embodiment of pure and intelligent friendship. The brotherly aspect of the character of Nicklausse, clearly belonging to this world and as comforting as a proffered hand, elf or imp whose lightness comes from the quickness of his blood and who is a son of the earth rather than a nebulous progeny of the clouds. The "easy as A-B-C" aspect that also distinguishes him, he who enlightens the others as though by an illumination taking the form of childish pranks, like the pupil who finishes his test well before the appointed hour and imparts to the rest of the class the answer to the problem, or like the player who—mute up to then—answers the riddle just when everyone is about to give up.

A boy at once easy to get along with, quick with his feelings, as he is with his perceptions, and whose support and advice are never wanting on any occasion—all this though he appears to be a scatterbrain and his actions aren't at all inhibited by the self-assurance of a mind that one may nevertheless assume to be suitably busy. A place that doesn't attract attention by its glittering or nobly austere facade, but where you feel comfortable because the things as well as the people there don't greet you as a stranger and, far from being correct to the point of becoming chilly, discreetly reveal themselves to be useful quite without any overly superior air as they are without any gloominess. The one characteristic proven, in the end, by my still-intact sympathy for Nicklausse and my disgust with overly sumptuous hotels is this: given, once and for all, that we must subscribe to the dictum according to which it is better to *be* than to *appear*, I have come to demand of objects as well as of people that they appear less in order to be more, and turn away from everything that presents itself in too solemn or too brilliant a guise, not only because too much of a glare always hurts one's eyes and association with someone who behaves like royalty or like a coquette is rarely cordial, but because very little appearance has become for me a proof of quality, an assurance, in any case, that my hopes will not be disappointed, that I haven't been cheated, and that the thing or person contemplated, like a machine with power in reserve, will certainly hold much more than the little—or the least—it promises.

How exciting it is, always, when the runner who, up to then, seemed too far behind ever to catch up, emerges victorious. Such a moment grips you because it is a revelation: the straggler who didn't seem to have anything going for him wins out over all the others, the hidden god appears in all the radiance of his strength, a moment comparable to the point when the masks come off, when the imposter steps forth abashed, and when the face of the world suddenly seems changed because one single thing has turned out to be the opposite of what one had thought. When I despise values flaunted with an excessive ostentation or values that have just now been acquired, is it perhaps because I would like to spare myself the possibility of a similar discovery? The lightning bolt of a naked breast jutting out from the horseman's costume in which the heiress has disguised herself, the stupefaction of the tramp who wakes up a king and—on a less strained level—the feeling you have of extraordinary luck when a coveted object, far from disappointing you when you enter into possession of it, turns out to be superior to what the logic of any sworn expert or accountant permitted you to suppose.

A sensational turn of events, in sum, for which the rest of the plot merely prepared the favorable conditions; an unveiling that is the veil's reason for existing, instead of being no more than its final negation; the raising—in a "transformation scene"—of a facade whose only virtue is to show up as unrefined the beauties that no matrix of this sort protected against prostitution. That a day will come when I, too, will sing my great aria, perform well, receive the ears and tail like the matador who, sword and little red flag in his hands, has just attained the highest peak—this is a vow that I often catch myself composing. My ambition, of course, remains contained within more or less reasonable limits (since the models I have chosen for myself for the general conduct of my life have never been the greatest), but there is an ulterior motive in this: with respect to the judgment that may be passed on me, it must be understood that I am not of so average a class as not to be in a position, at times, to equal—even surpass—the best; already, certain people, at least, necessarily suspect me of performing below my true capacity, for lack of doing my utmost, and are saying about me: "If only he took the trouble . . . "; the opinion of a single person, if need be, can suffice to make me content, if it is someone I place high enough to accord to his vote the value of a consecration and if I have not too illusory reasons for seeing it, not as a vaguely benevolent approbation, but as a sort of sponsorship.

I am therefore divided among several desires that seem at first sight to end in contradiction: the legitimate wish to situate myself in a high rank without, however, posing as a candidate for the highest (whether because I fear, in my eyes as in those of others, the absurdity of an ambition too visibly disproportionate, or whether the idea of being a man in a high position inspires me with a sincere repugnance); a more reckless pretension to being a person of whom those in the know, who can read between the lines and don't need anyone to dot their i's for them, expect a distinction that would be useless to hope for from the stars of the first magnitude; a childish wish to place myself under the aegis of a master of vast understanding, in whose eyes I would assume the position of the younger brother he should support, or the right arm on whom he could lean, or the favorite disciple, as Saint John was for Christ. What I would like, in other words, is to remain in the background while at the same time being virtually first and foremost—without fame but, for the shrewdest, crowned with laurels—consecrated, finally, by a man of genius to whom my enlightened devotion or my understanding, more penetrating than any other, would in return be precious. To be at once the scrupulous sort of person who sizes himself up without complacency and the forgotten one confident of an immanent justice, the modest creature and the proud one sure of his right to be less modest, the devoted follower and the vizier without whom the sultan's authority could not be asserted—this is my aim, in the end, and the resolution of that contradiction which is perhaps merely a mask with which I would like to disguise (the true incentive, then, being *duplicity* rather than *duality*) my version of playing it both ways at once: if my value is actually superior, people will appreciate it all the more because I have gone unrecognized and because there will be a false judgment to rectify; if it is with good reason that I make no claim to anything, people will at least have to acknowledge that I am someone who never overestimated his own importance and who thus displayed an unusual wisdom. However it turns out, by not drawing attention to myself and remaining curled up inside myself, I will have managed not only to escape the possibility of failure, but also to avoid compromising myself or laying myself open to the blows of fortune, as happens in our game of who-loses-wins to those who are too manifestly lucky. Deliberate calculation, inborn prudence, and an almost organic propensity to occupy (like a child buried in his mother's breast) only the modest compartment of an area completely my own join together, therefore, to temper my pride and discreetly determine its appearance, like the rider of a horse he has so well in hand that no uninitiated person would suspect that the mount was a bundle of nerves, capable of sending the horseman flying at any moment.

It would probably be better not to try to fathom which one predominates here—wisdom, superstitious fear, or a certain sybaritism disguised as indifference; if I keep to my role as a person determined above all not to deceive himself about what he is, then too rigorous a concern to measure each of these components of my behavior would risk conveying me into a speculative area where—as a matter of self-respect as much as intellectual scruple—the desire to conclude (and to find, if possible, an *elegant solution*) would take precedence over all other considerations, so that my thrust toward a greater exactitude would in the end work to the detriment of the truth. But, nevertheless, I feel discomfort and some regret at leaving this question hanging; it is irksome not to be thorough in an examination of conscience and I also don't tolerate very well the sense that I have left an unresolved problem behind me, once I decide to pose that problem myself: in domains that changed over time—childish brainteasers being gradually replaced by subtler puzzles —I have for a long time taken a keen pleasure in deciphering enigmas, and perhaps it is merely my laziness (implying a disgust for any effort not justified by the hope of a result of some importance) that has little by little deflected me from benevolently playing Oedipus as I did during the period when my brother and I were so passionate about small problems to be elucidated that we not only set about establishing predictions based on facts collected from the racing newspapers but together wrote, for our own use, a *Journal des Concours* entirely devoted to games imitating those that so many dailies, and so many periodicals for adults as well as magazines for children, offered their readers, in some corner where a "diversion" took the place of news, information, or literature of any kind whatsoever.

My brother and I, who have by now attained, even passed beyond, the stage of maturity and have more or less forgotten that there exists any difference in age between us, are separated by a gap of four years. When we amused ourselves with exercising our perspicacity—for love of the art—on useless objects and, in a parallel way, stubbornly sought the key to the great mysteries that present themselves to the curiosity of every child, this handicap of four years placed me on a level far below his; quite a long time before me, he had found out, for instance, that Father Christmas was only a fiction, but he was prudent enough not to let anyone know about his discovery, judging it wise to conceal from everyone (even from me, who played the role, with him, of confidant or coadjutor) the fact that he no longer believed in a fiction by virtue of which he received toys every twenty-fifth of December; by some means I don't know about, he had also penetrated a little family secret and discovered, without saying anything about this either, that the person we had been taught to call "sister"—so that it would be clearly understood that she had the same rights as we did to our parents' affection—was in reality only a first cousin being brought up with us; and lastly, he was enlightened earlier than I about part of the enigma of sex and had reached that first stage of knowledge which consists in being aware that a newborn child was formed in its mother's womb and that it is because of this that we have a navel.

The delight in entering, through successive unveilings, the reality of things. Conceived on the same principle as those books of plates in which, for teaching purposes, the external and internal anatomy of the human body is revealed, the thin advertising leaflets that we brought back from the first Salon de l'Automobile—the one in which was exhibited, still covered with dirt from its long trip, the car that had done the Paris-Peking rally—showed us, stripped bare in each of the series of colored and captioned diagrams, the structure of the vehicles manufactured by the De Dion-Bouton and Panhard-Levassor companies: body, chassis, engine and details of engine parts as well as of the transmission system, a collection of plans and overlays in superimposed layers, arranged in such a way that, flipping through the leaflet and going from the simple exterior view to a succession of views in section that were more and more limited and elaborate, you went farther forward at every page into the heart of the machine.

To study these leaflets and give yourself the illusion that you possessed a knowledge of mechanics almost equal to that of an engineer was only a game which you didn't give another thought to once the leaflets were closed again. With each page turned, there was certainly the joy of making a discovery and the pride of acquiring a few scraps of knowledge about how the car seats were upholstered, about the delicate assembling of the cogged parts that formed the differential, and about the functioning of the basic pieces of equipment, the magneto and the carburetor; but this was still a superficial pleasure; here were not the real problems, those whose progressive solution was indistinguishable from the motion of life itself, so that the boy who had advanced far enough in them gained the right to be described as a "man of the world."

At the time when I saw *Tales of Hoffmann,* with its three tales related to the romantic theme of the unhappy lover who drinks in order to forget and of the consoling Muse enveloped, as by incense, in the fumes of his drunkenness, three tales whose single, enigmatic pivot is much less the singer Stella than love seen as having a threefold aspect (as passionate fixation on what is only a

pure image such as Olympia the dummy, as alienation of self in carnal delirium as with Giulietta the thief of reflection, as erosion of one's being by an
exhausting exaltation of the feelings, as for Antonia who dies from her own
song), I am not sure what stage I had reached in that initiation whose end
may be considered as having been attained when, after much time and many
different adventures, one begins to perceive that it has no end and will only
be completed when one has experienced, not death, but decline and then de-
crepitude, which follow so closely upon one's period of ascendancy. I don't
know if the schoolmate who appointed himself my mentor during a good
part of these early years had yet taught me how one could transform into an
instrument of consuming bliss the organ hitherto exclusively employed in the
satisfaction of what in the language of children is called the *petits besoins* [*lit.,*
little needs; call of nature] and if this companion (the very same who, one day
when we were out walking, had defended me against our teasing fellow pupils
when they claimed, in a vexatious general outcry, that I had *"fait pipi dans ma
culotte"* [peed in my pants], whereas I had only splashed myself while wash-
ing my hands at a fountain or quenching my thirst)—I don't know if this
friend, more experienced and more diligent than I, had already taken it upon
himself to explain to me the mechanism of the act of love, in the guise of the
following apologue: a little boy and a little girl show each other their organs
and when the little girl asks him, "What's that?" the little boy says to her, "It's
a finger. And what's that?" to which the little girl answers, "It's an eye," and
the little boy concludes, "Hey, let's play put the finger in the eye!" Can I even
be sure that at the time when the transvestism of Nicklausse attracted me so
I really knew girls were different from boys other than that girls wore skirts
and their hair was longer? If I did know, it was only in a very theoretical way
(from having seen my little niece when she was being washed and dressed in
her baby clothes or, when I was taken to museums, from not having failed to
notice that the female figures did not have that appendage which, among the
men, was generally hidden under a grape leaf). At this uncertain stage, I was
not yet very far removed from the time when one of my most cherished desires—the first of this kind, perhaps, that I recall having experienced—was

to read the *"texte intégral"* [unabridged text] of the *Contes de Perrault* (reference to which I had seen in some bookstore advertisement) because I had
imagined that in this unexpurgated version I would have a chance to learn
something about how women became mothers.

Except for the great revelations about the body—the revelation of solitary
pleasure and then of the complete act of love—it is by scarcely perceptible
stages that one progresses in this kind of knowledge. What one knows does-
n't count for much compared to what one sees, and still less compared to
what one senses. To have *seen* this, to know how to *do* that—this is certainly
what matters, and more than in any other domain, here pure science takes a
backseat to applied science.

As we were still trying to find our way—our eyes covered as for a game of
blindman's buff—along the tortuous paths of theory, the discussions I had
with my brother every day were fueled for a while by the story of exploits attributed to a character of his invention: a little girl named, I think, Marcelle,
who was very sharp and whose usual jokes consisted either of pissing in front
of the boys or of showing them her split pantaloons (or her behind, for quite
often she walked around with her sex and buttocks naked under her skirt).
The stories about Marcelle—whom we discussed as though she were a real
person whom we knew—were a sort of password between us. At that time,
neither my brother nor I had ever held within the field of our vision the sex
of a pubescent girl or one approaching puberty any more than that of a young
lady or a woman; we viewed the imagined pranks of Marcelle with a mixture
of amusement, admiration, and sympathy, but I wouldn't venture to say that
we would have liked to have a kid of this sort within the circle of our friends
(though with her a working knowledge of a number of things would have
been so easy!) because the fact is that we were both quite shy children, preoccupied with love but having very innocent loves ourselves: little girls seen
from a distance or barely approached, such as the adolescent we fought over
in a spa in the Vosges, or those two sisters we said we were in love with during an earlier visit to a Flemish beach, my brother taking the older one and I
the younger, whom we had dubbed "Faust" because of a little toque she wore,

and of whom I recall only how, with her sister, she burst out laughing when she saw me come in last, by far, in a children's race organized on the occasion of some festival or other.

For my own part (and without my being able to remember whether my brother was with me when the thing took place), I recall with a certain distinctness the circumstances under which I saw, for the first time, a girl's sex worthy of being designated by a coarser word than the word *vulva* or any other more or less scientific term applicable to the organ by virtue of which a woman is what she is—the sex of a girl developed enough already for the question of decency or indecency to be brought up in connection with her and for the display of that part of her body which it would be unseemly to name, whatever name was used, to constitute a spectacle of a nature to disturb, if not the man I have become, at least the little boy I was then. This girl's sex—the first I saw that was charged with enough erotic potential for the word *cunt* to be able to be applied to it—appeared to me in the sun of a summer day, on a beach of fine sand swarming with people at bathing time. I can't say precisely whether this happened at Ramsgate, a very crowded beach in the county of Kent, or at Biarritz at the beginning of the 1914–18 war, when we ended up there as semirefugees, my favorite brother and I having left with our sister and her little girl at the beginning of the Germans' advance on Paris, then my mother coming to join us along with our older brother once the latter returned from England, where he had been staying for several months in order to practice his English. Chronologically, the vacation at Ramsgate (where I see myself in a Norfolk outfit with short trousers) is located approximately in the month of August 1913 and therefore predates by scarcely more than a year the withdrawal of our household (except for my father) toward the Spanish border, to the wealthy town where they bought me my first suit with long trousers; the possible error is not great, therefore (despite the step up where clothes are concerned), if it is the damp sand of Ramsgate rather than that of Biarritz which I choose retrospectively as pedestal for this vision; the reason for the choice is that something exotic, non-French—and more likely Anglo-Saxon than Iberian—remains attached to the vague image I have retained of the girl in question. She was a tall, thin little girl whose breasts had not yet budded and whose body was still hairless; standing in the water, which reached halfway up her legs at most, she had just been swimming or diving in the sea and the bathing suit she was wearing—white or some very light color—had become transparent; it seems to me that over her shoulders, a little hunched from apprehension about the onrush of the next foaming billow, fell her wet hair—skimpy hair, rather long, perhaps gathered into braids, but certainly not opulent. For the first time, therefore, I was seeing, practically nude, a girl who had to be about the same age as I (twelve or thirteen, depending on whether the setting of the story was Ramsgate or Biarritz) and who, though not yet nubile, had nevertheless reached a stage in her bodily development such that she could no longer show herself unblushingly in a state of nature. What probably surprised me the most, when I had the godsend of this spectacle, was that I wasn't at all excited. I gazed with curiosity at this sex, reduced to a simple cleft in an unattractive flesh about which nothing indicated womanliness except for that almost abstract split which presented itself to my eyes much less as an object of desire than as a strange thing, a thing whose outcropping into broad daylight seemed so unexpected and so obscene that—if it hadn't been for my contentment at *having seen*— what it would have aroused in me would have been disgust more than anything else. It is probable that if, in any circumstances whatsoever, my gaze could have rested on the nudity of a fully developed woman and if this woman had been in the least desirable, I would have felt the effect of her attractiveness and been engulfed in ecstasy and confusion; but I was at the time much too young, and too naive, to be in any condition to perceive the woman in the little girl and she herself, though already fairly tall, too visibly still under the age of puberty for the appearance of her sex through the wet web of the cloth to be more than merely incongruous. Clearly, anything that belongs to the domain of the erotic always has two sides to it: attraction soon changes to repulsion, fear is close to desire, and it is difficult to distinguish, among the mysteries of the body, those that rank as marvels from those that are merely ignominious (before I learned that the same gesture repeated a certain number of times in the proper rhythm could lead to the miracle of climax, it was with an admiration not unmixed with horror and disgust that I

had seen my brother cause the skin of his penis to slip down in such a way as
to uncover the glans, his virgin's unwashed glans, in order to show me that he
was ahead of me and now capable of "uncapping").

Beyond this darkness, sometimes diaphanous, sometimes muddy, which
we prospected eagerly, impatient to extract its essential wealth from it and little given to being squeamish about what we managed by chance to bring to
light, there was puberty, that is, the moment when we could regard ourselves
as virtually men and when (it seemed to us) our eyes would be totally opened,
like those of Adam and Eve after manducation of the apple. For the time being, there was only, for us—anxious for virility and for that premonitory
sign, the *mue,* which would deepen our voices after straining them oddly—
that innocuous thing they called "growth," which served our mother as the
explanation for so many of the little complaints that might chance to afflict
us: a little stiffness or headache, poor digestion, a slight rise in temperature—
venial ills for which growth was generally blamed.

Our heights measured with our backs to the wall and marked with a pencil line, exercises with barbells in the evening under our father's direction,
precautions against the "heat and cold," cod-liver oil, Manceau syrup, phytin
[a white, nearly tasteless powder used as a general stimulant]—all this, clear
as day and posing no problems, was associated with growth like the garden
that had been rented in the rue Jasmin so that we would get some fresh air
and like the gymnasium in the rue Pierre-Guérin. Personal observations of
and experiments on our own bodies, the race toward puberty, competitions as
to who would be the most completely a "man of the world"—all this, too,
concerned our physical beings and their development, but seen from a more
abstruse perspective, limited to what we only talked about to each other, what
did not even appear in the notebooks or on the isolated sheets of paper that
we covered with our handwriting or that we used for drawing. Contrary to
official knowledge, traditional knowledge admits of transmission only from
mouth to ear and we were, all in all, fully esoteric, expecting from puberty, as
from a philosopher's stone, our transmutation.

If every initiation is sanctioned by trials, I must acknowledge that the sessions in the gymnasium at 5 rue Pierre-Guérin as well as the ingestions of

cod-liver oil provided them for me in ample measure. I faced them in the most mediocre way, and it might be even better to say that I didn't face them at all. Would my instructors have had more success if it had occurred to them to represent these unpleasant events as formalities that no one could avoid if he wanted to become a *man* in the sense in which I understood it? I would hesitate to suggest this, so great was my disgust for cod-liver oil (which they made me take, I recall, from an egg cup with a closed bottom, of white china threaded with pink or blue, which disgusted me even more than drinking it from a spoon) and so strong was my horror for certain of the exercises one had to perform under the direction of the physical-education teachers.

The class, in the rue Pierre-Guérin, usually began with quite simple movements—as in Swedish gymnastics—movements I consented to with fairly good grace because they could be carried out without pain and, being executed firmly on one's feet without the use of any apparatus, did not give occasion for vertigo. This was the neutral part of the class, the part I would happily have seen prolonged but which, as I knew all too well from experience, would be brief. Next came exercises with barbells or Indian clubs which also had nothing fearful about them and were even rather amusing because it was pleasant to feel one's arms weighted and sometimes pulled along this way by what they were carrying as though beyond their own impetus. The work on the *parallel bars,* already more athletic but still almost at ground level, represented a way of putting oneself in motion that was without any viciousness and was so situated, in the organization of the classes, that much more terrible drills were generally excluded on the days when we did this one.

Aside from the gymnastics that used pieces of equipment and other controlled maneuvers in the course of which my perception of the void by which I was surrounded and the idea of a possible fall (even beyond the actual fear I had of breaking my neck) caused me a frightful anguish, the principal evil was what my brothers and I called the "Chinese torture," an exercise for making one's shoulders supple and developing one's thorax which was practiced on the *rib stall,* a series of horizontal bars attached to the wall one above the other, on which one placed oneself, back to the wall, holding on by one's hands and feet, in a position I can no longer reconstruct in detail but of which I recall that it was very painful, since one had to push one's shoulders as far back as possible, the teacher helping by pressing hard with both hands. In the blue-green light of the vast hall, with its glass roof, I'm sure my grimaces were scarcely less dreadful than those of a slave tied to a cross, when it was my turn to undergo the "Chinese torture."

With all my being I rejected the suffering I had to submit to, my back glued to the rib stall; but this rejection came to nothing: groaning or stoical, there we were, deprived of all help, without the means to steal away or even to cut it short.

No physical pain resulted from the exercises on the equipment and on those in which the question of vertigo came up; there I struggled only with shame and fear: fear of falling, shame over my awkwardness, shame over being afraid and yielding to that fear. To climb the pole or the knotted rope was nothing, either. The smooth rope demanded a greater effort but, clinging tightly with one's hands and legs, one felt passably safe, all the same. Negligible also was the *sliding board:* using either poles or ladders, one climbed up to the platform, then returned to the ground by hurling oneself, for a brief descent, onto a toboggan consisting of an inclined plane made of a broad waxed board; this was not supposed to be a feat of strength but a pure recreation alternating, from one class to the next, with the *giant stride* during which, clutching ropes that were attached, at the very top of the gymnasium, to a disk capable of rotating, and ended, at their base, in a sort of short ladder with three or four bars allowing one to hold on better, several of us at a time would turn round and round, running first then abandoning ourselves to the motion of the merry-go-round thus formed when the speed became sufficient so that, the centrifugal force exerting its effect and we, the satellites, tending to move away from our gravitational axis, the ropes were led to take a position closer to the horizontal and we—the satellites—to spin for a certain time without any possibility of contact with the ground. Things became more complicated, however, with the *estrade,* a sort of broad platform much higher than I was from which, one after the other, we were made to jump, at first forward, then backward (which, barring an accident, I could never bring myself to do, so much did my flesh creep at the sensation of the yawning emptiness behind me and the idea I had that I would not fail to bang my chin on the edge of the platform); worse, still, was the *trapeze,* nauseating with its pendulum movement that did not stop while you turned upside down, as they ordered you to do, so that for a moment your head was down and the slim cylindrical bar of wood on which your two hands were closed seemed to transmit all down your forearms the aerial uncertainty of the ropes. These latter two exercises perhaps offered the advantage over the "Chinese torture" that I could, to a certain extent, escape doing them (remaining inert and as though paralyzed by a fear that I didn't have to simulate); but what I couldn't avoid in any way was the humiliation with respect to myself and to the others: to have "withdrawn from a competition" (as they say in racing language) and to know that I had behaved like a "wet hen," no more no less, to hear the teacher declare mockingly that my "rear end was too heavy." During at least the entire first part of each class, I was uneasy, asking myself whether we would have to perform any of those detested exercises that day; thus preoccupied, I moved about without any enthusiasm and displayed only a feeble application even to those exercises I had no reason to dread, some of which I would even have enjoyed if I had not been wondering anxiously about what the rest of the class might contain that was physically unacceptable.

Making no effort to do anything, except to make as little effort as possible, I attended the sessions but only participated, in short, at arm's length, without ever really involving my body in them, unless compelled and forced, or —to be more precise—sometimes allowing it to be involved in them, but allowing this despite myself (as one suffers an illness) and never involving myself deliberately. Under such circumstances of almost total apathy (when I hadn't actually withdrawn), any progress, even the most minimal, was strictly out of the question; a docile and even fairly studious pupil where school matters were concerned, I would have to rank myself, where gymnasium matters were concerned, in the category of the dunces from whom the most one obtains is that they give proof of being present and whose attitude, as for the rest, is an obstinate refusal, a negation assuming the form of the inertia and muteness of a stone.

If I was always an awkward boy who seemed encumbered by his arms and legs, or unsure of them, I must say there was nothing congenital about this; what has to be blamed, I think, is not a defect inherent in my physical constitution (which appears normal to me insofar as the word *normal* can correspond to anything definable) but rather a certain softness against which my instructors were not able to take action early enough or with enough energy. Would it be accusing them unfairly to reproach them for having allowed me to acquire such bad habits in the gymnasium, whereas there they had an excellent setting in which to correct this character flaw and, most likely, could easily—at least in this particular area—have neutralized its effects with a progressive training such that I would have learned, little by little, to triumph over myself?

To back out right at the beginning, not even to try (for fear of not succeeding or merely out of indifference): a mixture of pessimism and laziness, the one laying the basis for the other so that a vicious circle was created. Was the leap from that height, which seemed so far up to me, so very difficult that my chances of success were almost nil and it was therefore natural that, convinced of my failure and without courage as soon as the preparatory run toward the jump began, I made only a vague symbolic attempt? Or did it quite simply demand an effort that I, defeated beforehand because this way the matter could be settled more quickly, declared myself incapable of producing without even having tried to engage in the experiment? Pessimism and laziness: was the first truly profound motivation or merely an excuse for the second? Could the latter be the terrain outside of which the former could not develop, given that if I must speak of myself as someone who, in large and small things, has always tended to become discouraged, the reason for my despondency is not so much my fate as a human being, considered in itself, or any one painful situation in which I might temporarily find myself, as it is my absolute certainty that I lack the energy required to be equal to what—generally or specifically—destiny requires of me? Disregarding a certain superficial pessimism that amounts to predicting the worst in order not to be disappointed and is also akin to superstition (never to rejoice in one's fate because that would risk attracting bad luck), there is something inside me that should perhaps more fairly be called "defeatism": what is the good of going to so much trouble for an undertaking that can only come to nothing? Useless for me to run any risks or become in the least anxious about anything, since, even if the game is worth the candle (which is doubtful anyway), I know I am powerless to attain the goal. I despair of myself, in the end, much more than of things, and what appears insurmountable to me is not so much the obstacle in itself and all the various difficulties it represents as the apathy that makes me the equivalent of an invalid and is the reason, for instance, why I decide not to climb a mountain all the way to the top, stopping as soon as I sense the approach of the moment when I *will* suffer from vertigo, as soon as I foresee that I will be hampered in my movements at the very instant when, so long as one is in control of oneself, one will not run any serious risk (ordinary fear, in other words, being more powerful than vertigo, since even before it actually seizes me I am afraid of becoming prey to it, and dread the fall, with its completely prosaic reality, that might result from this diminution of my faculties). Undoubtedly it is too late, now, to go back; it won't be in the period of my decline that I become less timorous and I can only brood, as over a shameful thing—without hope of being cured of it, for the ill took root too long ago—over my ridiculous ineptitude at all sports, whether the luxury sports (tennis, at which I am worse than anyone, skiing, which I have never gone in for) or what one could call the "useful sports" (swimming, horseback riding, driving a car, boxing). Certainly there is nothing particularly serious, in itself, in the fact of being a dreadful swimmer (capable, at best, of a few strokes), a pitiful horseman, a nonexistent driver (received my license when I was eighteen but never drove after that), and totally helpless when it comes to fighting. For anyone who is anxious to make an impression this is quite vexing, and knowing how to ride a bicycle can't be, from this point of view, more than a meager scrap of consolation; when one remembers —as I do—having fallen a number of times during a single riding class, consumed by a distress aggravated at each fall by outbursts of laughter (coming from a tall, lanky Englishwoman who rode bareheaded in a masculine outfit as though to demonstrate clearly that anyone who wished to could be virile), one is not proud of oneself if one progressed no further than that in one's equitation, among other violent exercises. But these deficiencies, apparently, are venial, because when I think about it, there isn't much chance that I will be shipwrecked, fall in the water, or have to swim across a river, also not much chance that I will be obliged, even on a trip somewhere, to get from one place to another on a horse the handling of which would demand real equestrian skill and because, however quick one may be to take offense, life remains possible even for a person who doesn't have the pugilistic talents of an Arthur Cravan, as long as he renounces the pleasure (supremely wholesome though it is) of playing at being a righter of wrongs everywhere and at every hour of the day; as for cars, though people use them constantly it scarcely bothers me that I don't know how to drive one, because I can leave this to others and tell myself that if I should have to learn, there will always be time. A charge more serious, however, than these deficiencies, in which it would seem nothing very important is involved, is the fundamental weakness of which they are the symptoms: not to have taken it upon myself to overcome the apprehensions that paralyzed me, to have allowed this sort of impotence to settle deep inside me, is an indisputable sign of cowardice; the subject of a remorse and a piercing regret, as may be a youthful mistake for someone who—now completely ruined—thinks of that early mistake which, far from representing only a misstep after which he quickly regained his balance, led him insidiously (but decisively) into the path he should not have taken. *Cowardice* and *youthful mistake* will perhaps appear to be big words to use in connection with those little evasions that were habitual with me during the gymnastics classes at 5 rue Pierre-Guérin in a glassed-in backyard. Yet I am sure that such words are required: it hardly matters that my cowardice bore only on trifles, then, and that my youthful mistakes were neither misdemeanors that could send me to a children's court nor even the sorts of acts that cause their author to be regarded as a bad apple without, however, thereby exposing him to any legal sanction; I know very well that, by shirking this way, I was behaving with the same faintheartedness as I did each time it might happen that, having attained adulthood, I eluded, out of fear, the performance of a duty whose correctness and gravity I was quite aware of; and I also know very well—whence this *piercing regret*—that it was through the accumulation of such trifles that I acquired the habit of never exercising my will and little by little settled into that cowardice which I believe, up to now, I have succeeded more or less in masking (even while crying it from the rooftops, as if to appear to sin through excess of scruple), though I can't be sure there won't ever occur, for me, circumstances such that—past all sense of shame—I will allow it to burst into broad daylight.

In that hall where, as in other similar places, a dancing class (attended, for her part, by my older sister) was held certain evenings of the week, I therefore got off to a bad start and neither of the successive directors—not the first, who, it seems, came to the point one day of telling me to do whatever I wanted (to which I answered politely that I wanted to do nothing) nor the second, driven to use more energetic methods—succeeded in pulling me out of my rut. If they could have instituted actual sanctions against me (even if only the sort of punishments people inflict on you in school), would they perhaps have managed a semblance of discipline? But in such intermittent classes as these, both of them (the brutal Hercules as much as the fat, smiling potbelly) had no recourse and they would have needed, in compensation for the impotence in which they necessarily found themselves, all the severity my parents didn't have in order to overcome my unwillingness by means of appropriate retributions and to put things back in place.

Simple indifference, a natural propensity to do nothing, under our first director; fear, positive repugnance toward the painful things he commanded us to do, under the second, who horrified me. "He's common," said my mother, whereas my maternal uncle—more indulgent toward athletes, perhaps because during his adventurous life he himself had worked with his body, appearing in circuses—said: "He's a good fellow." It didn't matter much to me whether vulgarity was a predominant trait in this gymnast or whether his deep-seated loyalty overshadowed his clumsy bearing and his indelicate manners; I was not comfortable in the presence of this large, strong man who seemed to allow no means of evasion either for himself or for anyone else and whom I had often heard extolling "willpower," which meant a good deal more than a mere swelling of the biceps.

His massive fighter's body, his broad, rather pale, and perhaps slightly bilious face, his little mustache without points (a circumflex accent set between his lips and his nose), his smell, about which I only know that it existed and I didn't like it, but which I can't define (the stale odor of food? of sweat? or something more profound?), the ability my elders attributed to him to "control himself" (otherwise, what might his rages have led to, terrible disruptions!) — I can't see which of these physical or moral characteristics I might fix on to describe his person more concretely than as an image without thickness, without any value even as caricature and almost as alien to reality as were, for instance, to the great flabby, overhanging mass of swollen yellowish canvas which—at the time of the first Salon de l'Aéronautique—struck me with an anguish I concealed even though it was difficult to bear, certain satirical postcards published when another French dirigible, the *Patrie,* was lost, and which depicted the military balloon racing away, its mooring lines broken, while in the upper-left-hand corner a North Wind with the face of a bearded old drunk blew full cheeked.

How, then, am I to describe him, if I wish to invite him to appear here as one does someone involved in an incident as a witness if not a protagonist? And where should I pick him up, at what point in the fairly long period during which he numbered among the acquaintances of my parents, who respected him because of the indisputable integrity he had until the day when his exemplary willpower was undermined by the taste he acquired for drink? Should I depict him in civvies, as he was when he tormented me during the years preceding the other war? But I don't even recall, any longer, the clothes he wore when he inflicted his lessons on me. Should I describe him as a soldier, with the sky blue jacket and kepi of a second lieutenant or infantry lieutenant, at the difficult time when his men (according to what we learned) nicknamed him "the Boxer" because his ready punch made him so unpopular? But thus outfitted—and already, in actual fact, half out of our orbit—he no longer has more than an uncertain relation to my gymnastics teacher. Why not, given these circumstances, try to apprehend him indirectly through an event that I did not witness myself but that was imprinted on my imagination more than any detail experienced with the senses and illustrates better than anything else the capacity for decision, and the control over a body as agile, if need be, as it was powerful, by which he impressed me so? An event

that, at the time when it occurred, was the topic of quite a few family conversations and caused me to regard its hero as a kind of superman; an event
that, in truth, can be contained in very few words and by now seems very banal to me.

The wife of our physical-education teacher was, if her rather colorless appearance has correctly imprinted its image upon me, a sickly looking Italian
Swiss with a white, perhaps freckled complexion and hair tending somewhat
toward the reddish; neither ugly nor pretty, but rather graceful because she
was so slender, and generally dressed in black or in dark colors, which given
the pallor of her skin made her look like a half-starved orphan or young widow. The couple lived—on the first floor, I'm quite sure—in the same building occupied by the gymnasium, and it was there that this long, fragile creature, whom people were astonished to see paired with such a colossus, gave
birth to twins. The thing very nearly came to the worst possible end: the par-
turient suffered a violent hemorrhage—so violent that, according to my
mother, "the blood ran under the door"—and if this woman, whose face was
so pallid that one wondered how a body as manifestly anemic could contain
so much blood, was to be saved from this critical situation, there was not a
second to lose; everyone admired the coolness and the sportsmanlike qualities
of the husband, who, going off in quest of some medicine or some other
means of rescue, jumped directly, it seems, into the stairwell by leaping over
the banister in a single bound and came back carrying the desired object
when it was thought that he had scarcely left the house.

The champion with a thousand resources devoted to the cause of the
Good. The certified rescuer, like dogs such as the Saint Bernard and the New-
foundland. The tough workhorse who, in the severest weather, performs his
task. The baritone with powerful lungs who, however, does not know what to
do with himself on stage once his aria is finished. The soldier without helmet
or coat of mail, arms dangling after the blows exchanged. The knight-errant
with scowling face whose strong hand I feared. The one I regarded—because
this was what my family did—as having high moral qualities but whom, in
his heavyweight uprightness, I knew to be pitiless and whose entire being,
what was more, disheartened me. No less than the prowess of his dive into

the stairwell, what remains associated with him, for me, as though he were
the one primarily responsible for it as well as the one who set it right, was the
very simple horror of that business of the hemorrhage.

I would be a poor loser if I tried to question the aversion inspired in me
not only by the vulgarity of the appearance of this man who impressed me so
terribly, but also by the very strength he possessed and his iron severity, in the
presence of which we all felt like very small boys. From this distance, I am obviously led to believe that, far from functioning as an example, the almost su-
perhuman power I attributed to him contributed, instead, to making me
withdraw, in the same way that the image of an overly formidable father can
incite certain children, not to emulate him, but to seek a refuge in a sort of
nonexistence that excludes, for the present and the future, any idea of standing up to him. But is it still true that, faced with a cruel father, some children
—the weak ones, such as I—assume for their whole lives the habit of avoiding anything reminiscent of the crash of a clay pot against an iron pot [*le pot
de terre contre le pot de fer:* meeting more than one's match], whereas others—
those not marked by the same original defect—choose the opposite path: to
harden themselves and, even if only out of hatred, endeavor with all their
wills to prove their virility. It was therefore not because of that exemplary ath-
lete with his forbidding exterior, or because of the shocking fact of knowing
him to be paired with a creature as frail as was his companion (a union that
might make one ask oneself if the spilling of so much blood was not due to
the element of paradox implied by such a conjunction); it wasn't anyone's
fault, nor was it a result of circumstances, that I allowed myself to glide down
a slope of cowardice, first shrinking from that dizzying exercise or leap which
would have demanded too much effort of me, then backing out of one thing
after another and in the end shirking everything that required the involve-
ment of my body (I'm not even saying: that required my body to confront
real danger). And having gotten off to this bad start, I gradually came to be
—one defeat leading to another, for cowardice only tends to spread—what I
am today: someone who somehow or other succeeds in creating an illusion
and to whom (at best) the less severe would perhaps be justified in conceding
that he does not lack a certain facade, but someone who, very precisely, is

nothing other than that facade and would be reduced to zero if life's hazards led him to have to depend, in order to be capable of anything or even very simply to live, only on his own energy; someone for whom literature is merely a sort of railway siding (because adventures that take place on paper have no physical consequences) and whose only attempts at action assume the form of a vague ideological militantism inducing him to adopt a semblance of a position from time to time on the humanitarian problems of our era; someone whose more and more pronounced taste for the theater—whether he loves, as a fervent adept, the beautiful Italian performances of opera, or whether he takes his memories of the theater as material for reflection—corresponds to his need to find a diversion, an area where he can be enthusiastic the whole day through but where this enthusiasm remains gratuitous, when all is said and done, and where even the most tumultuous torments of passion surge forth only in effigy.

It is therefore the austere surroundings of that gymnasium, separated by a simple courtyard from the main body of the building on one story of which the Swiss woman had bled, it is this hall with its floor covered by thick carpeting mats, furnished with various pieces of equipment and rigged all over with means of ascension such as ladders, poles, knotted ropes and smooth ropes, that I have chosen as the setting for what I am describing, today, as, in sum, my original sin. A sin that did not consist of improperly eating the fruit of the Tree of Knowledge but rather of shirking everything that made life something other than a Garden of Eden; a sin that was an act of disobedience also, but even more an evasion, and which is serious in the sense that, being a sin of carelessness, it is a diminution of the self, a dead loss, a failure—something that rebellion is not.

Aside from the heavyset individual who presided over all this, and his two acolytes (a wiry little brown-haired fellow with the awkward gait of a tumbler, who had an Italian name, and a tall blond man with a rather elegant figure, both more easygoing than our Samson, tormentor and savior of his Delilah) I recall nothing, to all intents and purposes, about those who, on the days the class was held—Sunday mornings and one weekday afternoon, I think—found themselves assembled there with me during one full hour by the clock for the performance of that ballet. There was a tall, dark boy from Algeria whose impetuosity was like that which people assign—perhaps generalizing erroneously—to the Barbary pirates; like all the gymnastics pupils he lived in our part of town. I also remember a sickly Austrian boy who must have been about my age and whose intelligent, sad, little monkey face, all white and wrinkled, was pocked with freckles. Were there girls among us? I can't really say, even though I vaguely recall one named Yette, a robust, cheerful girl whose working outfit consisted of a sailor suit of knitted or woven cloth; one had only to look at her to know she wasn't afraid of anything, and I would have done well to profit from her example!

It would be useless, after having been tempted to blame my teacher, for me to search the attitudes of my fellow students or my brothers for something that, wounding me, would have tended to made me withdraw once and for all. Perhaps (as seems natural) I was mocked for my fears and my clumsiness? If this was so, it was almost certainly not malicious: assuming there was mockery, it never went in a direction such that I was hurt by it and the whole of my character might have been affected by it. At that time, anyway, I felt nothing in me bristle at the idea of losing face: the little kid I was had only a quite imperfect concern for his honor and scarcely worried about morality either. If he had any at all, it didn't go beyond the vague principles with which his parents indoctrinated him and what he was taught at catechism. If he was able to feel touched to the quick or his vanity satisfied, it was always in connection with mere childish matters or purely superficial things: the profound humiliation I experienced—and expressed in a great scene with tears and shouts—one day when they made me try on a "quartermaster" suit that came, I think, from La Grande Maison and whose trousers, with their flap, seemed to me to resemble the sort of diaper cover one put on babies; the pride in being "Julian Lechim" the Animal Tamer appearing alongside "Siriel Piar" the Virtuoso, when we played traveling sideshow and my brother Jacques was the barker introducing us, the younger ones, as two sensational attractions: my brother Pierre, who actually intended to take up music, promoted to the rank of Hungarian violinist and myself, who didn't know how to do anything, assigned, for some pointless reason, the role of tamer of wild beasts; the bitter mortification I felt and the devastating sense that I had behaved like a boor one day when they made me apologize to a little boy for having said to him, when we were together in the Bois and were playing, "You're as green as a green apple" or for having shown, in some other, equally uncharitable way that his very obvious poor state of health had not escaped me.

Instead of the desire to impress by doing better in a competition with others or the simple horror of seeing oneself outdistanced, what, almost from the beginning, I allowed to establish itself in me, then, was a strictly external vanity—that of the little boy who accepted being no good at gymnastics but couldn't tolerate being dressed in a way he felt was unworthy of his age, that of Julian Lechim full of himself in his role as animal tamer whereas Michel-Julien did not hesitate to show, in the rue Pierre-Guérin, a ridiculous faintheartedness, that of the young boy out for a walk more ashamed that day of having been guilty of a lack of good manners than he was every week when, publicly, he behaved like a crybaby and a sissy.

If I complain, today, of being someone who is nothing but a bit of facade and if, even while fearing to see that piece of wall collapse, I aspire to the dignity of the man who may not be brilliant but who can be relied upon—where the simplest human relations are concerned as well as in his main activity—the source of this lies, probably, in a twofold motion produced in me by that fault whose pitiful consequences I had to obliterate one way or another. As I sank down into a hopeless deficiency when it came to those very matters concerning the body and courage which I believe to be so very important precisely because they are so very elementary, I tended to replace the great virtue that I lacked by secondary qualities situated in more comfortable areas: a knowledge of my heart, since I lacked the essential strength that allows one quite simply to have a brave heart; the capacity for disinterest, since I didn't have enough violence in me for anything at all to seem really desirable; a homesickness for distant places, though I am so cowardly in the presence of what touches me closely; an openness toward events whose theater is the mind, for—however bold one may be in one's thinking—there is no occasion to grapple savagely with these events, as there is with those of the real world. As, then, I turned away from what I knew to be the solid core of things and, for me, the difficult area, I was led by a moral concern all the more fastidious because I felt myself to be fundamentally offending to avoid deception and also not to make a display of anything that was overly promising; yearning, nevertheless, to adorn with a certain prestige that body over which it would have been better to possess some mastery, I tended—despite my lack of taste for frippery—to compose for myself a figure behind which I could hide everything I felt to be contemptible in me and by means of which I could acquire for myself a little approbation; but I used this subterfuge (if indeed there was any deliberate artifice here) with a sort of honesty and fashioned this figure in such a way that I could clothe myself in it without too bad a conscience. An individual whose goal, in his vestimentary appurtenances, is to achieve taste and distinction, without anything too bourgeois or anything slovenly either; his dress must indicate that he is not an ordinary person and that he knows it but does nothing to accentuate his difference and, especially, does not sin through an excess of self-assurance; that reserved appearance which he has and which he readily makes use of (seeking to disguise as elegance his actual shyness) directly expresses his fear of seeing himself exposed and revealed for what he really is, at the same time that it points one toward the idea of a simple lack of confidence which has no basis and only shows an overly strict exigency in regard to himself; a correctness that, moreover, answers a sincere need to brace himself against his fear of knuckling under but indisputably includes an element of cheating since it gives the impression that, beyond this very neat exterior, there is perfect internal rectitude, and also suggests that a mystery—to which he alone holds the key— could well be hidden beneath this surface, too smooth not to be a sign of depth; also, something uneasy, preoccupied, and bitter in his face, which reflects the sad truth of the disturbance to which the individual is prey but just as clearly signifies the intense spiritual life of one who has nurtured not a few noble illusions and has recovered from them without, for all that, resigning himself to the fact that things are not more than what they are. A twofold movement, consequently, which on the one hand drove me to do whatever I could to throw people off the track successfully and on the other hand inspired in me (as though this were at once the counterpart and my only viable position of withdrawal) a strict probity: that of the man who, if he is never filled with an invincible ardor and self-assurance any more than he is seized by poetic fever, at least makes it a point of honor to pay to the last penny whatever he may have happened, by chance, to promise. An irremissible divergence which, literally, cuts my heart in two: my attachment to those various adornments with which I embellish my body the way a jockey does himself with his jacket or a torero with his "costume of lights" and by which—though I don't know how to do anything with my body, as I don't know how to dominate any creature whatsoever, human or animal—I endeavor to make an impression (without much success, for in order to manage this I would have to sport more dazzling colors); my attachment to the truth, which not only leads me to condemn myself on a number of essential points and deprives me even of the certainty that I would stand fast in my last retrenchment if I had my back to the wall, but comes along periodically to destroy the overly flattering ideas that I continuously invent for myself as to the intrinsic value and the practical efficacity of such adornments.

Facade, adornment: was it anything else that drew me when, toward the end of the 1914–18 war, I was vaguely tempted to enter the American Red Cross because of the khaki uniform, because of the ease with which one could provision oneself there with whiskey as well as cigarettes, and because of the girls one met there, who looked at once tightly buttoned up and rakish, women-soldiers who had nothing in common with the nurses, and who were fraternal rather than maternal, unlike that *Vivandière* in hussar-style dolman who sings in the famous comic opera, "Come with us, honey!" At that time, when the United States, having entered the war, was now more highly esteemed than England, organizations such as the YMCA or the Knights of Columbus also enjoyed a great prestige among many young people of my circle because the privileged individuals who belonged to them had a right to handsome uniforms without, for all that, being soldiers prepared to play at La Tour d'Auvergne for lack of being of an age, yet, for the Bara drums. Facade, adornment: it was this inclination, much more than any inclination for sports, that caused me, along with a thousand others, to join the Racing-Club de France, where I at first had the pretension of training myself for the footrace, then—toward the beginning of the period immediately following the war—tried my skill a little at rugby and played the forward second line for a season, on a team of juniors (I got winded quickly and, what was worse, I was skittish: every time I chanced to have the ball in my hands I hastened to pass it to someone else, impatient to be rid of it in order not to be "tackled"; I played, in other words, at being someone who played rugby in the same way that the year before I had wanted to play at being a footracer, this on the level of the pantomime or the gesture of pure show that one makes without really compromising oneself, remaining still on the edge of the true act, at a stage that—at best—does not go beyond that of random impulse). And, too, it was definitely not an excess of energy—such that I wouldn't have been able to feel comfortable with any spectacle unless it involved violence and bloodshed—that made me, later, a fan of bullfighting. What I liked so much about the character of the torero was unquestionably his courage or (to be more precise) the quite particular form this courage assumed in him: to expose himself in all his beauty, to risk darkening with his blood the figures of a geometry that was more Arab than Euclidian. The death of the bull and the man's confrontation with the horns—all in accordance with a specific protocol and specific canons—was in my eyes a tragedy, the only valid kind since it was true, unlike those proposed by the theater or any one of the other art forms. But there, too, I was cheating, contenting myself with remaining on the edge: for the spectator—even the one who, sitting in the first row, can easily imagine he is not at all separated from the action—the corrida is as unreal as any sort of aesthetic manifestation, because it's not a tragedy one lives through but simply a tragic spectacle one observes from outside, without confronting the slightest danger, the only risk assumed by the aficionado being to travel long distances time and time again and to leave relatively large sums of money at railway station ticket offices and in the hands of bullring managers and hotel proprietors for a series of mediocre or faked events before having the chance to be present at a great day.

Since I have for so long accorded the corrida the value of an example (somewhat as I used to do the steeplechase) I can't possibly, now, join its detractors, who don't see bullfighting as anything but a histrionic sort of cruelty, whereas its ultimate signification is the imposition of a majestic order on primitive material, as one might expect where an authentically great art is concerned. What I find repugnant now is not the thing itself (with its undeniable substratum of barbarity beneath its seductive appearance) but my own attitude toward this thing: to enjoy as a dilettante a spectacle based on death and courage when I myself am so uneasy about death and so lacking in courage; to participate mentally in these herculean labors and feel myself borne along by a wind of heroism, not innocently, as in the theater (where it is understood that no one's life is at stake) but with the fierce exigency of someone who, being a lover of strong sensations and having paid for this, feels he has been swindled if the episodes of the drama he is witnessing—though he can, at the very most, only imagine the anguish exuding from the pores of the torero—do not allow him to pose as a superman by proxy.

Among other passionate enthusiasms that have colored my life over the years, I have, therefore, finally eliminated my love for the corrida, as I am now in the process of eliminating my love for Verdi's operas, astonishing lyrical edifices (both musically and poetically), no longer clinging with the same blindness to these all-too-easy means of intoxication and having little else but suspicion concerning magic potions thanks to which—without moving an inch—we believe ourselves to be demigods trifling with death or men with hearts so swollen with desires that whole crowds can hear them beating. The famous names of Luis-Miguel Dominguin, Manolete (whom I've never seen), and, in earlier times, Belmonte and Joselito—who succeeded the two stars of my childhood, Machaquito and Bombita with their strange nicknames—have lost, for me, the emotional charge that made them comparable, for the zealous churchgoer, to the name of some great saint, or, for the romantic lover, the name of a certain woman, and if, hungering for moments of splendor, I still enjoy mingling with the public, whose rustling transforms into a living organ the vessel of an opera hall, whatever my delectation there is no longer anything in it I can feed on: the paradox of art is that, being valuable as an allusion to something that goes beyond its closed world, the highest art turns out to be that which excites us too deeply for us not to experience as powerless to satisfy us precisely this art which has made us more demanding and given us the desire for something beyond art.

Eliminations now in progress: my love for Verdi's operas; a little tune to sing (one of the sort that "keeps going through your head"): *Un au-delà de l'art, un au-delà de l'ère, un au-delà des lyres, un au-delà dès lors* . . . [something beyond art, something beyond the times, something beyond poetic talents, something beyond starting then]. But, as the actual consequence of the fact that I have just gone on an extended tour—by that quasi-supernatural means of displacement referred to in the expression "airway"—that took me, this time, after Martinique and Guadeloupe, almost as far as the Iles de la Vierge and then to Marie-Galante, and to the Saintes (visiting them by sailboat), and interrupted my nausea in the purring of these pages, shouldn't I use the interval thus created to readjust my viewpoint and recognize that—despite certain stray impulses as testified to by this very trip, devoted to studying problems that arise in the French Antilles as in every place where men of different colors live together—I am nowhere near having eliminated everything that assumes the appearance, in my eyes, of the grand aria under the starry vault or the fancy-dress ball in the duke's palace?

The period before my departure had, in fact, been punctuated by moving images produced in me by theater performances or manifestations having to do with opera.

On the stage of our Académie nationale de Musique, a German Salome, her white throat richly timbred and her face tantalizing, rolls over and over almost naked, a melody incarnate making one dream of an art with positive coordinates, such as eroticism can be, and not of a futile magic in which everything operates only symbolically. On this stage, now darkened for the meeting in the cemetery in *Un Ballo in maschera*—an opera whose plot is moved forward (if one thinks about it) by the coloratura in male dress, a comic-opera page in the role of unwary advisor or overly talkative confidant whom nothing marks, at first sight, as the messenger of death—a pale figure veiled in black hesitates, vacillates, sways to the left, to the right, opposite prompt, prompt side, like a mad butterfly bumping into things; his voice—emerging from the most exquisite milling machines—brushes against us, penetrates us as might an anxious soul forcing entry into our hearts; in the last scene of this opera (as I saw it put on in Paris by the Teatro San Carlo of Naples) masqueraders, hooded cloaks, people in black velvet masks, and plumed savages move about in a splendidly lit place which is not so much a stage as an infernal grotto unconfined by any background since what one sees —in an infinitely receding space—is the very Hearth of Dance, a trap for our gaze, which cannot discern where the fictional architecture takes over from the real architecture and which allows itself to be led, without ever reaching the end of it, through a space that is carved out among the many columns and proves to be, as far as our eyes may see, filled by ever more dancers. At the Théâtre Sarah Bernhardt, *La Dame de Chez Maxim's,* in which another sabbat—the sabbat of the licentious actress full of sex appeal and spirit—abolishes all distance between the theater and life, as did the singer in the sumptuous costume of a rather vulgar biblical princess; this, in a spectral 1900, with a liturgy of outmoded locutions, bourgeois witticisms and precepts mixed in with guttersnipe quips. In the nave of the smoke-filled Greek temple which is the Eglise de la Madeleine, before the performance of the *Requiem* dedicated to the memory of Manzoni, the mouth of the soprano—whose breath will uplift us any moment now, like the breath of a majestic angel—purses for a second in a mimed kiss aimed at a lover or husband we divine but can't separate out from the part of the crowd toward which the movement of her lips is directed, a kiss that is all the sweeter because, thus sent out into the void, it encounters nothing that might stop us from appreciating, if not its taste, at least its intention, and, as the song's prelude addressed to an invisible listener, can appear, to more than one, to be personally meant for him.

In a bedroom in the real world, late one afternoon, I looked on—at the same time as all of that—while a girl I did not love and who did not love me pinned her black hair up on top of her head with a quick and precise gesture, facing the mirror, in a style I had never seen on her before and which, crowning her delicate mulatto profile with an oblong mass, gave her the satisfaction (reprehensible, because she was denying herself) of resembling an Egyptian. And a short time before—rather distressed, because I felt I was caught in the trap of an amorphous adventure into which, without circumlocution, I had been invited by this same person and found myself in the situation of a gambler who knows that the dice are loaded but also knows that he will not be able to stop himself from playing—seated on the edge of a bed in another hotel room, I was leafing through a child's book, an illustrated spelling book, along with its owner, a simple, honest Haitian boy I had gotten to know during my first trip to the Antilles and who, having become a voodoo priest after having been the leader of a choir in a voodoo center in one of the poorest neighborhoods of his capital city, was now touring Europe with a company of dancers and was counting on earning enough from this engagement to open his own *hounfor* once he was back in Haiti; in the childish manner he owed in part to his flirtatiousness as a scarcely disguised homosexual, in part, also, no doubt, to his nature as one inspired by the gods, my companion—playing the good little boy—was eager to show me that he was profiting from his trip to learn to read, and that he was doing this from the spelling book he had been given by a "gentleman" who had also given him a large map of Paris published in the form of a page that unfolded; I didn't know whether this erstwhile ragged sprite had invited me to accompany him to his room and then to sit next to him out of simple friendliness, to make me welcome in his lodgings and have me admire the progress he had made since joining the music-hall troupe, or whether the ulterior motive of a seduction that could result in a calculable profit was one of the reasons for this invitation; distressed as I was, I was more moved than I should have been by the two of us reading this picture book, on each page of which—or nearly—appeared animals such as one so often sees in children's books; it wouldn't have taken much to let myself be carried away, like a cork, on the current of an adventure that would certainly have been a great cause of confusion for the mediocre libertine that I am but would, perhaps, have deflected me from a more banal intrigue about which, without knowing that it would induce me, for a rather long time, to see myself, where my emotions were concerned, as a boxer broken in two by a low blow or a bull nailed alive by a bad thrust, I nevertheless had a presentiment that, starting up from just about nothing and not promising much, it would hurt me all the more because it contained nothing of the sort of illusion contained in that friendly reading of the spelling book; this was only a vague thought that disturbed me for a few minutes without crossing over the boundaries of the possibility that was being contemplated, and very recently, with frank pleasure, I saw once again my companion from that other late afternoon: passing through Paris, from which he was preparing, when his tour continued, to leave for the South of France, he came for a family dinner at my home and told me about the amazing circumstances surrounding his birth, describing to me how he came into the world "feet first" (here the narrator, throwing his chest back, extends his two arms straight in front of him to show the position of his legs), his mother—who died before she could raise him—having given birth suddenly on the steps of the "cathedral" of a town in the north of Haiti and a storm (which the narrator at first describes as a "cyclone") having broken at that very moment as though to proclaim that the son of the poor Negro was truly one predestined.

A girl who wanted to be an amber-skinned Thaïs instead of a dark-skinned Aïda and whose physical attractions I can now admire quite coolly, feeling as I look at her a sweetness unmixed with any friendship; a hirsute and sophisticated boy I find touching in the devotion he shows to his brand-new wardrobe and his schoolboy's spelling book as well as to his gods imported from Guinea. These two figures, who continue to move me when I remember the scenes that centered on them, come back to me illuminated by the same stage lights as their contemporaries, who appeared before my eyes as I, the spectator, sat there tranquilly, the first group more serious, the others lighter, as though, by summoning me to respond, they wished to notify me of something essential to my life: that Salome, so well formed to give the expression "vision of art" a meaning of the same order as, but more weighty than, the meaning in the advertisements of the smutty newspapers and who calls upon me, without subterfuge, to question, again, my entire conception of beauty; that page, death's emissary, expressing himself in frivolous terms, who may be sphinx, siren, harpy, or any other creature whose ambiguity goes beyond the imprecision of the sex and is a sign that he belongs to the intermediary world populated by angels, demons, and other messengers from heaven and hell; that maddened creature wanting and not wanting, making its pendulous way again and again, between the struts of the night, from one term to the other of love's alternative; that masked crowd filling a theater platform which has deepened to become a universe into which, every frontier having been abolished between what is real and what is fiction, one's gaze plunges vertiginously; that same Last Judgment crowd when, seeing the drama crystallize in the steel of a dagger, it unmasks itself with a single gesture. In her unenigmatic way, the little woman of Chez Maxim's also has a lesson for me, for she teaches me with a simple twirl of her tucked-up skirt that in art as in literature, nothing is worth anything unless it comes across, *leaps the footlights,* and strikes one in the middle of one's chest, the way a prostitute's solicitations awaken a sudden desire. As for the kiss sent out silently by the soprano in the *Requiem* as she stood in a very historical evening gown in the church choir, is there any need to comment on that to explain what it was saying?

The water maid with large metal ankle supports who, her pitcher of water on her head, came to me from Pakistan by airmail; a female colossus, the Demeter of Cherchel seen in Algeria at the Galland Park museum which is also populated by nereids and by Europa lolling over the bull's spine as though among cushions on a couch; at the aquarium of Castiglione, where there are also morays, the figureheads and the forward part of the *lampare* on either side of which is sculpted a mermaid blowing into a trumpet, her tail split into two long scaly branches, tightly braided serpents; the great Italian angel encountered at every step in the twilight of Tuscan cathedrals or the harsh glare of exhibition rooms; white against the azure sky, the tall headless female one sees—close to a broken phallus—on the island of Delos, an immense space choked with broken marble, encircled by an intensely blue sea with its fat billows of foam, where there is a "dragon's den" open, perhaps, to a few creatures akin to those dryads among whom Jean-Jacques Rousseau dreamed of finding his love; the London thyiad, the Lady of the Lions, whom —quite illogically—I hoped to find again, like a phoenix, one beautiful Venice evening at the *Fenice.*

In a meadow very reminiscent of old France, white turkeys, peacock, pale barefoot shepherdess sitting sewing or knitting on a rock, we landed late one afternoon, Guadeloupe scarcely more than an hour away and thrust back into the far distance by this brief flight that had carried us, the pilot and me, from Pointe-à-Pitre to the island of Saint Barthélemy, a tropical Elsinore with its nordic, sometimes princely looking peasants, its cows, its palm trees, its two-sided roofs painted oxblood red, its deeply indented coastline, its schooners at anchor in the port of Gustavia. Having up to then traveled only on airliners, I was discovering the great joy of arriving in a marvelous country after a landing made in uncomfortable conditions that allowed one to imagine what a "heavier than air" flight must have been like at the time of the pioneers.

The machine that transported me had belonged (as I was informed by the professional who now used it to convey passengers like me) to the famous shoe manufacturer Bata. During our flight, as my companion was naming for me the islands we could see—Antigue, Montserrat, Redonde, Nevis (which the Spanish called Nieves, meaning "snows") and then Saint Christophe and Saint Eustache—I was as attentive to the various maneuvers as I would have been during a flying lesson and amused myself by reading on the control panel a sheet of paper on which—filling in here and there the blanks deliberately left in the printed text—were typed particulars indicating the plane's characteristics. Without understanding much about it, I took some pleasure in reading this and as I did so I was no doubt rediscovering, several dozen years later, the pleasure I used to take—when I was collecting postcards of airplanes, filing them in a thick album—in initiating myself, as I supposed, into the mysteries of aviation, still quite new then, by means of the brief explanatory lines placed at the bottom of certain of these cards published a little later than the others, and about which I particularly appreciated their air of being documents for specialists, an air they owed to these notes, which were in truth quite vague but constituted enough of a guarantee to eliminate the idea of any fraud similar to that which I had observed in the case of other specimens from my collection, created by presenting a very small number of images under many different titles, the caption differing from one card to another only in the pilot's name and, sometimes, the photograph being reproduced in reverse, so that "Védrines in full flight" became, for example, "Garros . . ." even though the same monoplane, which was flying toward the left edge of the postcard when it was piloted by Védrines, now flew toward the right edge.

Although I received my true baptism by air during the "phony war" (when I was a serviceman in the area of the Sahara and one of my barracks companions was a sergeant aviator who took me up, one Sunday after lunch, in the biplane with which he taxied for our commander) and although I have since then traveled quite often by plane or hydroplane (even flying, when I made my first trip to the Antilles, in the all-too-famous *Latécoère,* which disappeared in the Atlantic on its return trip) I had, in order to understand what was exciting about mastering such a means of locomotion, to go from Guadeloupe to Saint Barthélemy entrusting myself—for lack of any regular connection between those two islands—to a pilot regarded as no less skillful than he was adventurous and whose resemblance to the companion of King Artus was perhaps to be explained as much by this sky rider's rebellious streak where our social norms are concerned as by his Breton origins.

The opposite of the "great jockey," whom my brother and I prized not only for his equestrian abilities but also for his wisdom and almost ascetic seriousness, the aviator is a daredevil, a rowdy, and it was probably during the 1914–18 war that he showed himself in all his brilliance as hothead, given the examples of men such as Navarre, Nungesser, and other military celebrities whom high-school boys like me were thrilled to see in great places like Maxim's in the rue Royale or Harry's in the rue Daunou (at that time called the "New York Bar") or else in Gerny's in the rue de Port-Mahon or in a microscopic bistro like Kannett's in the rue d'Antin which numbered among its female clientele a woman named Jiji, sister (according to her) of the illustrious Védrines, and where I was delighted, one day, to hear the ace of aces, Navarre in flesh and blood, chatting with the woman who owned the place while I myself sat at the bar. For the sports star adopted as a model of a species of saintliness—a conception still belonging to childhood and smacking of its catechism—a very different sort of character was consequently substituted at the time of the First World War, and not only because it was now the lofty feats of the champions of combat aviation and their frequent harebrained or desperado exploits that were featured in the newspapers but because, as I grew older, I was attracted to a different type of hero: the more I aspired to emancipate myself, and the more specific my sexual ambitions became (the image of a fraternal woman—so to speak—with whom one is on an equal footing, gaining more substance now than that of the maternal or purely ideal woman adolescents dream of), the more I detached myself from the figure of the sportsman who has complete command of himself and turned my gaze toward the figure—much less conformist—of the free spirit who laughs at all the rules and, physically, shrinks from nothing.

Just like those adventurers of the Far West shown in certain illustrated stories in the children's magazines—such as, perhaps, *Le Jeudi de la Jeunesse*—ordering, in a pine-board saloon which they had just entered with their pistols at their hips, a cocktail (at that time I pronounced it *"coquetaille"* and thought it was, not a mixture of variable components, but a particular spirit) or sometimes a whiskey or what must be a most refined beverage—if indeed it exists outside the imagination of a writer for children—"strawberry champagne" (as light and fresh as the design featuring an enormous rose that embellished the back of the black satin blouse worn by Buffalo Bill, the horseman with the vast felt hat and the musketeer's thin goatee, when I saw him at the Champ de Mars caracoling with his rifle in hand, star and impresario of a troupe that included cowboys who were carbine rifle marksmen and horse trainers, Cossacks who sometimes flipped over along the flanks of their mounts and galloped with their heads almost touching the ground, a group of whirling dervishes, gymnasts performing the exercise called the "human pyramid," and lastly some Redskins, whom one saw attacking a stagecoach and whom, at the end of the show, I so greatly wanted to view close up that I got lost in the crowd and was found—it appears—at the edge of their camp, not overly dismayed at having remained separated all this time from my parents), the aviator of the years 1914–18—at least the sort that my schoolfellows and I dreamed about—was at once the knight-errant, the outlaw, and the man whose only form of relaxation was the sort of excess symbolized by a bout of heavy drinking.

Master of his art, insensitive to fear, and, for both these reasons, deserving all our respect, the war ace was more like a pirate than a soldier; he was, in sum, a skyrover, and, just as the searover ought to dissipate in debauchery a good part of the booty coming to him by rights, the aerial huntsman, during lightning-quick joyrides to the rear without asking anything of anyone, or-giastically dishonored the laurels that, in default of more substantial prizes, had fallen to him as his lot. Between this passion for combat and this passion for pleasure, there was more than one correlation: it was with the same mo-tion that the aviator hurled himself now into the deadly region where in the midst of the enemy projectiles he performed evolutions in themselves risky, now into the equally stormy zone of alcoholism and of sexuality, as though an essential characteristic of his were an indiscriminate scorn for the various lim-its set by a sense of self-preservation in most people and as though a single—though multiform—burning cloud represented the only milieu in which he could breathe.

Although it is unwise, for the person who doesn't have what it takes, to try to play the hothead (for he will assume only the superficial aspects, as I did, imagining myself to be made of somewhat the same stuff as the aviators be-cause I spurned school discipline to go get drunk in bars), it is important for everyone to dare, at least, to break at some point or other the circle in which prudence and respect for custom has enclosed us. Whether one person makes little of his situation, his comfort, even what some will call his honor, for the sake of a passionate love whose object may or may not be worth such a sacri-fice (this hardly counts in such a case); whether another abandons himself body and soul to some vice and becomes a gambler, a drug addict, a pederast, with a supreme scorn for the harm it may do him; whether yet another—bas-ing his position, not on a personal whim, but on a view of things that appears to him to be an interconnection of solid reasons—stakes his life on a card such as social revolution or devotes his existence, in total disregard for the im-mediate consequences, to attacking a certain prejudice that he loathes, pro-moting (in both cases) what is not generally recognized over what is consid-ered the norm—all these individuals, the proponents of pure pleasure like the champions of a higher reason, those all too unloyal to themselves as well as the uncommitted, have in common the fact that they are fighting a heavy battle against the Goliath of current morality and do not hesitate to confront a real danger: that of destroying themselves, of exposing themselves to disrepute, of ruining their health, of disappearing prematurely or simply dying after having gone without so many of the joys they might justifiably have desired. Fierce as they are, they evince—each in his own way—an audacity that is sufficient to situate them beyond the limit of the ordinary, whereas I myself (who believe I am capable, if really necessary, of standing fast when life is at stake) can't bring myself to make any gamble and prove consistently to be without the strength to risk—as one throws down the gauntlet—my life or its tidy order *expressly*, unfit as I am (even though always on the verge of it) to seize my freedom with all that it comprises of hazard and remaining the spectator behind the barrier of shadow, the enthusiast in the first row who sees things from close up but is not in the heat of the corrida and even goes so far as lazily to give up to fans of more modest means the seats in which one roasts in the sun in order to loll, like a sybarite, in those that are in shadow.

In the course of that worldwide conflict during which I was so dazzled by and paid such attention to the exploits of the aviators while concerning myself very little with so many other soldiers just as brave but consigned to more vulgar modes of butchery, combatants in the mud whose subjection to a stricter discipline expressed itself, whatever their rank might be, in their outfits, so much less fanciful than those of the men of the air (not yet clothed, as they are now, in a special uniform, but wearing, with greater license, the badges of the branch of service to which they had belonged before being assigned to aviation), I was passing, in school, from the "first cycle" to the "second cycle"—being about to enter the ninth grade when the war broke out—and attended the lycée or the cramming school with decreasing zeal almost up to the day of the armistice, which occurred just after I had secured (by a hair) my baccalaureate in philosophy, to which I would add other academic degrees only after many years and one or two false starts. At the same time that I was climbing these steps, I was also climbing the levels that, rising from the LITTLE BOYS' to the MEN's department, took me from the so-called tennis type suit of white-striped blue flannel (the jacket and pants bought ready-made at

Biarritz in a shop selling articles for the beach and put on only when I was dressing up) to the made-to-measure suits turned out for me—soon without anyone else intervening in my choice—by branch stores such as the High Life Tailor and then by an obscure bearded tailor in the Bourse area, classic city wear at last becoming my informal as well as my formal dress after the transition represented by the use, during the week, of informal sporting costumes with breeches covering the knee and, some time later, English- or Saumur-style riding breeches worn with any sort of jacket, which I regard- ed as an already appreciable form of progress toward the adult manner of dressing.

To have to shave, to smoke blond tobacco and drink American drinks, to attend music halls with promenades, to exchange (rather shyly and awkward- ly) a few boy-girl kisses or caresses, so that one no longer goes to confession because now one has little secrets that the priests don't have to know, to go out alone in the evening and sometimes come back only after obscure galli- vanting, to be connected (by links, in truth, as tenuous as they are innocent) to girls of loose morals, these—along with the move from 8, rue Michel- Ange (where we had experienced our first nighttime alert over Paris: a zep- pelin, we thought, and everyone ran to the windows in the hope, disappoint- ed in the end, of the fine fireworks display which would be created by the aerial battle that could not fail to take place), with the selling off of the old apartment which offended my nascent snobbery and our establishment in a more comfortable place, at number 2 in the rue Mignet (from which we were thenceforth to hear, from time to time, the sirens, followed by the "all clear," of the firemen and the shooting of the antiaircraft batteries set up in the Au- teuil racecourse on the site of the famous dairy)—these were a few more lev- els up which I allowed time to carry me and which I will ratify as the most visible of those whose ascension, as it appeared to me, I made throughout that period during which, separated quite early from my two brothers, who had been mobilized into the artillery, I soon felt the reins slacken, being, on the one hand, removed from the influence of those two older brothers and, on the other, less restrained than ever by parents who were now too worried about their sons in the army to keep a close watch on the one who was not threatened by any immediate danger.

I have mentioned the close relations that tied me to one of my two brothers, the one who seemed headed for a career as a virtuoso on the violin and who, when he temporarily became an artilleryman, proved to be a courageous fighter and also an excellent horseman, as though it had been important to him to show that our old ideas about the heroic nature of the metier of jockey was not entirely a piece of childishness. I would be lying if I suggested that I missed his company; too exclusively concerned with the pleasures that I was —though not without anguish, vexation, and mistakes—gradually discovering (having gone only a very small piece of the road as yet), I had eyes only for that brilliant panorama unfolding before me and, if I looked away from it at all, it was only to gaze at my own exterior, bent as I was on appearing in that pageant with as much elegance as I could, given my small financial means and that confusion of my limbs which is simply my lack of decisiveness expressed in physical terms; proud of a life whose dissipation seemed to me very chic and in which setbacks counted for little (for, at the age I was then, one feels time stretching out ahead of one), enchanted with that life, whose most serious fault was probably the fear of finding myself much too short of money to be able to start in again the next day—and no doubt that impecuniousness was itself the main reason I finally gave up this way of life —my days were very full, however empty they may have been objectively, untroubled in any way by the thought of my brothers at the front (except for an artificial sort of compunction) and containing no yawning hole favoring an exploration of myself which would, perhaps, have inclined me to measure how much vanity there was in my restlessness and led me, by the detour of pessimism, to more humane sentiments. I can't deny that, mingled with the admiration and friendship I had always felt for the brother about whom my mother and my sister delighted in reporting certain instances of mischievousness in his early childhood (how he asked the schoolmistress, in grammar class, "What is the etymology of the word *underpants*?"; how he combed his hair every night before going to bed so that, he said, he would "be handsome" in his dreams), this attachment to my brother Pierre who, formerly as gifted in classroom competitions as in those that took place in the schoolyard, had later proved himself in the field of music, was passionate about many moral and religious questions, viewed intercourse with women only in the light of romantic love of eternal dimensions and dedicated himself for the time being to his vocation as soldier with a sort of cheerful self-abnegation, there was now a tinge of disdain: how different this brother, whose valor and intelligence I did not question, appeared to me, fighting his war so simply, from those cavalier pirates who, one could readily believe, only assumed such huge risks in aerial engagements in order to pay for their right to complete freedom; how tame he seemed, taking no more than his regular leaves and, far from running around the streets when he came to Paris, finding all his restorative in the small, quasi-familial circle of people we knew from the parish, not even from the neighborhood! It would therefore be inappropriate for me to lay a great deal of emphasis on the good feeling that persisted—and still persists in many areas—between my brother and me; what I can, however, accept as undeniable is that—despite the power that is still exerted on me by certain individuals who are surrounded with disquieting sparks or whose life, having reached a particular point, then glitters, becomes iridescent, alters, warps, acquires (if it did not possess it already, even if only by reason of a lowering of social position caused by birth) a direction comparable to the mysterious moment when, in many melodies of Mozart and especially of Verdi, the current bends, slips dizzyingly toward *something else*—I have up to now placed my truest affections where, in one way or another, a trusting relationship could be established such as exists between two brothers—or on the part of a younger brother for an older—and my need for which is most likely rooted either in a longing for the early years during which my brother and I together, he barely a step ahead of me, went in search of at least a theoretical solution to the lofty or trivial problems one poses oneself when puberty comes, or in a disposition whose deeper nature escapes me and which I see simply expressed in the high value I now place on that search conducted with a companion closer, obviously, than any father or mother could ever be (since he has become our accomplice) but respected as much as one of our ancestors could wish himself to be.

The word FRATERNITY—which follows in red the all-white EQUALITY, itself preceded according to protocol by the azure of LIBERTY—is perhaps, therefore, the most alive of these three words for me, the one that (without claiming to make it the ultimate magic word) I would most readily freight with these precise, biographical references I prize so greatly.

A tacit agreement among several individuals who do not need to be of the same stock (nor of the same sex, nor of the same generation) to form a species of secret society; an open solidarity with the mass of people (whatever may be their occupation, their country, or the color of their skin) represented by people of goodwill, FRATERNITY oscillates from one of these poles to the other, their distance apart being more than a simple question of quantity, and I feel —for the moment—incapable of opting either in the direction of an attachment to an infinitesimal number of persons with whom everything happens implicitly or by innuendo, or in the direction of a communion that is vaster but, because of this, more diffuse and valid only when expressed out loud and constantly translated into action.

Whatever the size I give, in the end, to this circle of relations in which community of origin does not matter—and it is not necessarily out of the question for me to admit to it representatives of species different from mine, at least as invited guests (one New Year's Eve, friends found me dead drunk sleeping on the floor of their vestibule with the family dog, a fine German shepherd to whom I felt tied by a familial sort of affection, and some fifteen years later I chanced to address friendly gestures to some caged monkeys I saw in the Jardin des Plantes where a few of us from the Musée de l'Homme were walking, after a hearty lunch such as we were accustomed to eat once every week when we came out of the swimming pool on the rue de Pontoise, drinking considerable quantities of beaujolais, whence my condition that day: a true return to childhood or to nature, as on that New Year's Eve during which too many rounds of drinks exchanged had put me on the same footing as a quadruped and that Sunday when, awaking at home after another drinking bout, I evinced some surprise, if not offense, at the fact that the maid had not taken the cat with her to Mass)—whatever the basis may be, if I succeed in getting beyond my present indecision, upon which this fraternity rests, a fraternity which I know is, in any case, quite distinct from the fraternity of pure chance that is too often that of blood relations, it seems impossible to me to eliminate from it the element of gratuitous choice, spontaneous gift, unconsidered (and, if need be, preposterous) motion toward another living being, without which it would be no more than an abstraction just barely good for carving on the walls of buildings, printing in ethics or history books and embroidering on the banners of gymnastics societies.

I will discover these particular references, capable of giving visible substance, for me, to the idea of fraternity, here and there in the jumble of stories I decided so long ago to note down, stories often multifaceted which, I would say, I held onto the way one saves objects as evidence, even though I did this (in the case of more than one) without really knowing what they would become evidence of and what, in the end, would be their most important aspect; without having recourse to childhood memories, always dubious because too fragmentary and malleable, I will find at least one of these references if I turn to those of my stories that, lit by the uncertain glimmer of a war which I never more than vaguely touched, concern the several months during which I had some, however little it may have been, experience of military life, a group life that everything—beginning with the uniform—strives to imprint with an esprit de corps and in which it is difficult anyway, even for the most refractory, to avoid the camaraderie of the small clan (reduced to the volume and, most often, the duration of that transitory training).

As a soldier in the 1939–45 war, I have some very short daily duty sheets which of course do not provide the motivation for any epic story but could, if the opportunity presented itself, furnish the substance for a travel story since their more significant element is the stay I made in the rocky portion of the Sahara during seven to eight months, the greater part of which elapsed in a truly desert region, in that somewhat cenobitic collection of buildings designated by the name of "Base 2" as opposed to our "Base 1," situated about one hundred kilometers away in the largish village of Revoil Béni-Ounif, which represented our only contact with what is conventionally called the civilized world. In that unit, whose exclusive activity consisted in carrying out tests on what in the language of the general staff was known as "substance Z" (in other words shells and other terrestrial or aerial devices loaded with toxic products), my modest functions were those of the artificer and scarcely went beyond the limits of a bureaucrat's work or, at the very most, a scholar's; to have charge of the munitions book, to record the distinctive marks of the cartridges and fuses (some with fins) used in the firing or release of bombs, to be at once the warehouseman and the accountant of all the varieties of objects of destructive properties that we were assigned the duty of testing—this was in effect my main occupation, to which was added, each morning, the role of water distributor, when the tank truck arrived from Base 1 and I had to divvy up as judiciously as possible (trying to reconcile the colonel's instructions with the troops' quite contrary desiderata) an always insufficient quantity of liquid among the laboratory, the kitchens, and the bathrooms. I was, in sum, overseer of fire and water, and this, in the majesty of the middle of the desert; so that, as I strolled from reservoir to reservoir holding in my hand the long pole with its quadrangular section that I used as gauge, I could have imagined without much effort that I was something like one of those thaumaturges, controllers of storms or rainmakers, described in myths.

In the rather motley group we formed (since, along with people coming from France, as I had, and other reservists belonging for the most part to an artillery unit quartered in Oran, there were several career NCOs attached to the staff of our center, Legionnaires working at the radio station, a detachment of native North African infantrymen, and a few *mokhaznis* appointed to the camp's permanent guard, troops joined, during a certain time, by some Englishmen from the RAF) the chemists represented, among the French-speaking military, a sort of intelligentsia whose members, with few exceptions, hardly mixed with the other soldiers (whose duties, anything but scientific, gave them no occasion, anyway, to have contact with the laboratory). I myself was theoretically attached to this little body of intellectuals and technicians, having been called up, like them, to the Twenty-second BOA (which we obviously enjoyed calling the "Boa") and having met them in Paris at the time of our initial gathering at the Palais de la Mutualité, our company's depot, before we were dispatched—by train, boat, train again, then truck—to this remote spot where almost everyone was bored and sought a semblance of entertainment in playing bridge. Now, if it was true that I used to have the idea of becoming a chemist, at no time in my life did I have the least fondness for bridge, and this alone (without mentioning the special position I occupied because of being attached to the general staff) would perhaps have been enough to deter me from the exclusive association with these early partners, to whom, though some were certainly excellent friends, I did not feel allied by any team spirit, where either our work was concerned or our leisure time in the evenings.

Fate having led me to assume, by disguising me as soldier, a more or less new costume (since I had experienced only a brief period in the barracks when I was younger), playing at being a soldier the way a child amuses himself with a dress-up outfit represented the simplest solution, and it was therefore those of my colleagues who seemed to me "in the know" from a military point of view—those whose responsibilities and manners made them most capable of playing opposite me—to whom I felt gradually drawn, as though among them I would discover my most agreeable playmates if not my best friends.

With the career NCOs (of whom one was a native of Oran with a Spanish name who displayed an alarming virtuosity when he pretended to be the victim of an alcoholic delirium in order to frighten one of our roommates all too prone to believe that the isolation, the sun, and the drinks sold at the mess, which was under his management, could only cause a number of us to suffer fearful sunstrokes) I was on very good terms, as I also was with the corporal of the Second Etranger in charge of the radio station, a lad of very correct bearing with whom I enjoyed chatting about the ways and customs of the very particular corps to which he belonged. But, whether pen pushers in kepis or perfect mercenaries whose only law was their discipline and whose only faith was their worship of the Legion, these professionals were, each in his own more relaxed or more rigid way, neither more nor less than guard dogs. Even though of all my associations in the camp they were the only authentic soldiers—and no doubt it would be more accurate to say: because of the very fact that they were 100 percent soldiers exactly circumscribed by the limitations of their duties—it was with a partner of a completely different sort that I finally performed my comedy, a reservist older than I, who had nothing professional about him and even enjoyed recalling that he was there, really, only as a "guest."

The name of this older man, who surpassed me not so much in the number of his years (since the difference between us was not very great) as in the fact that he had fought in the other war, came straight out of one of our old chivalric romances. Yet there was nothing about him that seemed at first sight to correspond to a name of such ancient nobility except, perhaps, his appearance, which was that of a worn-out actor and led him to resemble someone who had escaped from another age or, more accurately, who belonged to no particular epoch or condition, a look one sometimes sees in the city on the faces of experts in so-called accommodating roles, men too habitually accustomed to making themselves other than they are to retain in their physical appearance those particular characteristics that would allow an individual, even if we were to see him stripped of all clothing, all uniform, to remain most often someone we could to a large extent situate socially.

With this companion, who commanded the "first of the second" (the first 75-caliber gun, of the four that made up the second of our batteries) I immediately felt in sympathy; his Legionnaire-style peaked cap with its buff covering, his gaiters of unbleached linen, and the ample cavalry coat furnished him in Oran by the store at the Eckmühl barracks, his awkward, rather lopsided deportment—like that of a horseman whose bearing relaxes as soon as his feet touch the ground or like that of someone who has been strolling around for a long time without any precise destination and begins dragging his feet—his whole picturesque exterior (apparently not at all calculated and, as far as his clothing went, not dependent upon any recourse to fantastic accessories except, perhaps, the gaiters of unbleached linen similar to those that I too thought proper to add to my outfit before leaving Paris), above all that face with its thin, unobliging lips contrasting with eyes as lively and sensitive as those of certain animals, that tanned, hairless face cut by thick eyebrows the same silvered black as his crewcut hair (which sprang up densely as soon as the cap was removed) and, giving piquancy to all this, an accent I knew, as soon as we met, to be from the eastern region of the Pyrenees—these various traits immediately seemed to me the descriptive signs of a figure prepared to let himself be swept up by the imbroglio of the war as he would be by that of a commedia dell'arte.

Close to the beginning of his *Mémoires* (of which I once read with enthusiasm the first chapters though I confess I never finished the reading project in which I finally got bogged down and which I never thought, as an adult, of taking up again) General Marbot devotes some affectionate pages to the memory of the person he calls "my mentor Pertelet," a seasoned soldier of long standing who took him under his wing when he was just starting out in the military profession. As far as I myself personally am concerned (as, of course, I am working on something akin to my memoirs but never found anything whatever at the bottom of my knapsack to indicate that I was destined for the career of general, or even for the dignity of a reserve officer), I was not taught very much—if I honestly try to add it up—by that older man whom I nevertheless like to regard as having been for me what the veteran Pertelet was for the young Marbot and to whom I too feel I should address a cordial thought. The gustatory pleasure of herring roe preserved in cans ("Bonbons!" he called it, this caviar of the meagerly paid soldier, as salmon roe are the caviar of the middle class); the pure joys of a friendship that had come about by chance, true, but was confirmed by certain shared tastes including, along with the liking for herring roe and other barracks-room delicacies, an inclination to spend our free Sundays strolling in the desert; the morality circumscribed by that camaraderie and reduced more or less to the laws of a trade-guild capable, in its highest form, of standing the test of fire; if to this I add a disgust for bourgeois philistinism (in a rather Ecole-des-Beaux-Arts spirit) I believe I will have covered the basis for the friendship between my mentor and me. No doubt the most substantial thing I learned in his company was the potential value of living this way in company with another, the understanding between us no longer being based upon sharing the same sort of ardor, as in the friendships of our younger days, but on the small joys we appreciated together and which we knew we were almost the only ones—at least under the conditions of the experience—to be able to appreciate this way. A friendship that is based less on a complete harmony than on affinities difficult to calculate and, though free of disturbance and violence, has some of the characteristics of a love affair in that, like the latter, it needs no other justification than the fact that it exists.

Whether it exists between very young people or between men who have reached maturity and left far behind them the age at which one romantically appeals to a secret society sort of mentality, there is scarcely any friendship that completely forgoes signs of recognition and does not seek to affirm itself through gestures of a ritual nature. Like all human affections—starting with love, which, in its various forms, is rooted in the mysteries of biology and is only secondarily a mode of social relations—friendship needs a certain formality, which will be more than a simple obedience of the laws of courtesy, whose principle, in the end, varies little from one milieu to another (since it is always a matter of showing the other person that one sees him as *fellow creature*) and will tend in a more or less concerted fashion to demonstrate by ceremonial acts—performed in addition to the trivial exchanges of civilities required by politeness—that a particular bond has thus been established between two or more people united by a reciprocal affection. In the same way, friendship will often be based on certain details of appearance or behavior that will act in the same way as a password and, inclining one to think that they correspond to something more general of which they are merely the outer blossoming, will appear symptomatic of the possibility of an amicable relationship.

If I myself was a bit of an outsider in relation to my fellow soldiers in the Twenty-second BOA and beyond that was also anxious to avoid the exclusive company of that "intelligentsia" overly convinced of its own superiority, my friend, too, occupied an isolated position within the group of noncommissioned artillery officers, since he was the only one of them who could be described as an "intellectual": as a civilian, he had actually worked as a designer and architect attached to a government service in one of the most famous cities in the Moslem part of Africa. Not only were we therefore in some sense displaced in relation to our respective entourages but because of our vocations we both felt, almost to the same degree, a commitment to the continent of Africa, and this differentiated us as much from my comrades the chemists from the mother country as from his comrades the artillerymen, who were inhabiting the region of the Oran only by chance. This shared attachment to a land different from our native land no doubt represented—with all that may be involved in loving things that are situated elsewhere—the most serious basis for our mutual sympathy.

It seems to me we hardly ever spoke of this. Our relations were more or less limited to being table companions surrounded by many others, so that ordinarily the conversations we had were disjointed and general, amid the din of the mess hall. Droll or indignant comments on the latest thing the colonel had done that day; teasing remarks about one or another of our officers or colleagues; occasionally some memory from the past: Sunday excursions in the back country of Morocco on his motorcycle, my trip to Black Africa and the various summers I spent in Spain, comical episodes from our artistic life, his activity as artilleryman in the other "war to end all wars" and his hearing, which had been perceptibly dulled by the discharges of the 75-mm guns— our chats rarely went farther than that, and except for frequent diatribes against everything opposed to our ideal of freedom, scarcely ventured into the areas of morality or politics. About me, he knew that I was married; about him, I knew that he was divorced, incapable as he was of allowing himself to be in the least restrained. Search my mind as I may, I am almost certain we never exchanged any other confidence.

This friendship, though not effusive (perhaps because it did not go beyond the limits of a pleasant companionship, as fragile as most relationships one forms away from one's own country), nevertheless had what I would call its "good times" before disappearing behind the screen of fog pulled down by the defeat and the years of occupation, a period at the beginning of which we would send each other news from time to time (vague news in which current events, too intense not to be thenceforth the touchstone of every friendship, only intervened very distantly), referring in our letters to memories of our

season in the desert without being able to be sure that we were always thinking the same thing and finally, my own indolence playing a part, ceasing to
write altogether. One of those great moments of communion—which at the
time made us think we had rediscovered for our own use the marvelous ton-
ic of fraternity—was a beautifully limpid, dry night we experienced, after an
evening spent chatting (and drinking a little, only just as much as was proper) in the room my friend shared with a few of his assistants from the artillery:
as a way of honoring this companion from the Pyrénées-Orientales department, I decided that before separating we should all dance a sardana, which
we did as best we could under the starry sky in a rather chaotic round which
(for lack of an orchestra and because of the total ignorance of my partners, including the Pyreneen himself, concerning Catalan music) was backed up only
by my own vocal accompaniment. It was not hard for my imagination to
transmute this nocturnal gesticulation, executed as conclusion to a barracks-
room party, into a mystical dance of Corybants or something approaching it.

Our other great moments were in the sporting atmosphere of the shooting
sessions that we had, when the nice clean barrels would launch their toxic
projectiles at the sheep which some *mokhaznis* in rubber suits and masks—
stiff golems or deep-sea divers—would afterwards bring by truck to the laboratory, where their viscera would be examined for a voluminous report on
the results (satisfactory or not) of these massacres, a first rough version of the
fate to which men were eventually to be subjected.

At daybreak we would set out in trucks for the firing range, which was
many miles away, for if the shooting had taken place too close to our buildings, the wind might have blown the poisons we were spreading back on us
or toward connecting points. For me, these outings did not seem to have to
do with war but, instead, recalled the railway trips I took with my teammates
to the Columbes stadium during the only year when I played rugby. In the
same vehicle as I, the artificer, there were other people belonging to the general staff, notably one of the Belgian legionnaires from the radio station, the
one who told how in Indochina his comrades and he ate boa meat, finding it
excellent food, and who toward the end of our campaign offered to remain

alone with the *mokhaznis* to guard our Base 2 (abandoned during many months of the year because of the torrid heat) as long as they left enough wine for him.

Ordinarily, my place was alongside the officers who were directing the gunfire, positioned up on a building whose terrace shook under our feet when the din reached its height. Once suitably stunned by the first detonations, I found it rather agreeable to be swept up by this outburst, a short distance from the guns but not so close to them for an impressionable nervous system to experience too much pain from it. The spectacle—a real battle scene, with flames and plumes of smoke, the gun crew busying themselves about the gun commanders who lifted their right arms and then lowered them as they shouted "Fire!"—was also one of the most exciting imaginable and, knowing that one risked nothing, one was all too likely to forget those other living creatures—the unfortunate sheep—who paid quite vilely for the operation: invisible, because very far away (and also penned behind low walls), they were only a theoretical target, reduced to the post that showed where they were and that we were delighted to see (though this actually happened only once) so precisely struck that it flew up into the air. Witnessing these shootings, I understood the pleasure to be found in handling high-quality firearms effectively and how a person who is not completely disabled by fear does not necessarily have to be a sadist to find some joy in the activity of war.

This, however, was only small-scale warfare except where the sheep were concerned, and my enthusiasm was not even great enough to make me forget altogether the horror that had always been inspired in me by things that were too noisy: detonators, firework bombs, ships' foghorns, cathedral bells heard from too close by, everything that explodes too suddenly and makes one jump or whose powerful vibrations seem to be heard not only by the ears but by the belly and the whole surface of the raw-nerved body. Whereas my duty —according to one of our main officers, who never had the slightest idea I was shirking it because he stayed at an observation post situated near the targets—was to run to each gun that "misfired" and immediately put aside the cartridge that had not exploded, I contented myself with counting up the car-

tridges that remained after the shooting was over—these had to be the defective cartridges, since the entire contents of the crates of ammunition were
put into the breeches. The sin was venial, no doubt, and I could without remorse disobey the instructions of a finicky officer; but I have always wondered what more serious defections I might have been capable of if a real
shooting had been involved—let's say, to be more precise about it: a reciprocal shooting, with fatal results on both sides—and not this sort of shooting
which only the animals we were using as targets could have taken for anything but an exercise. I still recall, with a bad conscience, those "misfires" due
to the fact that the capsule that was supposed to make the cartridge explode
did not detonate when struck by the hammer, a negative phenomenon rather
disconcerting to the novice: his entire body tense, he was already preparing
himself for the recoil of the detonation and was left, in the absence of that
detonation, in the situation of someone about to tip over into a void suddenly opening before his feet (or someone abruptly stepping down because of a
change in level he did not anticipate), at the same time that the initiating gesture of the gun commander in charge of the firing, since it was not followed
by the expected noise, came the completely gratuitous—and dizzying—start
of something that did not continue.

Coming back from the shooting, our mess was always very lively; we ate
and drank with an appetite even keener than usual and spoke loudly, not only
because the dry, excruciating noise of the 75s had deafened us but because the
gunfire had given us all the feeling of taking part in a heroic action. My mentor was pleased with his team, which he felt was well in hand after several sessions of shooting, homogeneous, and in a condition to acquit itself properly
if he had to come under fire with it. I always listened attentively to what he
said about the war he had fought and especially (for I thought I could learn
from it) his experience of fear, since he in no way hid the fact that he had
been more afraid and had had more trouble overcoming his fear after being
wounded, just like a bullfighter who loses confidence after a serious accident
because he can no longer believe he is invulnerable. It was during one of those
conversations inspired by our artillery sessions that he suggested to me—like
a landed proprietor inviting his guest to shoot a few rabbits with him in his

warren, a courtesy the guest can't refuse without the risk of appearing to be someone who does not deserve such friendliness and who would be better avoided in the future, or else like a host lending his wife or daughter to a stranger passing through, who can't decline the offer without a serious infraction of custom—that he suggested to me a sort of "honorary shot" which I would fire in his place at one of the next sessions.

The team of several men commanded by my mentor included, besides the gunners, a gun layer and a shooter. Positioned to the right of the gun and standing in profile in relation to its axis, the shooter was supposed to manipulate the small rope that actuated the hammer (holding the rope in his right hand and pulling it toward him, then releasing it, which would cause the hammer to strike the detonator placed in the center of the cartridge) after which, the shot having been fired and the barrel of the gun having first recoiled on its slides and then returned to its original position because of the spring action of the braking device—a system whose principle I had known about for a long time because when I was just under fourteen, at the start of World War I, I had read an article in *L'Illustration* about our 75 gun in which some optimist stressed the superiority of its hydro-pneumatic system over the spring brake of the German 77—he had to use both hands to maneuver the lever that opened the breech and caused the ejection of the case. A pair of simple enough operations, so that for one to be known as a good shooter one only had to perform them fast enough and with sufficient regularity (something I obviously did not have to worry about, since my "honorary shot" would be a single one and the titular shooter would immediately step back into the spot he had been obliged to give up to me). In order to earn a perfect score, the noninitiate was merely required not to forget to maneuver the lever, something the neophyte (it seems) usually neglects to do, stupefied as his is, being new to it, by the powerful detonation.

The prospect of substituting myself for the shooter and firing a shot frightened me almost as much as that of a real and imminent baptism of fire. To take it upon myself to do it was already a difficult resolution and as I made up my mind to it, I felt like a brave soldier offering himself as volunteer for a dangerous mission. To go through with the thing after deciding to do it was yet another stage to be passed and I did not manage it without first losing my nerve (declaring to my mentor with a small, rather pitiful laugh that I did not feel in top form that morning, although everything had been arranged the night before). It is clear to me that I would have wriggled out of doing this thing altogether (a brilliant feat of arms for me, since I have only very rarely been able to subdue the convulsions of my poor carcass) if I had not been afraid that in so doing I would lose face in the eyes of my friend with the beautiful name from an old chivalric romance and would no longer be able to count myself, even in an honorary way, among those he judged worthy of being his seconds in case he went into action.

It was at one of the last sessions (when I came to the point of saying to myself that if I let my failure of nerve stand as a permanent thing I would be very ashamed for a long time and would regret, yet again, having retreated before something that involved no risk but was merely unpleasant) that I made up my mind—the shooting had not yet begun—to announce to my mentor that I felt ready that day. The night before, I had decided nothing: because the act frightened me, I preferred to do it as though unexpectedly, so that up to the last minute I could take refuge in the idea that since I hadn't committed myself I could just as well decide not to do it. Of course it all went very simply and even the thunder whose violence I was so dreading was not as awesome as I had thought it would be. Maybe I had cotton in my ears? In all honesty, I can't recall if I had thought to take that precaution and I also can't say whether, as I pulled on the little rope, I stuck my other finger in my left ear—the one closest to the point where the explosion takes place—as custom would have allowed me to do, according to my mentor (who unfailingly though delicately made that gesture himself at the moment when he gave the order to fire by lowering his right arm). What I do remember, however, was that—naturally—I neglected to go on and open the breech, too proud of myself and in too much of a hurry, after all, to get away from the gun.

The man who gave up his spot for me so that I could fire the gun and then immediately returned to his post to work the lever (as though my omission had been anticipated) bore a name that could have been—and perhaps was, or will be—the name of a bullfighter; he was of Spanish stock, like so many

of the men from Oran at our Center, among whom there was also a mason I
once heard singing the flamenco where he sat all alone in a corner of the barracks yard. Shortly after that great day, my mentor drew for my wife a caricature depicting me seen from the back pulling on the little rope with a light
hand, a flower held between the fingers of my other hand, with the gun sil-
houetted in the background. All in all, then, it was in an atmosphere almost
of family festivity that I underwent this practical initiation into the artillery,
an ordeal on which I could feast for a while (since I had, in however small a
way, triumphed over my nervousness) but which was soon to merge with other trifles from the time of the "phony war," leaving me with no diploma other than this pen-and-ink drawing, now lying in the drawer of a secretary
which is not mine, celebrating my "honorary shot" or rather the salute I
could have dedicated, as a farewell, to those months of isolation and friendship. It has been many years since I last saw that drawing, and I think in truth
it is best that it stay where it is, for I am astonished now that I attached such
great importance to those military games, which were no more than a comedy completely outside me, and that I was so dumbfounded, as though at a
display of miracles steeped in meaning, by certain other suns of our artillery
sessions, seductive fireworks that they were: the Saturn ring that one of the
guns spat out during the first firing, a sign of the Apocalypse traced in the air
in an incandescent swirl by the metal belt of a shell that had accidentally
come apart; a distant landscape of mountains that appeared once on the horizon in the direction toward which we were shooting, as though our ostensi-
ble aim had been to shell a mirage; a gun operated less quickly than the others and which had gotten behind, so that once the firing was over it
continued to launch shot after shot, as obstinate as a dog howling all by itself;
the bloody head of a ram (a truly sacrificial object) set down on a white sheet
to be photographed for documentary purposes, on the day of the last firing
session (when time shells were used, which made it more complicated and
slower than shootings with percussion-fuse shells), the weather being gray
and gloomy so that it felt very much like the "end of summer," when the casino is half closed and many of the summer people have already packed their
bags.

Except for two or three bombardments (passively endured, without there being any combat that required boldness and quick thinking) I was not to experience any other shooting, up to the end of the hostilities, but this entirely theoretical experience arranged by my mentor. As a soldier in the phony war and a civilian at the time of the Resistance, I preserved my body intact, but because it had never been put at risk it seemed unfinished to me, as though despite my age I hadn't yet reached puberty. True, at the time of the parade of the *Forces françaises libres* down the Champs-Elysées, along with many other Parisians, I had to lie facedown for several minutes on the sidewalk near the Astoria Hotel to avoid the bullets of the snipers on the rooftops; but that was really a picturesque interlude in the hurly-burly of a festival and too benign to be regarded as a baptism of fire. If I search for something that, lacking the real thing, I could substitute for it, the best I can do is to note that a few days before that belly-flop exercise, at the time when Paris was undertaking to liberate itself on its own, though I was not involved in any fighting, I had the opportunity (though accidental) to experience how space was suddenly metamorphosed by the immediate presence of danger into something real, with its three dimensions no longer mathematical coordinates against which perspective melted away but a well-defined frame in which I knew my body was situated and perceived no less intensely the proximity of other objects the sight of which worried me. Returning from the Musée de l'Homme about noon on the first day of the uprising, on the bicycle that had been my means of transport every day during the entire Occupation, I had just turned onto the Pont de la Concorde in order to go from the Right Bank of the Seine to the Left when I found myself between a puddle of blood (immediately perceived as human and freshly spilled) spreading out on the sidewalk to my right and, stopped on my left, a German armored car full of helmeted soldiers with weapons in their fists; for several seconds I was aware of myself as a body drastically exposed, unarmed, denuded, with the sharp sensation of the weight of my buttocks on the saddle and the force of my feet on the pedals, all spatial dimensions being summed up in the distance that separated me from the bloody pool to the right and the steel car to the left, recognizing that now time, too, was a dimension, one created by the motion of the bike activated by the effort of my knees and improving with each passing moment my position in the system.

Compared with the fear born of something one imagines (for instance, being in the hands of a police force such as the Gestapo and waiting to see what they will or will not do with you) there was something ambiguous and almost pleasant in my directly physical fear of being used as a target: this was an awareness of my body taken to the highest pitch, as occurs in a state of desire, where what is revealed at the same time as the superlative existence of another body is our own nature as organism, at that moment standing (or placed in some way, it hardly matters how) in a void occupied by nothing but itself and this other body, whose intoxicating reality, a reality that makes us feel we too are more real, it would seem impossible to heighten by even one more degree, except by unclothing it at the same time that we unclothe our own. The fear of bullets is also connected to the idea of nudity, since it reminds us—in a hostile way, but with the precision of an image that incites us to caresses—that wrapped up as it is in the materials that usually hide it from others and allow us to forget it, our flesh continues to exist, as vulnerable, sensitive, and naked as if no clothing enveloped it. Even for a coward (someone whose main concern is his own safety and who thus, except by accident, deprives himself of many joys because he does not dare pay the necessary price), mightn't there be something voluptuous about discovering that he is in this way nude within the superimposed layers of manufactured products that make up our customary carapace? There is nothing surprising, then, in the fact that many people derive a sort of pleasure from war that helps them to accept its constraints, at least if they have not been demoralized by too long a series of disasters; however atrocious war may be, it disguises them as something other than what they are (which not only represents a sort of adventure in itself but also makes it easier to be courageous, because in uniform one is less oneself than in civilian dress, the costume like the military life as a whole tending to transform one from an individual into a small particle of a collective entity) and it even draws them out of daily life when fear leads them to so extreme a renunciation that one cannot any longer even speak of solitude in connection with it. No doubt it would take a considerable accumulation of fear and pain to cause them to be disgusted forever by these too costly emotions and to bring them out of the abjection that consists in relying on outside events— not willed but suffered—to cause a change in one's life (an abjection that characterized me to some extent, since despite my fear of it, war, in 1939, when seen in a certain light, appeared to me as a sort of evasion and salvation, being, on the one hand, the only truly important thing that could still happen to me, and, on the other, a lightning-fast removal from my usual surroundings).

I speak about this war as though I had actually fought in it, whereas it is just barely permissible for me to say that I knew certain of its most harmless aspects (since, being a serviceman from an older age-group mistakenly assigned to a corps of specialists, I always remained outside the combat area) and it is easy for me to remember what it might have involved in the way of amusements, never having been led to experience its horror. I would probably write about it in a completely different way if I had done more than simply *brush with* danger occasionally: clearly there is no comparison between wondering, during a limited time, if the spot you are occupying will be flattened by bombs or if certain people will have the idea of firing at you, and experiencing, during long days whose end can't be known, the unenviable condition of being cannon fodder. If I deduce from the fear I had on one occasion of being "used as a target" what "fear of bullets" may be like, I am dodging the issue, because there is a difference between risking one's life and merely being in a position to see such a risk, as yet still imaginary, become actual.

This danger, never more than merely brushed with—as though, while I did not want to remain altogether a stranger to the war, I was at least anxious not to do more than touch it with my fingertips—is all I will be able to accept responsibility for, of that dirty business. Because a written request of mine to this effect had been granted, if a position warfare had begun in France, as almost everyone thought it would, I would have been assigned to an "Army Archeological Service" in the process of being formed on the very eve of the breakthrough that was to bring about the collapse. I would no longer have been responsible for distributing fire and water, but for inspecting the area of operations to oversee, insofar as possible, the protection of the monuments, to identify everything that might be brought to light by the rather special excavations represented by the digging of trenches and, if required, to obtain assurances from the authorities involved that the need for respecting such sites would be taken into consideration in planning the lines of defense. I found this prospect attractive, not only because in this way what was unwarranted about my assignment to a company of chemists would have been corrected, but because such duties would have led me to fight the war, in some sense, without fighting it, certainly exposing myself to some danger but only in order to play at being, not a soldier, but a spoilsport, dedicated in completely conscious absurdity to a militarily useless work and, thus, involving myself in the tragedy as a dandy who barely comes into contact with it, too detached either to run from it or to lend his help to it. Toward the end of the Occupation, I made a moral gesture: I joined the FTP [*francs-tireurs et partisans:* a unit of the Resistance] "on D-Day at H-Hour," using the pseudonym Gérard (in honor of the dreamer in *Aurélia*) and the regimental number 1092. To assume the risk of having to risk my life when the fighting started—this was the meaning of this gesture which, like everything else I happened to attempt in the domain of courage, remained rather ineffective: my activity as a partisan was in fact limited to handing over to someone named Marc, a few days before the uprising, a box of 6/35 cartridges that I had held on to after giving up, in compliance with the requirement formulated by the Germans when they first moved in, the cylinder revolver I had inherited from my father and kept in one of my desk drawers at the Musée de l'Homme. Then, coerced by a friend from the Comité du Théâtre, I occupied the Comédie Française at the start of the uprising with other members of the Comité, was very nearly involved in a rather adventurous mission (to do with some weapons that, for a moment, it seemed someone had to go and fetch from the Place de la République) but changed plans when the Front National, which had formed at the Musée de l'Homme as it had in the other institutions of the Palais de Chaillot, decided to occupy that building. When, ashamed of the inertia of the sixteenth arrondissement (where I was staying in a friend's house so as to be able to go to the museum without exposing myself to the dangers of a long trip across Paris), I returned to my own neighborhood of La Monnaie—where barricades were going up—to see what was happening there, I at last made a firm resolution to participate actively: a SITA truck for removing household trash was blocking the rue des Grands-Augustins and had to be moved, and I went down from my apartment to offer to help, something that, in my mind, was only a first step; but here again I only brushed with real action, because by the time I reached the sidewalk they no longer needed any help, and the next evening, all the bells, including the great bells of Notre Dame, began ringing to celebrate the arrival of the liberating troops. Thus, during the uprising as during the war, all I did was make a few gestures, none of which had any consequences and which I also performed as pure formalities, hoping that events would not take such a turn that I would actually have to fight. At a certain point, was it that things had turned out in such a way that this same individual who had dreamed of being a jockey when he was very small, though he was incapable even of performing his gymnastics properly, had progressed so little that when he was over forty he would still be trying (as in the fictional life of a game) to deceive himself by various ritual mimicries, semblances of positive action in which a person who tries to save his prestige despite his fundamental deficiency chooses to cloak himself?

Of this war, which I lived through from beginning to end without ever testing my courage in a decisive way (or rather, simply enough, in this way proved what a coward I was, since all that was required to put myself to the test was to want to do it), what I will remember, for lack of epic events or cloak-and-dagger story adventures, will be the moments of close companionship it allowed me to experience: the camaraderie of soldiers (somewhat of a fantasy) in the North African desert; the deeper friendship of the few men of my circle who, in occupied Paris, knew that their reactions were roughly the same and that even those who were less reliable had the minimum of loyalty that allows one to trust another person. All in all, I learned an important lesson about friendship from the war, and my firm desire, beyond mere vanity, not to appear blameworthy in the eyes of a carefully chosen group no doubt represents what I acquired (or finished acquiring) in the course of that period. But how far have I progressed if I do not have any golden rule by which I could determine *with whom* I should consider myself to be truly close and on what basis—firm enough so that the phrase "friends for life" has some chance of not being a mere empty gesture—a fidelity should be established on my part toward those who will stand before me like a moral conscience personified, a Dulcinea in whose presence one does not want to lose prestige? And can I even—if I examine this more closely—count on such a comedy of masks, since it leads me to realize that in order to have the strength not to fail, I need to find partners to whom I would be bound by a pact based either on the very strength I would like to acquire, or on things worthwhile only to the extent that it is henceforth understood that precisely with respect to them is one incapable of failing? A strange sort of acrobatics I am indulging in here, as I seek—like a music-hall oddball miming a fighting match all by himself —the jiujitsu hold by which I might triumph over myself by a simple pressure exerted in the requisite conditions with only my thumb and index finger, like those yellow-skinned men wearing ample belted tunics and short broad trousers whom, as a child, I saw in photographs confronting each other without violence in an unarmed combat whose consequences (I thought) might nevertheless prove fatal. Up to this day, it has never been in real-life confrontations but only in the solitude of dreams that I have seemed capable of mastering a certain hold or a certain secret lunge that would allow me to win as though it were child's play: bearing down upon a winged bull I was facing in front of the portals of the Musée de l'Homme, I observed, at the moment that I thrust at him, that he was no more substantial than a balloon animal, as though the only secret for abolishing terror and overcoming obstacles was the pure and simple decision one made to charge at them. I admit that it is hard for me not to think, sometimes, that with experience, things I am afraid of will melt away like the bull, which, falsely, had frightened me in the dream, and that even death will prove to have been no more than a bogus figure of fear when at last I arrive—sooner than I imagine, perhaps—at that "hour of truth." However childish these bursts of euphoria may be, I must nevertheless remember that a little courage is enough, in many cases, to change into a sand castle what one had made into a mountain, and that this inner power, which gives one such control over what is outside, is a matter of *willing* even more than of *knowing,* whence the futility of resorting to technical subterfuges if a firm will is lacking at the very outset.

A sharp turn similar to those that must be made at short intervals in a horse show leads me, therefore, to note a mistrust of knowledge likened more or less to a collection of recipes that are certainly worth something but cannot give the real answer. Now, to acquire knowledge is the object of one of my profoundest desires and the moment when something is revealed has for a long time appeared to me most disconcerting: how could I, with one stroke of the pen, cross out this passionate desire that probably fuels the most manifest part of my will? If it is of primary importance to show that one has a will of one's own, one must "know what one wants" (as the saying goes) and if one of the things I want most obstinately is very precisely knowledge, I have twice the reason—or the reason multiplied by itself—to persist in trying to find out what, in the last analysis, are the values that I should regard as enduringly mine and dedicate myself to serving with all my will. Such knowledge, of course, will not be a kind of magic capable of giving me the iron will I used to admire in my gym teacher; but at least it will help me not to waste my efforts, probably allow me to concentrate more effectively, and respond, in some way or other, to my desire to be a man who, knowing his limits, does not stray into paths at whose ends he would discover only failure and, avid to dissimulate, would inevitably drift into inauthenticity.

I will therefore sustain very firmly my wish to understand more about this idea of brotherhood, at once so bracing and so elusive.

There are noble brotherhoods, but there are also ignoble ones; if one cannot concede as valid, for instance, the sort of communion that may exist between two cops as they give someone the third degree, one must conclude from this that what is important is that thing *in* which, *through* which, one communes and not the fact of communion pure and simple. *Brotherhood,* of course, is one of the most moving words, but before one becomes moved, it would be an advantage to know which sort of brotherhood we're talking about: the brotherhood of cowards who join in eliminating someone weaker than they? Brotherhood in courage but for a cause that is at bottom idiotic or detestable? The brotherhood of criminals as close as the fingers of a hand? A brotherhood based on a shared inclination or vice? The good-natured brotherhood that reigns within a group of extroverts or a sports team? The brotherhood of a club which the vanity common to all its members tends to promote as a society of perfect human beings? Universal brotherhood, still only a slogan up to now? Even though *to fraternize* may be a better watchword (not only because it is a verb that evokes an action but because it implies an enlargement of the circle, an appeal to others, the conclusion of an alliance that did not exist before and, in a general way, the breakdown of all the different sorts of barriers that stand in the way of effusiveness) I don't think the idea of a communal brotherhood can be enough in itself, for the recognition by everyone of the simple fact that all men are zoologically brothers and associated by the similarity of their destinies would still leave unanswered these two questions: According to what terms and conditions should this brotherhood be lived? And what should we, all together, try to do with it?

If I were prepared to solve these two problems now, perhaps there would be nothing more for me to do but bring this book to a close after briefly setting down their solution. Does that mean that I would be able to sit back and rest? Not in the least, for then I would have to work at translating these ideas into action, and would certainly have to write, and write again, in order to formulate them in a way that was ever clearer, more communicative, more convincing . . . But I am far (as I know all too well) from having accomplished the long journey at the end of which I would be able to risk attempting some conclusions. All I can do now, more or less, is simply describe some friendships, at the same time allowing myself to present a certain number of reflections one at a time and to insert here and there, in fragments, something that will resemble perhaps that "enigmatic scale" that Verdi introduced, among other vocal parts, into one of the *Pezzi sacri* he composed when he was nearing the end of his life.

A serious sort of brotherhood experienced last December when I took part, as an observer, in the Congrès des Peuples pour la Paix [Peoples' Peace Congress] held in Vienna: it was a great moment (commensurate with the international nature of the assembly) but it was only a moment and I also lack the militant spirit that would let me pursue enthusiastically what I continue rather dutifully, with the desire above all not to disappoint those who very naturally expect me to be loyal to them. There are two terms, after all: what is seductive, and what one regards as the Good. Need I emphasize how much easier everything would be if one could find a legitimate way to make these two terms coincide all the time?

A frivolous sort of brotherhood, superficial and committing me to nothing, experienced as the chance result of a few encounters at a time when my health, the inclinations of my character, and my occupations allowed me greater latitude for some kind of night life: in an English bar in rue Pigalle, one Christmas night, a young British student was going from table to table carrying around his neck—like those necklaces of flowers with which the Polynesian islanders customarily decorate tourists—a toilet seat on which he was politely recording the signatures and addresses of everyone present, in order to preserve (I suppose) a tangible token of those hours of collective euphoria; another evening in the same bar (which for a long time I used to patronize now and then and from which, on my return from Béni-Ounif, I, soldier that I was at the time, came home once with two frightfully black eyes as a result of an impromptu boxing match in which I and one of my companions opposed four or five strangers with whom we had quarreled on the sidewalk), an Englishman with graying hair, very drunk, very lonely, and very sad, sent a bottle of champagne from his table—without the slightest scrap of conversation resulting from this gesture—to my wife and me and the friends who happened to be with us, three men and one woman.

It is fair to say that the more time goes by, the more I tend to regard with amusement these superficial and fortuitous encounters which at one time filled me with delight but which, I see all too clearly now, imply no solidarity and are worth something only to the extent that they express, in the most naive way, that it is intolerable to remain all alone and that to form even fleeting relationships with strangers, as long as one presumes them to be at all like-minded, is indispensable (at least from time to time) to anyone who does not want to suffocate altogether. With its daily torments and its police terror such that everyone had to ask himself what he would do in the case where someone was using torture to impel him to turn in someone he knew, the Occupation does its part to make me more exacting where brotherhood is concerned and has shown me the great value of certain acts that belong to an elementary code of living that has nothing (to start out with at least) heroic or brilliant about it: to share what one has with a person in need, to reject an advantage derived from the persecution of innocent people, to know when to hold one's tongue and when to speak, to protect those who are being hunted down, and all sorts of other actions tied to imperatives as simple as the dictum of childish morals that "you must not be a tattletale." But I nevertheless remain convinced that no true fraternization can be conceived that would be rigidly serious and judicious: what is, in its essence, an impulse of the heart must, by definition, jostle, even if only a little, the limits imposed by morality and reason.

To break out of one's matrix, to get out of oneself, to merge with people outside oneself—this is the simple, vague impulse that, without any passion for drunkenness as such, may lead one to enjoy drinking in bars just as one may also take pleasure in mingling with the crowd waiting for the arrival of the Tour de France without being a fanatical fan of bicycle races. Ordinarily lost in a mass that is hardly more (except when a certain exoticism heightens its colors) than something that moves as one moves oneself and against which one must avoid colliding, one will be delighted when even a meaningless bond is created that allows one to live in harmony with that mass or the handful of anonymous people who represent it. All the more reason, in historical circumstances such that almost an entire population displays its heartfelt happiness in the streets (or at least ceases to be morally holed up behind its walls), that this great formal stir and confusion will cause someone who feels in sympathy with what is behind it to experience an intoxicating multiplication of himself through his contact with others.

The end of a war will always be cause for rejoicing on the part of the people on that side, of the two sides, that can now say "fraternity" without falling silent when it comes to saying "liberty." After such trials, it seems to the winners that peace has solved all their problems; it is not simply an end to the fighting—a negative event, since it is no more than a return to normal—but the beginning of a better age, for which one departs from other bases: the wound has been excised, all one will have to do now is join together a little and, at the worst, give another little effort. The Second World War was followed, like the First (though more briefly) by a period marked by this optimism: the forces of evil had been conquered at last, and now a livable world could be built.

I was in Paris when the liberation of the capital signified, for many egocentric French people, that the war was over; in fact, it lasted almost one year longer, many men had ample time to get themselves killed, and I found myself in Dakar, about to return from a mission to Africa, when I learned of the fall of Berlin and the cessation of hostilities in Europe.

At that time it seemed, for the colonized peoples, that things were going to change: the proponents of racism had been crushed, democracy was on everyone's lips, and one no longer spoke of "Our Empire" but of the "French Union." Under the leadership of an inspector of colonies I had gone with two other specialists (one in human geography, the other in tropical agronomy) to study the means—of a liberalist order—by which to palliate, on the Ivory Coast, the manpower crisis that followed the elimination of forced labor. A trip that had obliged me to view Africa in a way completely different from the way I had before: what was in question was no longer the beliefs and secular institutions whose study had been the principal object of the mission in which I had participated a good fifteen years earlier, but problems that touched the very flesh of the people (living conditions in their villages and on the plantations, standards of living in general, methods of payment of contractual laborers, possible uses of their salaries and all sorts of other questions of the most forbidding sort for someone who had been led by, among other inclinations, a liking for the so-called primitive mentality to make a career as an Africanist; what I had to do—and I only succeeded with the greatest difficulty—was to rid myself of my romanticism, react as best I could against a turn of mind that (not to yield once again to the moralizing tendency that I must tirelessly make my *mea culpa*) I will call contemplative, and, above all, take a correct view of those miseries that one all too easily forgot because of the beauty of their surroundings, and, often, of the very individuals who suffered them.

As I was to take the plane the next morning for Paris, which I had left a little more than three months before, I had agreed that day to have lunch with two young men, one of whom I had met at the home of a mutual friend before he settled in Africa; it was a very simple good-bye lunch, with the amount of drink appropriate in the colony the day before one returned home. It was over dessert or when we were having coffee—as far as I can remember —that the radio announced the news, shortly afterward signalled to the inhabitants of Dakar and its environs with all desirable pomp by the noise of sirens and gunshots. Very quickly we found ourselves on our feet, listening with our brandies in hand as a record player broadcast the anthems of the allied nations, including that of the Soviet Union, which we accompanied in chorus with our three voices, even though we did not have the necessary linguistic knowledge to articulate its words. I was doubly happy, first because the great news had reached me in Dakar and second because the population with which I was fraternizing in the joy aroused by such an event was the black population of an African town.

My first concern was to go back, flanked by my two hosts, to the house called the Hôtel des Gouverneurs where I was staying with the leader of my mission and two of our companions, one of whom was the geographer and the other a planter from the Ivory Coast who had worked with us as local representative of that corporation in which a few rare estimable people, of whom he was one, rub elbows with a depressing number of brutes and swindlers. I expected that with my colleagues we would wander through the streets carrying with us a jubilation shared with the crowds of Dakar, and it was with this impulse, already completely fraternal, that I went to join them.

That the leader of our mission would come with us—something he probably would have been led to do whatever we decided, given our companionable relations—was out of the question, for, since we were leaving the next day, he had to devote himself entirely to the duties of his position. As for my two other colleagues, strolling around town was perhaps not the most direct desire inspired in them by the announcement of victory; yet it was in their company that I embarked upon that day which one could expect to be a great day. As for the first—a real workhorse with whom I had sometimes become irritated, given my nonchalance—what I appreciated, despite the tiresomeness of his rigorous rationalism, was his fundamental honesty and his resolute desire to improve in a perceptible way the fate of the peasants among whom we were making our investigations; I certainly learned a good deal from him in the course of our rounds, developing a more realistic view of things. As for the second—for reasons that are still rather romantic, certainly different from those that compelled me to respect the first—I enjoyed listening to him talk and may say that I spontaneously liked him very much because of his love of life in the bush and the men of the bush, also because of the passion he had for hunting elephants, an activity that appeared to him quite natural (since he had to protect both his own plantation and the crops of his people from the incursions of the great destructive animals) but to which he had an air of devoting himself with a tranquil ardor, much less in a spirit of obvious self-interest than of Crusoe-like adventure. The two men were as different physically as they were intellectually, the first being tall, lean, and angular, like a big blue-eyed Scandinavian (he actually came from the East), whereas the second, a little shorter than I, looked like a lively, dark Mediterranean (though I cannot say if he really came from that region). I wonder—not knowing really what I am about and being something of a flying fish or amphibian, a beaver, seal, frog or toad—in which foggy or sunny clime an uninformed narrator might situate me, for I have (unfortunately) very little in common either with the head of the large family who loved the rigors of mountaineering because "only when one is tied to the same rope as another man can one judge him at his true value," or with the bachelor leading his Negroes in the tracks of an elephant and sharing with them the game he killed.

There were quite a few people in the streets, but they were calmer than I had imagined: no delirium comparable to what followed the armistice of November 1918 or the liberation of Paris—a sort of July 14 with nonsimulated firing; nothing, above all, that allowed one to feel such a swelling exuberance that blacks and whites would in the end form, at least for several hours, one single, identical swarm in which social differences and divisions by color would be forgotten. Everyone walked, crossed paths with others, mingled, but it seemed that each kept his own thoughts to himself. Things being what they are (it only occurred to me later) under the sign of what peace, offered to everyone as a joint possession, could the Africans and colonials of Dakar have come together? Thrust suddenly into the euphoria of the dissolution of war, I though quite stupidly that the success of the allied troops could only be the source of one and the same euphoria for everyone and—without stopping to size up the tenacious belief in my privileged position implicitly evinced by my decision thus to play the great good-natured lord—I asserted my desire not to let this beautiful day pass without fraternizing with the colored portion of the population, an apparently normal consequence of the jostling and chance encounters of the street, for anyone who wanted to take part in it.

However, this day, which I thought would be the most open, the least confined, was not for me, in actuality, even a day spent outdoors, since I remained until quite late in the evening with some Levantine merchants who were celebrating the Victory with my luncheon hosts and a few of their acquaintances. Wiser than I, my two companions from the mission left us early and went off to the small bistro where we ate our meals to join an old Saharan officer—no fool and a rather good fellow—whom the geographer and I had met at Bamako and with whom we had traveled for nearly three days in the Sudan Express. By the time they left, I had already drunk too much whiskey to be in the least attracted by the idea of a peaceful dinner and preferred to remain where I was, like a gambler who is not persuaded by the most obvious losing streak to leave the gaming table as long as it is still materially possible for him to tempt chance.

The gathering I allowed myself to become swept up by was, in fact, only a very ordinary cocktail party that derived no particular dazzle from the historical conjuncture that had inspired it. We drank, danced, and flirted innocently with the ladies in an atmosphere that was really quite genteel and resembled a small family party. I don't know what drunken mood induced me to leave the large living room on the second floor and go down to the ground floor, where I found some pleasure in weighing myself on a scale that was part of the equipment of the shop; with me—also weighing herself—was one of the mistresses of the house whom I had made, for perhaps the past hour, my official partner and who (quite unfamiliar with any Eastern languor) was a good middle-class woman, a shade too loud, not at all unattractive with her pink-tinged white carnation standing out against her black hair and her even blacker dress. This took place among crates of merchandise in a courtyard or inner room that had the stale old smell of an Indian mail train and served as a warehouse, and after each weighing we began dancing again; since my weight was rather minimal, I think this test on the scale was really something of a demonstration to flatter my vanity. Later, having very platonically and lyrically paid court (as does someone who has alcoholic love in him) to a rather pretty woman—the wife, also brunette, of a minor civil servant or merchant from the interior—I discovered that despite my bacchanalian dizziness, my demonstrative galantry, and the childish pleasure I took in defying the law that forbids a respectable European living in the colony from mixing with Syrians, I was, in truth, very lonely. Reclining indolently because her leg was afflicted with one of those ailments that people make into something almost stylish because they are the price exacted by the tropics, immobilized in an armchair that had been transformed into a sofa by the addition of a chair or a stool, the beautiful Frenchwoman declared that she was no longer in any condition to dance and could pay attention only to one of the young men who had brought me there, saying she was in love with his eyes, so deep and so blue (something she could announce without fear of being taken at her word, because the man she was saying this to was, by vocation, as unsuited as could be to appreciating feminine charm).

In that living room where a number of people were moving about, between one and two dozen though I can't say exactly how many (just as, upon reflection, I can't guarantee that it was on the second floor that I should situate this scene and not on the ground floor, on the same level as the commercial part of the house), in this living room with its sham opulence where it seems to me some sandwiches were served, if not an improvised light meal, plates on our knees, and where probably (but not at all certainly, because it may be that yet another room was the setting for this edifying episode) we all adopted for a moment a position close to standing at attention and sang the *Marseillaise* with an old couple from Alsace, I felt, as I became more and more drunk, somewhat more in difficulty. The thread which I had been determined up to then to grasp in my fingers, not wanting to let go despite fate working against me, suddenly broke: quite simply, I stood up and walked across the room in silence with the demeanor of someone constrained to leave for a moment by a physiological need. But without even dreaming of pretending to make my way toward that private spot they call quite plainly the privy, I reached the exit with a steady step and—still possessed by the desire I had had since noon for some kind of fellowship—went out into the darkness.

Here I am, not surrounded by snow, wind, or bolts of lightning (like a Hoffmannesque character emerging, haggard, toward midnight one December thirty-first from the tavern within whose smoky walls he had left his shadow or his reflection) but under the incredible multitude of stars that tattoo the tropical sky. As I crossed the threshold, I probably breathed in a large gulp of air—like someone starting a long-distance race—and lifted my eyes romantically toward those stars which I sometimes wish I could eat, as though, absorption by mouth being the most elementary means of incorporating what one loves, it were natural that the desire one has for a thing be accompanied sometimes by an irrepressible cannibalistic desire. Unable to consume the stars, I probably breathed furiously and diligently at the same time, pinching my nostrils as though to squeeze more tightly the otherwise impalpable current of air created by my lungs, and exhaling noisily. I was probably also striding along rapidly in the very middle of the road the better to feel above my head that heavy burden of luminous pinpoints, sparkling too brightly to remain pure geometry, each of which seemed to derive its particular density and savor from the very violence of the attraction that all of them together exerted on me.

Of course, I was heading toward the center of town, toward what I supposed was the heart of the whirlwind, not feeling defeated after that party which, for me, had ended in disappointment, and wanting, to the exclusion of everything else, to attach myself to a seething crowd. The difficulty I feel as I try to reconstruct the fabric of these events without leaving too many gaps in it proves to me that from the beginning of the afternoon I had lost any exact notion of what I was doing; nevertheless, though I had no coherent vision, my own avidity guided me through the confused stages of my day, no less effectively in the unlimited spaces of the streets as within the confined perimeter of that house where I had just now been in despair: to blast through the barriers, to abolish the distances that separated me from other people—such was my pillar of fire and pillar of clouds in that zigzagging quest for a promised land.

Here I am, now, in the very midst of that exuberance I had been looking for: in the din of a square or broad avenue, I plant myself across from a large café with some sailors who are protesting because they have been refused admittance into the establishment. Disgusted at seeing that on a day like this anyone should dare to act in such a discriminatory manner toward men from the navy, I side wholeheartedly with them, posing, in my own eyes, both as an outlaw prepared for any conflict and as a defender of the indefeasible rights of human integrity. But our recriminations remain futile and at last we take off, without risking the scuffle that would surely have broken out if we had tried to force our way into that paradise of dazzling lights and noisy customers. Brothers from the *Potemkin,* rebels from Kronstadt, mutineers from the Black Sea, my companions the outcasts would perhaps fall from their heights, surprising me today as I ask myself if the halos they all wore and the Soviet national anthem I had heard that morning had anything to do with the fact that a rather tipsy civilian quite naturally threw in his lot with several of them, once the incident whose rather sheeplike victims they had been was over and done with . . .

The sailors in white uniforms with large blue collars and the civilian in tweed and gray flannel pants (for the weather is nice in Dakar at the beginning of May that year) have entered a dance hall, this time without encountering any opposition. After standing together at the bar and chatting a little with the barmaids, each of us goes off to try his luck. The sailors want to dance, but this poses another problem: no single women, and the stuck-up

chits who are here show no interest in anyone of lower rank than an NCO.
No doubt a few words will be exchanged, because my buddies with red pom-
poms don't hesitate to offer their services to accompanied ladies and even try
to separate couples on the dance floor by taking possession of the women. As
for me, I am standing near the platform where the orchestra is playing and
without a black velvet mask or Venetian hooded cloak am watching the spin-
ning dancers. Did I demand with a vulgar insistence that they play the Soviet national anthem? Did I incite a few of my humiliated, my insulted friends
(who were quite otherwise occupied) to make noisy demands along with me?
Did I go too far in demonstrating my solidarity with these rakish, guzzling
Volga boatmen with their Punch-and-Judy antics? A petty officer from the
navy, also in white but without the blue collar, tries to pick a fight with me
and invites me to step outside, which I agree to even though I know for a fact
that there is no difference between us to settle. To fight for the sake of fighting seems to me totally absurd and this is what I undertake to explain to him,
deliberately but firmly, assuring him that I have absolutely no intention of
avoiding it, that I am completely prepared to give him satisfaction, but that if
it is permissible to fight, one still needs to have a reason for fighting. As I say
this, I do not feel in the least inferior; it seems to me, on the contrary, that I
am in control of the situation and I am proud to observe that at least this
time I am mastering my drunkenness enough to avoid, with honor, a meaningless brawl in which I would definitely be defeated, and from which I
would emerge having made a fool of myself, my face covered with degrading
bruises. After having been Hoffmann the madman I become Nicklausse lec-
turing him and burst with contentment at the idea of such wisdom lurking
within the fantasy. Before the entrance to the dance hall, the petty officer and
I argue for a long time: I affirm with equal energy my willingness to fight and
my conviction of how nonsensical it would be without either protagonist
having suffered any insult. I play the roles of both witness and possible du-
elist, delighted to prove to myself that I have kept my head completely and
am capable of getting myself out of this idiotic business with as much dignity as composure. At last the petty officer calms down and yields to my argu-
ments: we take leave of each other like two adversaries whose appointed arbi-

trators have not reconciled but summarily dismissed them, believing that the conflict they were supposed to decide does not justify the shedding of blood.

So here I am once again wandering through the streets, still tormented by the greed that took the place of thought in me and whose profoundly benevolent nature had been strongly affirmed only a few minutes before when I had been able to make the necessary speeches, without retreating an inch, for my enemy to feel disarmed by such indisputable goodwill. I had left the liveliest part of town behind and was walking without any specific goal, only determined not to give up that night, as though something were waiting for me at the end of my sleepwalker's ambling. Seeing a lighted café, I went in. The place was sinister: a small group of colonials, men and women, were there celebrating the Victory in a family group, gathered around one or two tables which they left several times in order to dance. I sat in my own spot, drinking a brandy and water or something like that. These people paid no attention to me; despite one or two women with whom—if we had been able to break the ice between us—I would have been happy to dance because their physical appearance seemed pleasant to me, I found them vulgar and, wanting to talk to someone, settled for a Frenchwoman of about sixty who had to be the proprietor or a relative of the proprietors and who, occupying a seat near me, told me in a rather friendly way about the difficult life she had lived in Dakar, which had been her home for some thirty years now. This was undeniably a form of company, and equal in value to many another. Nevertheless, it wasn't long before I was feeling very lonely again.

Another departure into the night, and there is a good deal of obscurity in my memory about this next stage also. My stop in the little café, with no other human contact but that conversation about hard times with a woman tired out by too many years of work and life in the colony, had doused the modicum of satisfaction I had experienced at feeling so reasonable and at the same time so resolute after the storm of abuse at the dance hall. Also gone was the glimmer of reason that had allowed me to settle quietly a foolish quarrel arising from drink, so that as I persisted in walking along these streets I couldn't have been more than a drifting shadow. The only thing that could have compelled me to continue on my way instead of going back home to bed was my initial plan to attack the prejudices of the whites by fraternizing with Africans.

Did I encounter those three Negroes at an intersection? Or, when I approached them, had I already spoken to several of their fellows standing in the light of a crossroads to ask my way, though I don't know whether "my way" was to the African quarter, or the port, or the center of town, or was perhaps a simple, melancholy return to the house where my comrades from the mission had probably gone to bed by now after spending the evening chatting with the old Saharan officer? Or perhaps, realizing I was lost, had I merely wanted to find out where I was without asking the way to any particular place?

However it was that I approached the three Negroes, whether I went up to them right away, advancing in a burst of cordiality, or whether I approached them with the polite restraint of someone asking for information and, since the air was fresh under the stars and we were at loose ends now that the hour had struck midnight, we began a conversation and I was escorted by these people, who first appointed themselves my guides and then turned me over to still other hands—however it was, I told them I would take great pleasure in going for a walk with them. They did not offer the least objection to this and the four of us set off, they flanking me like tall, robust bodyguards.

Exactly how long did that walk last? Where did we go? And what did we talk about? Our conversation was probably limited to a rambling monologue during which I affirmed my desire for better understanding between the races, my love of Africa, and the very great esteem I had for Africans, who were closer to real life than Europeans. Most likely, too, my three attendants, not very open to the Platonism of my speeches, offered me some women, and I remember some vague whispered confabulations between them and some great black caryatids reposing on verandas and almost melting into the night, commercial negotiations, no doubt, that resulted in nothing. Soon, I believe, I was no longer speaking: I was simply savoring the joy of walking arm in arm through the soft shadows. Making full use of my vigorous supporters and moving my legs without thinking about it, perhaps I was on the point of dozing off when a violent punch on my chin recalled me to myself and, more than half dissipating my drunkenness, made me realize in a flash that my three attendants were trying to knock me out in order to rob me.

Thrown to the ground by the uppercut or hook to the jaw, I felt my ankles twisting as my aggressors tore the shoes from my feet without bothering, of course, to unlace them. Still quite stunned, I heard the three strapping fellows run off at full speed and found myself half draped over a flight of stairs as a stocky European in white shorts and a short-sleeved overshirt came up to me. He was a petty officer from the navy (did he tell me or did I see his gold anchors?) who, attracted by the noise, had scared off my robbers and was now helping me to stand up. Some distance away I recovered one of my shoes, abandoned in the panic flight; but I found that my wallet had disappeared from my right hip pocket, which had a large tear in it.

I put on my one shoe, brushed myself off, breathed in the smell of the greenery surrounding the vast building the sailor had been evidently assigned to guard, and answered his questions: no, I wasn't hurt, no bruises, just rather sore ankles. But what the devil could I have been doing with those Negroes? "I was taking a walk with them." "What? You were taking a walk with some Negroes? More likely you were getting yourself buggered!" I immediately responded by calling him a filthy name, we fought, and it all happened very fast: since he was stocky, as I said, it didn't take him more than a few seconds to deal me a second knockout and send me back down on my stairway.

When I returned to my senses all I could do was set off again, limping this time, since the only heel and sole I had for one of my feet were those of my sock. I was pretty much clear of my alcoholic fog, but drunk with rage. I felt no resentment at all against the thieves, who had laid me out quite neatly even though they weren't necessarily experts in the notorious Senegalese fighting that so excites the Sunday crowds in Dakar. Fair enough: since I had been stupid enough to trust complete strangers—as though Dakar, a black town, had to be a paradise on earth and not a port like all other ports with its underworld quite prepared to beat someone up—I could only blame my own naïveté if the loyal Othellos into whose hands I had meekly consigned myself had suddenly changed into perfidious Iagos; and wasn't it comical that after priding myself on managing things so well I had ended up getting my face pushed in after all and had also been relieved of the few thousand francs I had left? What I regarded as truly inexcusable was the conduct of that petty officer who was so convinced of the absence of any common measure between the black and white races that he couldn't conceive of someone going out at night with Negroes except for reasons having to do with sex, and this on a day when people were celebrating the fact that Hitlerism had been crushed! The only suitable retort I could make to this cop was by way of the cops: I intended to go to the police station and lodge a complaint against the shameful white man who had ignominiously insulted and struck me, in defiance, actually, of his own prejudices, which should have stopped him from displaying toward me a solidarity that turned out to be so fickle.

Walking with a quick step and a jerky one because of the imbalance created by my missing shoe, I turned into a long, very straight street. Despite the late hour, I encountered one or two people (blacks? whites? I have no idea) and asked them where the police station was. Protesting to a European civil servant against the vile action of another European who himself belonged to the official circles since he was in the navy appeared to me to be a duty I owed to the most rudimentary form of justice: wasn't it disgusting that on this day of all days, which one might have hoped would be dedicated to humanitarian sentiments, a responsible military officer should have shown with such bestial cynicism that for him Africans were still untouchables?

I was still walking along that drowsy street, so deserted it seemed interminable to me, and wondering if I would ever reach the police station. What was whirling around in my head now was neither global nor fraternal reveries against a discontinuous background noise of recollected scraps of the Soviet national anthem, but the plans of a grieving moralist who arrives like a prophet of doom proclaiming the abjectness of what he has seen. The contrast between my stocking foot and my shod foot transformed the one shoe that remained into a buskin and it was like a tragic actor that I proceeded toward the distant and problematical station where I intended to loose my thunderbolts. Perhaps I was beginning to feel a little worn out: my lower lip painful, my ankles slightly bruised, and my right leg retaining the smarting memory of one of the falls I had taken on the steps? Then again, perhaps I became aware of all that only later, when my anger had died down and I was resting?

Whatever the case, it was taking me a long time to get where I was going and my only idea, now, was to get there. Noticing a house that was wide open and brightly lit, with bursts of conversations issuing from it, I decided to go inside and try one last time to get someone to point out to me where the police station was. When I appeared before the men and women making merry there—with my clothes in disorder and perhaps the look of a blinking owl— their gazes turned on me, stupefied one and all: I was in the house of the Syrian merchants I had left some time before and my two hosts from lunchtime, like the Alsacian couple and the rest of the company, all standing, it seems to me, greeted this apparition, this unseated horseman wandering home limping badly and covered with mud, with the same eye as though I had been an emanation from hell as untimely as Banquo's ghost or the statue of the Commandant.

I briefly told the tale of my misadventure and forcefully stressed my desire to go lodge a complaint with the proper authority: that anyone should have thought I was a homosexual was something I didn't care about in the least (and I insisted on this point somewhat hypocritically, in order to show that I was broad-minded and not to offend my two hosts, because to talk about Sodom in their presence was the same as talking about ropes in the house of a hanged man); this having been said, it was intolerable that the mere fact of not keeping one's distance from Africans should be interpreted that way and I attached quite a different importance to this reaction, which proceeded from a scandalous state of mind, than to that business of blows unequally exchanged with someone who had hurled a term of abuse in my face.

Even though in their eyes my reasoning was probably less rigorous than in mine and they were in a better position than I to appreciate the absurdity of my appealing to a police inspector as though he were a supreme judge, my two friends decided to accompany me. Without them, I certainly would not have found the police station, which was situated elsewhere than in that street along which, wearing only one shoe, my eye cloudy, I had walked as though in a dream. A functionary with a fixed expression on his face listened to my statement and did not bat an eyelid when he heard me specify that it was not my first aggressors I was angry at but that petty officer from the navy who had grossly insulted me and struck me one more time. I probably looked crazy enough so that he did not pay much attention to the details of what I said and retained only what interested him in his job as cop—that a European had been assaulted and robbed by Africans—and I had obviously recovered only a very small portion of my reason, since I did not realize the inopportuneness of an action whose only result (if it had any) would be to bring grist to the mill of those who denigrated Africans whereas my intention had been just the opposite, to punish a racist. While I was making my statement, a sailor in a white uniform, large blue collar, and beret with a pompom on it came to complain that he too had been attacked, and displayed his hip pocket which had been torn just as mine had. Before signing my name below my statement (which a clerk had typed), I reread it carefully so as to be sure the meaning had not been distorted, but one may assume that these two complaints lodged during the same night would hardly raise the people of Dakar in the professional opinion of the inspector with the fixed expression . . .

Taking me home with them, my two hosts lavished attention on me: they bandaged my right leg and the man with beautiful blue eyes mended my torn pocket like a skilled seamstress; they lent me a little money and made me a gift of a pair of lightweight, comfortable black shoes with rubberized heels that came (they told me) from the American navy. Then they took me to my hotel, the Hôtel des Gouverneurs, where I arrived at about three in the morning and had just enough time to shave and pack my bags before getting into a car to go to the airport with my mission leader and my colleague the geographer. The latter was not the sort of man to have a high opinion of my completely gratuitous attempt at fraternization in the vapors of drunkenness, for his ideas, like his character—he was a member of the Communist Party and had fought as an officer in the FTP—predisposed him toward a brotherhood that was concrete in quite another way. As for the former, he was not insensitive to the ludicrous aspect of the whole business but pointed out to me— good diplomat that he was—that I would have been better advised not to involve the police because tongues tended to wag in the colony. As for the elephant hunter—who said good-bye to us at the airport before returning to his Ivory Coast—I don't know exactly what he thought, but I have every reason to believe that he was too experienced at taking action and too accustomed to controlling his reflexes not to regard as rather miserable a confused situation such as this whose only coherent principle, when all was said and done, was my lack of constraint.

As far as I myself was concerned—the first person singular, in other words the primary person involved, in this story of a grotesque escapade—I can see that everything happened as though some unknown administrator of justice, in order to punish me for having thus degraded myself under the pretext of fraternizing, had made use of the rapacious hands of those three blacks (probably full of scorn for the drunken white man abandoning himself so far as to claim he was the brother of men he knew nothing about except their color) and then the fists of a European military man (to whom this same drunken white man, so proud of his show of egalitarianism, was clearly not in any condition to furnish a model of humanism). Anxious to indoctrinate me, some Providence had perhaps taken advantage of my pointless night-prowling to prove to me the inanity of an effusiveness that doesn't go beyond a few symbolic gestures: a warm handshake, a Spanish-style *abrazo*, all of this dressed up with handsome smiles and pretty words. However sincere the sympathy that had for so long attracted me to people of other races and other cultures —and especially toward the blacks, ordinarily treated like poor relations in the human family—there is no question but that from the very start of this affair what was motivated by an authentically heartfelt impulse had been translated into action in the facile guise of a theatrical attitude: to fraternize with the population of color was a demonstration that could satisfy my pride but remained completely exterior, whereas true brotherhood would have required that in all modesty and lucidity—making a dogged and serious effort to help it defend its interests on the most down-to-earth and daily basis—I would take up the cause of the population that I had just seen for the first time clearly revealed in the Upper Ivory Coast when the geographer and I encountered a convoy of unskilled laborers recruited to go work for the planters in the south and when (the mask of exoticism falling from those faces, which were now merely those of tired men) that group—at first almost identical, as a crowd of people of color tend to be for a white person because of the shared difference that comes to the foreground—changed, as I looked at it, into an unhappy collection of individuals each of whom had his own nature and destiny that deserved one's sympathy and attention.

Does the fact that I now express such appropriate thoughts mean that I have finally stopped replacing positive acts (those that imply a commitment and, in addition, work toward a practical end) by pretenses reminiscent—making all due allowance—of the *desplantes* in the bullfighter's art: bravado moves intended to impress but with no effect on the fight itself and demanding less skill (even less courage) than the precision work that consists in unleashing the charge and then allowing it to take place without flinching, letting the horns pass very close before dodging them?

"No, I haven't stopped doing that!" I must answer that specimen of myself with whom I am far from done fighting like Jacob wrestling with the angel or that horseman Nerval speaks of, *who fought all night long in a forest against a stranger who was himself.* To do and to pantomime, to be and to appear—these are the opposing terms, the pole of value being opposed by that of prestige, as Illusion is to Truth, or Lucifer to the archangel, that archangel to whom I would be tempted to lend a sort of reality from the sole fact that I bear his name and of whom I saw, in Naples, a moving representation in the form of a picture entitled *The Devil of Megellina* because it is the most revered image in the little church of that neighborhood situated on the edge of the sea not far from the sanctuary of Piedigrotta which is a place of pilgrimage: in it, Saint Michael, wearing Renaissance armor, overwhelms a demon that resembles him like a brother and whose diabolical nature is indicated only by its bat's wings, corresponding—as they curve their shallow basins under the bowed head of the vanquished—to the feathery wings of the archangel extending their double canopy into the sky.

The clamor rising from the Auteuil racecourse over a disputed finish. The shouts of "To the guilloti'! To the guilloti'!" coming, among other cries, from a little boy who was running in all directions from one end to the other of the school yard one day when we were acting out the revolutionary days of 1793 at the coeducational boarding school. The scattered din in Naples during the festival of Piedigrotta, certain people carrying on the ends of fishing poles immense decorated paper hats which they tried to set down on your head by surprise, almost everyone tickling you in the face with long, comical feather dusters made of paper ribbons, and many children in paper costumes dressed up as fairies, princes, or other characters while loudspeakers broadcast songs that were to be the year's novelties. *Bravo! Bravi! Brava!* hurled in thanks to the singers in the Italian opera houses. A modulation with the power of the *ole!* shouted at the moment the matador transforms the nerves of the spectators into violin strings, at every level of the plaza. The loud noise of the Parade for Peace on December 13, 1952, in Vienna, when the Sunday crowd passed before the members of the congress of all shades of skin color and almost every country, placards and plywood doves standing out white against the cloudy sky and then floating in the light from the headlights, among the torches we were given so that we could have a turn holding them, all the while shaking our hands over the barriers strained to the point of cracking. The slogans chanted by countless lips all along the procession during the mass demonstration this past July 14, which the Paris police were not ashamed to stain with blood, attacking workers from North Africa who were milling about with other workers.

At the opposite extreme from these shouts all mixed in together and jostling one another, a woman's piercing cry—tragically isolated—which I heard when I was little in La Chapelle one evening when we were coming home from a family dinner: *"C'est une batterie"* [it's a fight], my father explained, meaning that a brawl was going on and using this word—present in *"batterie de canons"* [battery of guns] and *"batterie d'accumulateurs"* [battery of accumulators]—to express the action of two people who *se battre* [hit each other], just as the action of *mentir* [lying] can be called a *"menterie"* [fib], an analogy I was to discover later and which would make the terrible word *"batterie"* (through a sort of inner unburdening to which I would like to subject many other things that frighten me) seem airier than at the time when those people who were called *"gars de batterie"* [battery guys] seemed to me to be designated by this name because they were agricultural workers supposedly quick to quarrel and not because of their various jobs to do with *battage* [threshing wheat]. A man on leave squealing like a stuck pig one evening toward the end of the 1914–18 war ("I'm buggering him, Lieutenant! Lieutenant, I'm buggering him!") and dressed in horizon blue—field-service tunic, trousers, forage cap—and great black leather gaiters, a drunk of thirty-five to forty clinging to a streetlight on Avenue Mozart as though fiercely determined not to leave, as though no one in the world would be able to tear him off. Solitary cries that rise in my memory as death-throe ululations and can't be stifled by the great chorales of passion, enthusiasm, or harmony in which my own voice has managed, from time to time, to participate.

From the grandstand of the Auteuil racecourse (where I sat only once when I was about ten, to see the Grand Steeple won by the English horse Jerry M. ridden by the jockey Driscoll) I moved on, after a long interregnum, to the shadowy gates of the bullfights, then turned to *tribunes* [grandstands] of a completely different sort, as it became intolerable to me never to be more than a spectator (even if in close contact with thousands of others) and as I ceased to look upon all things with eyes thirsting for sensation more than anything else and came to discover that, from the point of view of positive action, the hero, the genius, and the saint are far from being the only types of men whose existences are justified: the sort of *tribune* [gallery] in which those who have been invited to be part of the *presidium* take their places at the start of a meeting and the *tribune* [rostrum] in the strict sense (and at the same time substantially narrower sense) from which one speaks on one's feet—like a conductor at his stand or a lookout in his watch tower—without succeeding (if I am the one who is thus on the spot) in transforming the human voice into a living link with the listeners. Too well aware of my shortcomings, I have never trod the wood of these platforms, upon which one steps up not in order to see but in order to expose oneself to view, without feeling guilty of a twofold imposture: that I am only there in the manner of a decorative figure even though these days I claim to be rejecting the values of facade; and that I am allowing myself to be treated as a "personality," as though I had the prestige that went with a famous talent or the authority of someone who has given proof of an exemplary citizenship. But from this new point of view, the fact that there should be such a great gap between the hero, genius, or saint that I am not, to my humiliation, and the man of some goodwill that I actually am can't matter very much: I recognized long ago that lending effective help was an almost laudable ambition, and there is no question that the world needs people prepared to exert themselves to their utmost as well as champions or those seeking high achievement. That I have until now avoided the three essential experiences—voluntarily risking mortal danger, killing, and bringing into the world (that is, staking one's own life, annihilating that of someone else as one does in war or insurrection, and causing a new life to come into being)—experiences to which may be added certain trials peculiar to our times—making a parachute jump, for instance, or submitting to tortures of which the "Chinese torture" of my childhood gives only a very distant idea!—is certainly a serious deficiency, but it has no significance except to me; if I manage to contribute something, however little, to help humanity reject its old tutelary relationships in favor of more fraternal arrangements, to come of age in some sense, what can it matter to others that my destiny—considered on its own terms, as though it were a work of art—may not be a masterpiece?

Everything would be played and would veer in this direction if it weren't for a straw in the system: resigned to a destiny that will not provide the material for any golden legend and convinced henceforth that, if this remains inconsequential to anyone else, what is dictated by the sporting spirit or appetite for difficulty does not weigh more in the universal scale than what one does out of pure love of art, I at least prize a destiny that in retrospect makes me *worthy of being loved;* now, is any favoritism granted, in any field whatsoever, to someone who quite simply is able to prove himself a steady sort of person? And if the most important thing is to have one's horse win and if working in a useful manner is worth more than consuming oneself in regrets for the ace one will never be, doesn't the example of sports teach us that efficiency unaccompanied by a beautiful style is rarely appreciated? No doubt I would not react with the same pleasure or the same foolish pride I once did to hanging about in the dubious quarters of foreign cities, such as Whitechapel in London and Limehouse, so disappointing a Chinatown, or the

Barrio Chino in Barcelona with its queer transvestite nightclubs and shops offering contraceptives of all varieties (with points, with ribs, shaped like clown heads or Napoleon hats) sold after being tested on a bellows apparatus with a red light that went on when the device had resisted sufficiently, or even—in areas both calmer and more remote—the outlying districts of Port-au-Prince of which certain corners occupied by rickety hovels, with porches held up by thin poles and as though mounted on stilts, evoked, when glimpsed in the night, the den of the hired ruffian Sparafucile in the last act of *Rigoletto;* no doubt I would no longer believe I was something of a "tough guy" or adventurer just because I walked around in ports like Le Havre, Marseille, Antwerp, or Rotterdam, which I visited when I was a child and which provided me with my first romantic vision of a maritime city. But if I have also gone beyond the period at which I was happy to find myself in a boat on a rather heavy sea (probably because then I had, cheaply bought, an illusion of mastery) and if the time is past when I imagined that, staying in an unfamiliar town, my contact with people and things was more real if I visited not only the parts of town where the monuments were but also the working-class districts, all these elements of decor or details of production retain a great power over me as though unadorned reality were incapable of uplifting me and as though a certain dose, infinitesimal if need be, of gratuitousness or fantasy were indispensable for me to take part in that match, with its heavy stakes, that is won or lost outside. Thus, in Vienna last winter, before I had altogether made up my mind to participate in that great human game in which one never hears the call "no more bets," I was moved and confirmed in my desire for action by two things coming together: the multicolored waltz of skaters frolicking near the hall of the Congress of Peace (as though to offer an image of the precious graces that war annihilates) and, the color of a midsummer's sky, the completely sensual sweetness of a beautiful gaze resting— with the dreamy rapture one can read in the eyes of bovine deities, water nymphs, and dryads—on those insouciant skaters.

"Look! Already the Angel . . ."

"Gentlemen, and *cric!*" ("And *cric!*" answers the chorus.) "And *crac!*" (The chorus repeats "And *crac!*")

The man uttering these words in musical tones was a Hindu employed as manager by the large white distiller of the area. This was taking place in Gros-Morne, where I had gone with a friend from Martinique to attend the wake of his old nurse.

"And *cric!* And *crac!*"—the traditional formula heralding the story the Hindu was about to tell to entertain the people who had gathered in the courtyard of the house to keep the vigil: the story of the thin young girl, thin "as the E string on a mandolin," said the Hindu, an expert (it seemed) in Creole oral literature.

As for me, I want to tell the story of Khadidja, or rather *my* story with Khadidja, a prostitute I met when I was a soldier in Revoil Béni-Ounif and who, though tall and slender, was not as thin as the thinnest string on a mandolin.

Khadidja bent Maamar Chacour, born in Algiers and twenty-three years old, according to the official records. Khadidja, whose first name was that of the Prophet's wife and who, after working in the red-light district of Colomb-Béchar, had transferred what little she possessed in the way of clothing and jewelry to a brothel in Béni-Ounif after a quarrel she had had with someone named Nadia. Khadidja, so imposing that the large Roman statue of Demeter from the excavations at Cherchel in the Galland park museum in Algiers reminded me of her when I contemplated it later.

Khadidja, whose form—with narrow shoulders, long slim legs, and wide hips—I inscribed in the diamond of the constellation Orion, which I had at one time taken for the Southern Cross (when I was discovering the tropics) and later (traveling in Greece just before the recent war) already identified with an absent form that preoccupied me.

"... Gentlemen, and *cric!* ... And *crac!*"

I hardly know the Creole language at all (delicate and nuanced behind its pidgin appearance), but my friend translated for me as the Hindu spoke, and the rhythm of his delivery and very subtle modulations would have been enough to charm me anyway, even if I hadn't grasped anything of the content of the tale. What formula might I myself use, being neither a Hindu from the Antilles nor a specialist in Creole literature, to introduce my tale, that of a very commonplace adventure imbued with a fair amount of cinematic exoticism but elevated, in my eyes—because of the contributions of several outward appearances—to the dignity of a lived myth?

"Rebecca" was one of the biblical names that struck me the most when I was a child because of the meeting at the water hole and the word itself, which evokes something soft and aromatic, like a raisin or a muscadine grape, also something hard and obstinate, because of the initial *R* and especially the ... *cca,* whose abrupt stringlike vibration I hear again, now, in words like *Mecca* or *impeccable.* "Rebecca": a woman with coppery arms and face, wearing a long tunic and a great veil on her head, with a jug on her shoulder and her elbow leaning on the lip of a well. "Rebecca": a name that opens like "rebel" and would perhaps end on the same muffled note as "impeccable" (already mentioned) if, as though in an increase in stiffness, it were not broken before the syllable with the mute *e* whereas the name associated with it— Eliezer—prolongs its murmuring, like that of a bubbling spring.

"Ergastulum," "cistern," "lucernarium": Aïda the beautiful and tender, the dark and proud captive, rejoins her lover, who is condemned to die of suffocation in the depths of a cave; Rebecca rests for a moment at the well where the dromedaries are watered and where the caravansary is situated; Gideon and his companions slip under cover of darkness into the camp of the Midianites, carrying illuminated lamps that they hide in jars.

"... Gentlemen, and *cric!* [repeat] And *crac!* [repeat]." The ergastulum for slaves; the *bousbir* for the present-day prostitutes of the military towns of

North Africa. At the Opéra, flesh-colored bodysuits clinging to busts with two protrusions but without apparent points worn by the priestesses of Isis or attendants of the pharoah's daughter imitate the naked torsos one could see and touch in a place like the Sphinx or any one of those houses, now outlawed, which in elevated language are known as "lupanars" whereas vulgarly they are called *boxons, bouics,* or *claques.* In rue d'Aboukir, two heads with Egyptian-style headdresses—caryatids without bodies, represented by their heads alone—ornament the carriage gateway of a building that one would no doubt be mistaken in believing to be a confrere of the homonym of the monster with human head and lion's body which was real enough to the ancient world but no longer is to us, except for the ruin surviving a short distance from the pyramids of Giza. When I said good-bye to her at the entrance to her den, Khadidja was wearing an ample white dress belted at the waist and a green muslin veil wrapped like a sort of turban around her forehead and hair; surrounded by the madame and a few of the other girls, she was sitting out in broad daylight, her back to the threshold of the courtyard on which opened all the bedrooms and other rooms of the single-story house; for the first time, that day, the day of my departure and therefore the last day of our friendship, I saw her dressed in Eastern fashion with her head covered.

Before she appeared to me, angel without rank and not yet fully tamed, in the form in which I knew her best—that is, in a *seroual,* those long, baggy trousers donned by most European soldiers and civilians in those regions, who liked to ape the indigenous fashion, and worn by her in imitation of their mates, who wear this as they would wear a suit of pajamas for the boudoir or the seashore—I had seen Khadidja in a blouse, loose top, or bright red pullover and a very simple gray skirt; dressed thus in Western style, she might have been taken—if it hadn't been for the blue decoration of symbols tattooed on her face—for a half-Spanish, half-Indian mestiza such as the stories of trappers or gold prospectors portray in bars built of wood planks. I recall being struck by her height, her long black hair, her fierce expression, and her poised bearing; but I don't see what subterfuge would allow me to recover her image exactly, unless it were by referring to another image as I did when, an adolescent in love with a young girl—whom her brothers and sisters called my "fiancée"—I would use one of the illustrations from my *Manuel d'Histoire* by Malet to insure myself, by summoning up familiar, catalogued features which seemed to me close to hers, against forgetting a face I was afraid I wouldn't be able to restore to life once it had fled from my mind: a profile of the young Bonaparte by Gros or some other painter of the time, a drawing that I sometimes traced, distorting it to accentuate its resemblance to the one I was endeavoring (and in vain) to dream of every night in order to prove to myself the authenticity of my feelings.

It is certainly possible for me to remember the worried and nervous look of Khadidja's bronzed face behind her tattoos, many of which were crosses and which were nevertheless distinguishable right away from their homologues used in the underworld. Were they family marks? Tribal marks? Ornamentation motivated by vanity alone? Whatever the case, they situated her in the very heart of her native milieu and contrasted, when one saw her rigged out as a suburban streetwalker, with that graceless mode of dress. Emanating from a twofold shadow—the poorly lit room where the dubious whiteness of her bed was displayed, my brain in which burns (like the little kerosene nightlight in my bedroom when I was a child) a lamp which, every day, imperceptibly grows feebler—I recall not only the unforeseeable riches of her body with its long, straight, sturdy legs, but also her slightly spicy fragrance, the soul of her skin, which was that of a goat girl rather than of a night person rubbed with ointments from the bazaar. These, however, are only isolated pieces of information and if the expression of these imprecise features gives an idea of what Khadidja *could* be, it in no way reconstructs the singularity of her body and does not introduce her specter, such as it would perhaps appear to me in the masquerade of a dream if it weren't the case that I (who used to dream so often) almost never dream, a sure sign of growing old.

In Colomb-Béchar—where before our months of complete isolation I sometimes went on twenty-four-hour leave with some friends because we had no other semblance of town within reach—I noticed Khadidja one beautiful evening in one of those nightclubs even more lugubrious than one might imagine from films about the lives of legionnaires or other colonists, but, since I was there only out of an idle interest in my surroundings, it didn't occur to me to talk to her. In my strolls around town I had already happened to sit down in one or another of these rooms with walls sometimes bare and sometimes painted with vague floral ornaments and filled with noisy soldiers (spahis or camel corpsmen) unless they were absolutely deserted except for the idle barmaid, and where, sitting at a table in front of some sort of liquid with my companions, I had all the time in the world to identify myself with the "living statue of funk" of which I had written in a letter one day when I was depressed and brooding about myself.

The only road that led to Base 2—which we soon took over as a battle-front in order to make the inglorious tests to which we had been assigned—was a route that joined the road to Aïn-Sefra several dozen kilometers from Béni-Ounif at a point where one could read, inscribed in thick characters on massive milestones, to the right "Aïn-Sefra," to the left "Dead End Road." When our trucks entered the fork thus destined (as the sign said) to disappear into the nothingness of the rocky plateau, it seemed to me that a very attentive fate had wanted to see expressed in black and white something I already suspected to some extent: the *dead end* insanity of my venture into military life. Later, settled in Base 2, I appreciated as another trick on the part of this facetious fate the arrangement of latrines labeled NCO TOILET, the point of which seemed to be to let the immense mineral landscape they looked out on know for what use and what users they were intended, while several yards away a similar structure bore the sign MEN'S TOILET as though it were important to prove to the desert itself that, though it might obliterate many things, it would never do away with hierarchy. Throughout the entire duration of a sojourn that almost all my companions regarded as a bitter joke, I truly believe I was impervious to the blues and the only painful memory I have of those months is the sort of moral disaster into which I sank, having had the imprudence of asking—out of a desire to be like the others—for a twenty-four-hour leave to go to Béni-Ounif, where I slept in a shabby room in the "Hôtel du Sahara" and, for the whole of that day, literally didn't know what to do with myself.

At Base 2 I tasted the presence of the desert, which is, if you like, only a void and an absence (the absence, at least, of all life) but in which the solitude one discovers—even if one is there with two or three hundred others, as I was in my camp of huts—is so intense that very little complicitous abandon is needed for it to change into fullness: not simply being alone, but *being alone in being* is what the desert makes one feel, for here more than anywhere else, one's consciousness of one's existence is confronted with the exterior in its purest state and becomes, having no rival, the very gaze of a God outside of whom there is no consciousness. The place where being and nonbeing—or fullness and emptiness—come together, the desert, at the same time that its nakedness deprives me, heightens the feeling I have of my own presence and makes me—as at certain moments when I am writing—feel alone in the world, nothing (when I am face-to-face with this nothingness) appearing to exist except as a function of me, as a dream I invent that can touch no one but me. In the place of meditation, which the natural desert is, as in the desert that surrounds me still sometimes when I sit down to write, I don't believe myself to be either more pure or more detached than in the moments when I take my part in the tumult of everyday life, nor do I ruminate with sorrow over the idea that I am separate; rather, I tend to think I have truly turned into a *microcosm,* as though the world reduced to the ideas that I manipulate or to an inert exteriority that I see, belonged, in all its mad diversity, to the solitary being I am, without any live intrusion preventing me from incorporating it into me so that everything may be contained in me.

Unquestionably, I took pleasure in gradually realizing that that expanse of rubble—which appeared to me more nuanced, richer in color than any landscape loaded with violent hues, so that in its heart I was able to come alive—was, far from being a mere dead surface, relatively populated. As I became familiar with the variety of Saharan desert known as the *hamada* (as opposed to the *reg* with its classic layers of sand) and as my eyes little by little became diligent at studying the details of the larger spectacle on which they had originally fed, I discovered infinitesimal plants that were paradoxically finding a way to survive in what I had at first taken for the very image of desolation; I also saw several insects, testifying to an animal life that, unlike the hostile kingdom represented by scorpions and horned vipers (happily less profuse than we are led to believe), one could observe without fear or disgust; by taking a long walk to a wadi where, we had been told, there were a few feet of earth cultivated by seminomads (which was certainly worth our spending many hours walking under the sun bathed in sweat) I even saw a few human beings: striding rapidly along, having started at some unknown hour, on his way to some unknown place where he would arrive at some unknown point in time, a man we encountered halfway to the minuscule camp which marked the end of our walk; near this camp, working a piece of yellowish, completely bare soil, another man behind a swing plow pulled by a camel the same color, the color of sackcloth with coarse, miserable darnings. Just as much as my view of the *hamada* as an area in which we would be the only living atoms except for a few venomous creatures, these tiny discoveries and our encounter with the two men overjoyed me, because of the very fact that (contesting the validity of my original idea) they revealed to me a certain number of presences in a solitude I had thought complete; however exhilarating it may be, the feeling of an absolute desert is probably so humanly uncomfortable that one can't refrain for very long from trying, secretly, to uncover the pulsation of a little life within this void whose virtue then becomes the fact that it confers an infinite value on the frailest apparition. Quite likely, despite my scorn for those who were bored at Base 2, I myself was less at ease there than I imagined, and I recall a strange event that was in some sense grafted onto another strange thing (my surprise at the sudden appearance of a little unexpected softness being joined by surprise at finding myself on the edge of tears at the sight of something that, anywhere else, I would have considered banal)—the emotion that seized me when, returning to Béni-Ounif in an automobile convoy after our campaign was over, I saw at some distance from the town a green patch of grassland that had grown up while we were away, almost supernatural pasture suggesting to us that this inland country (sterile not long ago, and so often vilified) was in truth a rich country off which, henceforth, we could feed ourselves heartily.

Among the North African prostitutes I had approached up to then, none had inspired me with an imperative desire to sleep with her, not even the one in Figuig to whose home we had gone one Sunday and who served mint tea with so delicate a gesture: the glass, slightly inclined, held out to you grasped between two fingers, the little one extending under the base while the tip of the index pressed against the rim. That girl who, seeing my shaved skull and my serious expression, had asked my friends if I was a dervish (a nickname that stuck), offered me very politely a little grain of mint and I was infinitely grateful to her for her attention, since I attach an immense price to those trivial gifts which, coming at just the right juncture, are a sort of proof that at a given moment the outside world has responded to us and are then preserved with a nagging fear that they will vanish like those astonishing objects one possesses in dreams and whose disappearance, upon waking, one deplores (before realizing that in fact the dream itself is the disappointing object one is so sorry not to hold in one's hand); but her face, with its hard, violently painted features surmounted by a sort of cylindrical cap, called to mind, not the majesty of a sibyl but rather the brutality of a cossack and seemed to have been so heavily daubed only in order to mask the signs of some kind of rot. At Colomb-Béchar I had seen other girls, some ugly, others endowed with that minimum of attractiveness that gives a prostitute a chance with someone: a little black woman, quite kind, who boasted of having lived with a sergeant for a while; a tall, robust Chleuh mountain woman; in order to enter the red-light district, however, one had to pass through a guardhouse where it was very difficult to avoid the prophylactic injection a male nurse had been ordered to administer to all those whose motives for venturing into that precinct were assumed to be something other than a tourist's simple curiosity, and such a beginning was not very encouraging.

It was during the period of uncertainty, slackness, and open laziness that preceded our embarkation for France—where the war was continuing without having, so to speak, begun—that I saw Khadidja again, one idle evening at our base in Béni-Ounif, with her hair still loose but this time wearing the *seroual,* which made her appear even taller and, despite her carnivalesque character, accentuated her qualities of savagery and determination. I'm not sure who had gone with me after dinner that night to have a beer in the *bousbir*—maybe it was the corporal in charge of the radio team, who, because he was a ranking officer in the Legion with a specialized occupation, was allowed

to eat with us, the NCOs of the reserve, at the Hôtel du Sahara. Blame me
for it if you will, but the fact is that I rather enjoyed the company of the professional soldier; the way in which he described the yearly festival at Sidi-Bel-
Abbès commemorating the Battle of Camerone was certainly enough to ex-
cite one's imagination: the flag bowing before that relic, the jointed hand of
the one-armed officer who commanded the Legionnaires wiped out in that
battle during the war with Mexico was a ritual whose air of being a pagan ceremony celebrated by people of another age or another continent certainly
wasn't evident to the man describing it, but his enthusiasm as he spoke (in the
tone of a priest explaining the mass and its deeper meaning) about this
homage paid to the body of which he was a part by the colored symbol of an
entire nation—as though the fetish preserved in the Legion's hall of honor
had an acknowledged priority over that unanimously respected emblem—
never failed to impress. This same corporal also talked to me about something
that is a rock of Sisyphus in the life of a Legionnaire: earning a little stripe
with difficulty, then losing it because of some overly extreme drunken episode
or some infraction of discipline; earning it back, then losing it again. At that
time, the Legionnaires did not have all the terrible renown they now have because of the horrors committed during the war against the Viet-Minh; the
main discredit associated with them was the rather ambiguous one entailed in
everyone's eyes by their status as mercenaries, and—even though it hardly
ranked them in the category of choirboys—one too easily forgot what was
implied among such men by the fact of being, in the full sense of the term,
professional soldiers. In my eyes, therefore, this radio team, of which I can
say, without misplaced pride, that they had a soft spot for me, was only a
small group of technicians, peaceful on the whole, good companions, and
more often induced, by the propensity they almost all had to get drunk regularly, to indulge in clownish pranks than in bloody rages. To be honest, I
should also admit to my lack of constraint and "back country" state of mind
at that time: these habitués of the border regions—whatever they might be
—presented me a great contrast compared to my companions the chemists,
almost all of them such homebodies!

Coming out of the Hôtel du Sahara, my friend and I decided to go and spend a little time in the *bousbir* before going to bed. We had hardly any choice of places in which to kill time beyond a noisy, smoky bar always full of more or less inebriated soldiers and one or another of those houses that were generally tranquil, where the girls did not importune you with overly indiscreet advances and seemed content if you emptied a few bottles of beer with them. At Béni-Ounif, the red-light district was not closely guarded as it was in Colomb-Béchar; there was more of a family atmosphere there and despite their dilapidation the rooms in which one drank did not look like sordid dives as they did at Béchar, where it wasn't hard to believe they were sets designed to create an atmosphere of disaster required for some film; on the contrary, they allowed one, stranger though one remained, to enjoy the illusion of being entertained in someone's home. I recaptured some sense of slipping into that distant intimacy a little more than five years ago when I was visiting the region of Blida and went on an excursion to the tomb of Sidi Fodil during the festival of the *mouloud:* inside the monument, hardly larger than a modest-sized bedroom, women squatted in long veils, their faces bare, warming themselves at small braziers in which they burned spices, in low voices exchanging thoughts that had to do with us, and thus gathered, without any men, around the saint's sepulchre, reminded me of the girls assembled in the living room of a brothel for the protocol of the "choice." I had something of the same feeling again on a visit to Algiers—that seaside city with beautiful arcades such as one sees at Genoa and typical of the large sunbathed towns that give me the impression of exoticism perhaps even more than more desolate spots (my sad drunkenness, the ambiguous feeling of fullness and isolation, being out of my element in the midst of an active life that remains foreign to me, the desire to play Haroun al-Rachid walking everywhere incognito)—when groups of the devout, all the more disturbing because these were townswomen, some of them smartly turned out, had taken up positions in the mosque of Sidi Abderrâhman near another sepulchre also surrounded by a multitude of flags.

Until then, I had always gone to the *bousbir* as a sightseer or a stroller or when on duty, which happened to me once, when my turn came to be the leader of the patrol that, after evening mess, was assigned to go around town seeing that the soldiers were behaving properly while off duty. In regulation dress, as I almost always was, except for my duck trousers (replaced this time by the pants I had drawn from my company's depot at the same time as the coarse cloth tunic that inspired Khadidja to say, a little later when we had become friends, "I thought you were a private," this direct confession being offered as an apology—unless it was meant to show me clearly that she was something more than a soldiers' girl—for having completely ignored me before I made advances to her), an empty holster attached to my belt and wearing on my head, not my usual forage cap, but a khaki sun helmet, I gravely made my rounds, flanked by two nonranking comrades belonging, like me, to the team of chemists, and spent a good hour or two strolling, as I chatted with my companions, down badly lit, roughly paved streets without forgetting to visit—in accordance with our instructions—the two places that could logically be regarded as the most likely to give rise to incidents: the rowdy bar where rounds of drinks were exchanged at a rapid pace; and the *bousbir,* ordinarily not very busy but capable of becoming the site of some agitation (as, for instance, during the time two traveling Frenchwomen were quartered there and did very well, since most of the troopers who happened to be in Béni-Ounif preferred, over the Muslims, these thickly powdered tarts, one a lean brunette, the other an opulent blond dubbed "the glutton" by one of my habitual companions). We lingered for a few minutes in the bar joking with the other soldiers, who teased us in a friendly way because of our regulation gear; at the *bousbir,* where everything was as peaceful as it could be, we hardly paused longer than was necessary to sample the glass of beer the old procuress had brought to each of us, anxious to maintain good relations with us, whom she already knew—or hoped to know—as customers and who that evening represented the police.

On the evening when, escorted by one of the men who ate dinner in the Hôtel du Sahara, which we used as a mess hall, I went to the *bousbir* mainly because that was still the place where one could be most at peace, how did I

—who was not tormented by any imperious need of an embrace and have always been wary of dubious forms of intercourse—come to spend the night with a prostitute of the lowest order like Khadidja? It is hard for me to say exactly, today. It no doubt seemed to me unpleasant to haunt the brothels, as I was doing, out of mere love of the picturesque, and, with my departure approaching, that it would be stupid to go back to France without having had any sensual contact at all with a woman of this country. Perhaps, too, no longer living (as I had at Base 2) in a barracks room containing a few beds, I might have dreaded returning to my quarters to sleep in the vast room assigned to the chemists? Since coming back from the desert, there was also a reigning spirit of voluptuous idleness whose inaugural sign had been the sight of the grassland turning green. Besides that, it is clear that from our first encounter I had been attracted to Khadidja and felt pleasure in rediscovering in Béni-Ounif this girl with her proud bearing who seemed to have nothing in common with the other girls except the exercise of what is considered almost everywhere to be a profession one should be ashamed to acknowledge. Will I not simply be yielding to a foolishly romantic temptation, when I say that I finally believe that if I was incited to depart from my long chastity and to do it in conditions such that I could have been left with some painful mark from it, the true motive must have been a little love for me on the part of Khadidja?

"Gentlemen, and *cric!* . . . And *crac!*" (One would have to be a fairly good musician, a rather expert linguist, and in addition be blessed with an adequate memory, to be able to insert here the song with Arab melody and Arab words that Khadidja sang when she strode across the courtyard in search of the bottle of beer that, being the good hostess she was, she had induced me to buy, though I had drunk a large number already; the modulated harshness of that cry—an encouragement to assault, a hymn to victory, or a witch's incantation—reminded me of certain proud songs proffered in their trances by those women I had known in Ethiopia who, inhabited or ridden by spirits worshiped under the name of *zar*, encircled their foreheads, like hunters or chieftains in ceremonial dress, with a strip of cloth or a diadem made from a

lion's mane; but if she had found herself among those Christians of the old
school, what spirit of town or countryside would Khadidja have been transformed into, if not the female spirit to which this song was dedicated:

> We gaze with admiration at her neck, her breasts, her elegant form.
> Her smile kills.
> Do not venture to think she is a woman!)

Among the grains of dust from our past that move us especially because of
the fact that their content appears out of proportion to its infinitesimal container (fragments of something very important which fate has left in suspense
or which, in order to exist, did not even need to have happened), among
those events so thin that one is almost surprised at having kept them in one's
memory but that gleam here and there in the hodgepodge of our life, I—and
probably others too—would number certain caresses that are completely innocuous, sometimes reduced to an apparently negligible gesture that nevertheless gives the illusion (but is it really an illusion?) that it ties you, just as
much as the act of love, to a creature whose name you don't even necessarily
know. Without any clear motive, fingers were clenched or laid softly on your
forearm, a palm was applied to the back of your hand or, during an indefinite
length of time, your arm wrapped around two shoulders, your knee pressed
by chance—and by the happy yielding to that chance—against another
knee. I, for one, place great value upon trivial effusions of this sort, perhaps
because I am not so much a man of passion as a man of longing: someone
who leaves things at a distance, in order to preserve his desire for them or his
regret at their loss; who because he is too weak to dare to take something,
only wants that thing and (without running any risk) makes sparest use of
that wanting; who lacks courage to the extent that he sees love as an interior
state in which to settle and not as an adventure, a drama, an *act;* who is always
seeking euphoria, never power or domination; who, instead of trying to appropriate something for himself, even if this entailed the ruin of the desiring
subject or the object desired, limits himself to constructing an object to day-
dream or brood about in order to revel in it; who remains a man subject to

whims, one who (almost without moving) always flies off toward unexpected countries. *You put a cross on each thing and you do nothing with it*, a female friend said to me in a dream I had many years ago.

(I did nothing—and also did not think for a second of doing anything—with the gentle Lumane, that slender, somewhat simian girl with very dark skin and prominent breasts who used to go to the home of Lorgina, the voodooist of the Saline quarter in Port-au-Prince, and whom I saw for the first time one evening when she was taken by the female *lwa* Grande Vélékété and, her features exaggeratedly twisted, went into convulsions for some time on a mat by the side of the leader of the choir, who was also foaming at the mouth and rolling his eyes up in front of all of us—initiates and noninitiates, men and women—who were there standing on our feet and were supposed to step over them—once over, once back—in order to attract good luck, and whom I then saw again on the evening of the "bedding of the yams," when the *hounfor*, loud with chanting and furnished with an improvised altar at the back, felt like a Nativity crèche, even more so because of those adoring shepherds, the men who, close to the painted center post known as the "midpost," stood motionless and quite proper in their duck pants to present some billy goats, future sacrificial offerings with necks encircled by leading ropes; many people were gathered there that evening and I was sitting very close up against Lumane, whose knee was touching mine; since I knew no Creole and she no French, we said not a word to each other; noticing that she sniffled, wiped her nose in her underskirt, occasionally grimaced, and moved around restlessly as though she were about to be possessed and were trying not to let herself go, I observed her from the corner of my eye with a sort of affectionate solicitude, waiting for that attack—which in the end never came—as though to help her if the spirit overcame her, and feeling in a strangely intense, profound, and self-evident way that I was her closest friend, even though that feeling was probably not fully reciprocated.)

On that night in Béni-Ounif when for me Khadidja ceased to be a creature without substance—a silhouette barely glimpsed against the background of a gloomy decor during an evening that was hardly more delightful—to choose her rather than another girl was a completely spontaneous impulse, as though my gesture in pointing to her had simply been the public avowal of an old association and as though no one at that moment could have dreamed of disputing it. As I speak here of a choice I supposedly made, it is even certain that I am giving a false idea: it all happened as though since the beginning of time it had been decided that that night I would share a bed with Khadidja. It is also certain that my desire to remain by her side was much stronger than any strictly erotic desire: I wanted that girl with a desire that I could call childlike; the actions we would perform were, in a sense, actions required by etiquette (since to spend time with a prostitute normally implies the execution of certain immodest actions) and, in another sense, the most natural and innocent expression of the desire I had for her. If one can—as I have wished to for a long time—experience love (in this case stripped of its halo of idolatry and purged of all odor of the confessional) as a friendship very simply pushed to the point of paroxysm, one that the effusions of sensuality would only be expressing with all the intensity demanded by an extreme feeling, then it was, no doubt, a particle of something tending toward such a love that I experienced in the basically venal adventure I had with Khadidja. Nevertheless, I can't ignore the fact that if the joy I felt at finding myself with her was almost as candid as my joy on certain Sundays at bathing in the pools that, at Figu-ig, serve to water palm groves and gardens, it was in a muddy sort of water, swarming with insects and frogs, that I took those great fresh baths in the oa-sis, and that with Khadidja I experienced whatever amiability and freshness existed between us all the more keenly because we were frolicking about, in fact, in waters just as filthy as those that covered the slippery bottoms of those pools.

Not without a feeling of shame, I must confess that on that first night it was with a cautious reserve that I made use of a companion of whom the least one could say was that any man at all inclined to be afraid, where love is con-cerned, of deleterious contacts would have had some reason to be mistrustful of her. Despite my months in the desert I wasn't moved by any mad desire, and I was therefore clearheaded enough, at least, not to undertake with my partner anything that exposed me too obviously to the risk of regretting it lat-er. An expression endowed with the idyllic charm that so often marks slang expressions designating obscene acts—an expression that, in fact, I had learned when I was in the army during the phony war—*"se faire brouter la tige"* [get one's stem nibbled] will allow me to indicate, in a euphuistic style, the service that justified in Khadidja's eyes my presence in the room where she retired to rest or exercise the esoteric part of her calling. Will I give an exact idea of the clear and naked honesty that governed our relations if I add that I reached the limit of my ecstasy—in all gentleness, as one comes in a dream—just as she was pronouncing the words "twenty francs" at the end of a conversation about money begun and pursued in the course of our dealings?

In Le Havre, I wrote, after a stay in the great Normandy port a full adult lifetime before this (I hadn't yet broken my solitude by marrying, hadn't yet rediscovered it by traveling—silly man!—in order to get away from myself by removing myself to a great distance and was experimenting with a style both too pretentious and too abbreviated to give a literary formulation to the confused things I was feeling, another way one can try to overcome one's isolation and one that I, for my part, novice that I was, would use with an awkwardness against which even today I must wage a struggle which experience has made, perhaps, more attentive and effective but certainly also much more tedious)—*in Le Havre, the ships, the dockworkers, the shady bars, and the brothels, madams in heavy makeup standing on the doorstep among the fish- and vegetablemongers.*

Day and night, on the beach and the esplanade, the healthy, salty damp of the sea, which makes one desire a vigorous love indulged with a naive, rather childlike sentimentality; in the town, the clamminess of a bath-house, the suspect force of dirty passions amid doctored alcohol, discordant music, the smells of bottled perfumes. The heart in silk stockings. (The next day, not departing from my theme—the low dive full of prostitutes—I took up this wretched image again: "The women wind off the skein of their closeted days by crossing their legs to show the silken mesh of their stockings.") *The mouth wants to be humiliated, or torn apart. There is no more gentleness or even purity. We no longer want* (when "I no longer want," committing only myself, would have reflected the truth) *the marine fragrance of algae* (which more properly should have been expressed as "seaweed") *but the odor of flesh in rut or bodies artfully pre-*

pared and rubbed down, bleached by the absence of daylight, fat with laziness and fatigue, and animated by one sole movement: that of the belly, which in this disruption of the usual hierarchy of the organs now assumes supremacy.

Here, I no longer have any liking for crystalline, clearly defined lines. (An undated note, extracted from my cards: "My liking for articulate, composed landscapes. Sometime in 1920, in Paramé, my scorn—very much à la Fantasio—for a wild sea that everyone was admiring.") *I no longer like either fire or ice.* (But if I examine my past carefully, did I ever really like the two terrible extremes symbolized by those two words?) *I now no longer like anything but what is amorphous, soft, lukewarm, damp. The monstrous vegetation of the algae, of hair soaked in sea salt and the salt of sweat. If I make love there is a storm and if there is a storm I make love.* (Nine years later, returning from Africa and on vacation with the family at a beach near Perros-Guirec: "Ebb and flow of love: one is thrust back, one is drawn forward, one is drawn forward, one is thrust back; in the end one makes love to stop this rocking which makes one so seasick.") *The very stars have become mouths—only colder than the others—and I would like to devour them.*

The voracious heart.

No more shadow, no more stratagems of light and crystal. Bodies dense and tightly embraced in their living fullness. To make contact. If I possess one of these bodies, for a time the whole world will belong to me. (As the year came to an end: "Fearful love: to clasp a part of the outside world in order to have the illusion of deflecting its laws. The desire for a shared love: to be the entire universe for a fraction of the universe, so as to be able to believe that your end will be the end of the world. We make love the way certain people say their beads during a storm.") *Delicate meanderings. Eddying of forms. Pressed thighs weave arabesques without pain—just the bitterness of temporary joys—and hands slip from dampness to coolness, from coolness to pungency. The dissolution of bones, gnawed away by the personal life of the sexes that hide like sea monsters spying their prey with a tufted eye: sharp grass, carnivorous flowers.* ("Oh whale! Oh siren!" sang the followers of old Maman Lorgina once in honor of the gods of the sea.) *Disjunction of limbs and ideas, portraying the last spasm, when our heads will turn over onto the other side of the world.*

With the authority of an island queen (such as exist only in the imagination) requesting the shipwrecked European to rid himself of his possessions, which will become her plunder, my companion had said to me: "Take off your pants!" and—like that shipwrecked fellow or perhaps the centurion suddenly shy in the presence of the patrician woman who notifies him that he should undo his tunic before yielding to her for the sum of a few asses or several sesterces—I had stripped off the military clothing whose banality satisfied my vanity as though the very modesty of the uniform were enough to turn me into the prince or god who, assuming a crude outer appearance, mingles with common mortals. Khadidja having earned her night's pay and I my rest—I who had momentarily transformed myself (on the same metaphorical level where I clothe myself out of modesty in the goose-pimpled skin of a shipwrecked man or the sweating skin of a centurion) into a sailor who has been swallowed by the waves and who drinks from the belly of a nereid the sap that will assure him some sort of survival—we had slept until dawn in the large iron bed. Then I had left her, in truth without leaving her altogether, going to my barracks to wash, shave, and put in an appearance but in no way like someone who, the line drawn at the bottom of the smutty paragraph he has just written with a girl, and more or less nauseated, goes back to where he lives.

The society of single men we had formed during our stay in the desert (grouped, for better or for worse, as in any society, according to rank, birthplace, work, all of this overlapping with instinctive attractions or repulsions and the hazards of all sorts that produce cliques) was about to break up. The radiotelegraphists of the Second Etranger were to be the first to leave, returning to Bel-Abbès, and since I had been (I think) the only one of the reservists to associate with them in any consistent way, they amiably suggested that we all have lunch that day—which must have been a Sunday—at the Hôtel du Sahara. Along with their leader, my buddy the corporal, there were two or three Belgians, one of whom, formerly an officer in his national army, had the reputation of being a great drunk whom his passion did not prevent from being always very skillful and scrupulous in his work: a quick and accurate radiographer when he was sober, this calm, taciturn man who rarely showed his face lost nothing of his dexterity (they said) in the most terrible bouts of drunkenness resulting from his solitary drinking sessions, but simply used his left hand at these times instead of his right, which he usually used; he was the oldest member of the little team, whose youngest—also present at lunch— was a boy still barely out of his adolescence, baby faced and smiling, and with an expression at once so naive and so reserved that one wondered by what odd conjunction of circumstances he could have ended up in the Legion, whereas his first occupation (and probably his only one, given his age) had been that of violinist.

Throughout the meal, my hosts were anxious to show that, mercenaries though they were, and consigned more or less to the category of outcasts, they were not hardened, crude soldiers. Since I, for my part, wanted to demonstrate that I didn't attribute to them the customs of the Swiss Guard or the Iroquois Indians, our exchanges were marked by a reserve greater than the conversations that took place every day among chemists when, at the table, we listened to our star performers compete at tall tales or irreverent descriptions worthy of a satirical weekly, then, drawn in by one of them, would sing together *L'Artilleur de Metz* or some other popular song appreciated by the soldiery. At dessert, one of my hosts simply intoned, in a very dignified and serious way, *Bel-Abbès, berceau de la Légion,* a romantic, sentimental song in which the greatness and the service of the Legionnaire are celebrated in elegiac terms. Treated this way, I was as gratified in my snobbery as though I had been admitted into the most exclusive sort of club or some distant initiatic brotherhood.

After coffee and a chaser, we were free until evening, so we had to do something and the *bousbir* was obviously the most likely place where we would be welcome. I was the one, I think, who suggested going there: I had to return my companions' courtesy in one way or another, and to pay a visit there would, more importantly, give me an occasion to see Khadidja again without seeming—in my own eyes as well as in hers—too clearly to want to be with her again when scarcely half a day had passed since we had separated. Even if they had wanted to, I'm sure my companions would have refrained from taking such an initiative, desirous as they were to make a good impression on someone they considered not just any NCO, of whom they had seen so many, but an intellectual, even a scholar; and it was (paradoxically) because of the occupation of professional soldier to which their setbacks had reduced them and the fact that they were seeking, if not to make one forget it, at least to give it the most correct appearance possible, and because of my own quality as a person who had done his studies like a good bourgeois and was anxious to avoid any appearance of superiority or pedantry, that if one of us behaved like a hardened, crude soldier that afternoon, it was not any of that group, specialists in one of the numerous lines of work that come together to create modern-style massacre, but, in the end, the educated man.

Of course I went straight to the place where I had the most chance of meeting Khadidja: the room where, served by her, I had drunk beer the evening before, in a single-story house that did not open onto the street but stood at the back of a courtyard bordered by other small rooms where other people—apparently all soldiers—also came to drink slender bottles of beer before putting themselves in the hands of some unfortunate woman to relieve their boredom or rid themselves of the completely carnal obsession that was torturing them. Khadidja was there, unoccupied, and it was in her company —to which, perhaps, was intermittently added that of one or two other girls —that we ingested the beer I was so determined to offer them. The great burst of tenderness (the desire to fuss over her, envelope her, protect her) which, the night before, had uplifted me so when I was preparing to go to sleep with her, indifferent to the fact that her graces could be bought and sold, now turned into a need to play the part of the generous fellow, who not only spares no expense and therefore gains in popularity, but, in the cordiality that induces him to give excessively, throws all sense of jealous appropriation to the winds and goes to the extreme of buying for others the pleasures that can be dispensed by his woman (whom, in doing this, he in truth claims as his possession since he thus poses as the master, the only one entitled to bestow her). "You'll have to excuse me, Sergeant! I get an erection on the thirty-sixth of every month," the senior member of the Legionnaires confided to me, declining the offer I had made him, the oldest, the placid ascetic whose drinking binges were legendary, of a turn with Khadidja. This offer met with the same lack of success, in the end—even though the new beneficiary would have consented, without having to be entreated too much, to shut himself up in a nearby room with the immodest Berber (whose possible poisons, I was forgetting, I myself had been afraid of)—when I again tried to make a display of altruism by addressing myself, this time, to the youngest, the violinist, whom his comrades teased amiably about a virginity which hadn't been breached by his life as a professional in remote garrisons.

My guests went off rather early, not having the same reasons I did for lingering and being, in addition, summoned back to the barracks for those various trifling occupations that fill a soldier's Sunday: mending jobs, a letter to write, a card game, even simply a pipe to smoke or a bottle of red wine to drink while listening to time pass as the old one did, the one who, from the beginning of this life, seemed to aspire to nothing more than a sort of nirvana, the methodical and patient practice of drinking taking the place of wisdom.

Alone with Khadidja, I returned to the room where I had left her only a few hours before and which was no more than the dwelling place for a large bed with uncertain springs. Until fairly late in the afternoon we took a siesta there and Khadidja did nothing to change our repose into a bacchanalian romp that would certainly have resulted in a substantial profit for her business. With great courtesy—as one goes to some trouble for a guest without there being anything servile about it—she asked me, when our siesta was finished, if I would like to take a bath, and when I said I would, brought a zinc tub of the most classical style, filled it with warm water, and then, when I had gotten into it, so blissful that I felt no shame at letting myself be handled this way, like a baby, soaped me from head to toe with great care, energy, but also sweetness. Always, after that—in Béni-Ounif, as well as in Saïda when the train taking us to Oran stopped there for a few hours—it was a pleasure for me to go wash myself in the Moorish baths: a contentment that certainly had something to do with satisfying a desire for comfort as well as for hygiene (to rid oneself of that almost moral filth that coats the soldier's skin even when he is not in a warm country and which, it would seem, only an indefinitely prolonged immersion can cleanse) but also with the idea of recapturing, in the warmth of those vast halls as peaceful and pleasingly ornamented as a mosque, a drop of the well-being of body and heart that had been bestowed on me the day I had simply rested in Khadidja's room like a traveler stopping over at a caravansary. Rebecca, the young girl with the pitcher (and perhaps large earrings?), Eliezer, the camel drover. Nineveh, a terraced city, in the thick plumes of smoke exhaled by incense burners like locomotive smokestacks. On the poster one used to see so often on the walls of train and metro stations, the elephant carrying (with his trunk?) a banner on which one read the slogan: "I only smoke Niles." The flight into Egypt, the night spent in the open air, with no other sleeping alcove than the belly of the ass. The elephant Saïd, who lived, I think, at the Jardin des Plantes. Lacking any of the sumptuousness of an oasis despite its name, the café Au Palmier de Lorette, in the quarter known as Bréda when it was mostly populated by women of loose morals [*femmes galantes*], who are to the ladies' men [*hommes galants*] what the courtisan [*courtisane*] is to the courtier [*courtisan*], more or less, and where there now stands a residential hotel I know of that goes by the curious name of Modial Hôtel, as though at the time it was baptized with a view to public appeal there was some hesitation between the drawing power of frivolous fashion [*mode*] and that of a global [*mondial*] sort of effulgence.

When, as a schoolboy, I made my way as best I could through Latin texts and, except on rare occasions, derived from the study of these word puzzles no literary joy, I liked Ovid better than anyone else, and especially "The Golden Age," which opens the *Metamorphoses*. *"Aurea prima sata est aetas . . .", ". . . stillabant ilice mella"*: shallow contours of a poem explicated in class, probably learned by heart, in any case read and reread savoring the long succession of syllables as a dilettante would have, but of which I no longer have in my head more than this almost nonexistent residue, in other words (when I think about it) not much less than the dust, almost impossible to gather up, into which the golden days I am relating here—a historian masking his ignorance with digressions rather than rhapsody—have resolved themselves with the passing of time.

As though one of the trees in Land-without-Evil or Cockaigne of which Ovid speaks had sprung up invisibly within my reach to feed me with its honey (instead of rising only today, and as a pure allegory, on the dung heap with which my brain has fattened itself from one reading to the next since my earliest school days), what was installed in me that afternoon, which ended on a note so different from the spirit of the braggart, the guy in the know, in which I had begun it, was a philter imbued with a succulence and a beneficent power different from the beer with which Khadidja—female Ganymede in Egyptian dancing-woman's pants—had slaked our thirst. I now felt for this swarthy sommelier an affectionate gratitude for the way she had treated me, she who, without ever forgetting her twofold profession as prostitute and hostess, at least knew that mercenary love also involved its own protocol, that hospitality had its rituals and it was precisely to the extent that a whore proved scrupulous in the performance of such rituals that she preserved her dignity. For this body, to which my own had been closely joined during one whole night though without there being a total pairing between it and me, I began to feel the simplest, most positive desire: the desire a normal man normally has for any woman whose physical appearance attracts him. It seemed to me imbecilic to have thus made love, to all intents and purposes, without making love, inhuman to have used this girl with a discrimination that had led me to travel with her only part of the way along a road whose pratfalls I was afraid of, scandalous to have shown such reticence toward someone who had just demonstrated to me that there still existed in our day—at least in certain regions—something analogous to what sacred prostitution must have been in the ancient world. The devil take my greedy caution, incompatible (it was flagrantly obvious) with the handsome impulse of generous cordiality that had moved me a short time before! Whatever was going to happen would happen: I could not leave things where they were with this creature whom I hadn't regarded even for a second as an object, the way, ordinarily, because of the very fact that they are offered or offer themselves, one is led despite oneself to regard prostitutes or those nocturnal strollers whom I much later heard described by the melodramatic term "women of midnight" by a woman from Guadeloupe who was visiting Paris for the first time.

The ebb and flow: one opens up and then closes again, by turns. That evening, when I returned to the *bousbir*, it was high tide for me. Not that I was in a physiological state different from the sluggishness in which so many enlisted men in the phony war found themselves mired, to their surprise, a sluggishness they felt was humiliating to their vanity as men and chose to ascribe to the deliberate addition of some chemical ingredient to the table wine. I was, quite simply, charmed by Khadidja and wanted to experience with her, unrestrictedly, whatever could be experienced. For years I had been mulling over a remark made to me long ago, *You don't dare go all the way with your desires,* by a man with whom I had a passionate friendship (the same one who said he prefered the substantive *God* to any other word in the language, whereas a painter to whom we listened somewhat as though he were an oracle claimed as his key word the adjective *eternal* and I the verb *transmute*); for years, too, I had been brooding about the condemnation hidden behind this other remark, *and you don't yet know the woman whom you will pillage and plunder,* concluding a letter I dreamed was sent to me by the wife of a poet I see only at long intervals but who is one of those older than I whom I have always loved and admired the most.

For some time already, a number of my comrades the chemists had also wished to make an excursion to the *bousbir,* quite without any intention of taking up with any of the girls there (for this, they were too delicate!) but in the same spirit that they would have toured Bagdad-by-night if they had happened to be in Iraq or the-heart-of-Isfahan if fate had led them a little farther East. Because they knew I had often gone into these neighborhoods, where only a few of us had been up to now, I could not decently refuse to go there with my less initiated comrades and the know-it-alls who had appointed themselves their guides, for they would have attributed this unexpected abstention to some sort of desire to cold-shoulder them by keeping to myself; besides, it was an excellent excuse to return to Khadidja again as though by a happy chance. I must say, however, that I wasn't really pleased to be going in a group, like this, to a place where I wanted only to display a certain deferential civility toward those who lived there, even if in my eyes it was the most dismal of whorehouses. As I had to, unless I was to disobey the laws of comradeship, I put the best face on things: as irritated as I might be by what was intolerable, in itself, about such a visit in a corporate body, I settled with my entire escort of rather tipsy reservists in that room whose orientalism seemed copied (but in a manner even more provincial) from that of the Place Clichy and which replaced the room that in France is called a *salon* in similar establishments. As they drank their beer—that real horse-urine that was served up in the guise of mead by my Valkyrie, without helmet other than her black hair—my companions, sitting in a circle, sang in chorus many barracks-room obscenities, I remaining silent as I listened to them with Khadidja at my side, as though we were the host and hostess by a tacit agreement among all of us, without there having been anything expressly premeditated about it. My group, in the end, displayed more tact that I had expected, offering up its crudenesses in the manner, not of boorish louts who think the coarsest kind of talk is the proper thing with girls but of boys accustomed to enlivening social groups and thinking it absurd to wait to be asked to perform their usual numbers; I think I can add that they also sang—quite inspired, and to the delight of Khadidja as well as that of her companions—the North African song that was one of our favorite pieces and that dates from the other war: *Ai! Ai! qu'il est joli mon p'tit paillasson de nuit* [oh, my pretty little tart]. It was that evening (I think) that Khadidja, after going away for a moment, suddenly put into my right hand—murmuring to me that she had just found it—a silver pendant of a pattern standard in North Africa: the famous "Southern Cross" sold, in different sizes and forms, everywhere to visiting Europeans and especially soldiers who, quite often, wear it on their chest as they would a badge. With the discretion almost of a player at hunt-the-slipper or of a child passing a stolen sweet to another child, Khadidja presented me with this jewel, a sort of diamond shape whose four sides fell inward—curving in toward the center of the figure—and whose lateral points, like those on the bottom, ended in bulbous swellings while the top one was crowned by an open circle allowing it to be hooked up or suspended. My first thought was that this object had been, not really stolen, but surreptitiously picked up after being lost by one of my companions; yet, once I had made inquiries the following day, I knew that this quite large and delicately worked cross did not belong to any of them and that I could therefore keep it without troubling myself further, having no idea how it came to be in Khadidja's hands after having left those —more industrious—of the artisan who had fashioned it.

During this gathering—which, except for the noise, had nothing baccha- nalian about it and ended, in fact, without any of my companions choosing to go into a private trance behind closed doors—Khadidja wore in her ears large loops apparently of gold which I had not seen on her in the afternoon and which could just as well have been a gift from a customer coming after our midday siesta as the impatiently awaited fruit of prudent savings, jewelry ordered long ago and delivered between my two visits. She kept these earrings on when we lay down, proud (I think) of the brand-new ornaments that mar- velously framed her face incised with tattoos. Too exclusively attached to the purely natural ornaments of which her body boasted, no doubt I would have accorded these only the attention merited by a commonplace refinement of dress—scarcely more striking on her, the vagabond with the beveled face, with the long, bony feet, than on another woman—if blood had not sud- denly begun flowing from her right earlobe, abundantly enough to spot the pillow on which her head rested, wholly offered up to my gaze since the body that was crowned by this head when standing on its feet was now lying down quite flat, and I was looking down on it from my own prone position, cover- ing hers without too many gaps or too much inexactitude, just as one geo- metric figure can be superimposed by another which one wants to demon- strate to be identical and just as my memory, madly, seeks to coincide with the whole of this picture—of which I am the painter but also one of its two models—as though the actor I was could, by doubling himself, become the retrospective witness—or voyeur—of the whole scene.

(*I can't love anyone, so I love myself,* I confessed to the girlfriend of a friend of mine one night when I was drunk and she and I were walking up the av- enue de l'Opéra together arm in arm; did this statement, more humiliated than cynical—concluding one of those inebriated Dostoevskian confessions that were habitual with me but that I detest today as I detest everything in me that reacts like a sentimental drunk—contain a distant trace of the occultists' theory about relations between men and women: that because Eve was formed from a rib of Adam's and is therefore nothing more than man's very affectivity, his sensibility exteriorized and opposed to him, a man loves himself when loving a woman and returns to his original unity when he thus joins the portion of himself from which he was separated? If I must find in my affirmation anything other than the whimsical notion of a drunken man getting something off his chest, I would be more inclined to believe that just then I was thinking of an image I cherished for a long time, of moral conscience childishly represented as a foreign authority more or less analogous to the sort of guardian angel that keeps watch at night standing at the foot of our bed to observe and judge us in the intimacy of our sleep, in the same way that the conscience keeps watch, motionless, in our head to observe the soul which—like its homonym the little piece of wood in the soundbox of the violin [*âme:* soundpost, soul]—is also ensconced there as though in the sonorous emptiness of a vast cupola; when you love only yourself, you must at least love yourself enough to have the respect for yourself you would have if you loved someone who should at all costs not see you fail, and in this case the distinct entity which is this angel or this conscience stands facing me like some Dulcinea who causes the lover to tremble at the prospect of losing his prestige. Of old Karamazov's three sons, it was Alyosha the gentle one, the mystic, to whom I had been compared—in the parlor of a Russian baroness, as he walked about completely naked, on his head an old helmet, crunching an apple—by the youthful companion whose girlfriend I adopted for a confidante one fine evening on the avenue de l'Opéra: *We are the brothers Karamazov . . . We are all sensualists . . .* he declaimed in a barker's voice, identifying himself with the violent Dimitri and assigning the character of the proud Ivan to the one we admired the most of all of us, whereas in the latter's studio—in a drunken speech sustained by the leitmotif of *I am the strongest swimmer in the world . . .* —what he had described for hours on a day of lyrical dishevelment was a voyage that he alone, against everything and everyone, had made across legendary oceans; and as for this pseudo-Alyosha whom a prostitute from Figuig would take to be, possibly, a marabout—which, in her language, probably meant a priest—wasn't it the case that the interest he showed at this time in gnosticism and also his skull, shaved for the first time at about this period like a polar dome—which, combined with his bearing, always a little stiff, marked him with a strangely monkish appearance—caused him, who behind his armor of untimely frost was more than anything else a spineless fellow and a dreamer, to be dubbed a little later, half seriously, "the Areopagite" by the master of that studio during a walk in the course of which the fanciful companion who had chosen to see me, ridiculously, as a double of the youngest of the three Karamazovs was himself compared to "Lucifer"?)

Her face a little contracted—whether because she was in pain or because she was frightened by her benign hemorrhage—Khadidja, with a quick gesture, took off the two earrings, one of which was colored the same thick red that I saw trickling down onto the pillowcase; as a wound deep enough to need to be tended, that insignificant injury moved me and what I saw was a tragic princess breathing her last in the wavering light of the flames as I pressed bloody Khadidja against me in the gloaming.

On this occasion (if it really was "this occasion," for I have great difficulty grouping all these occasions according to their exact chronology, tending perhaps to condense, as though to obey the classical rule of unity of time, what in fact was scattered and, for instance, falsely placing Khadidja decked out in her earrings among my comrades who had come in a jovial gang if several days and not several hours separated the bath taken after the siesta from this visit in that case made only when no one could any longer not know that I had established my quarters in a place different from the barracks)—on this occasion, which I would like to situate in a precise way in order to enclose within firm limits the reality that manifested itself here and protect it more effectively from disappearing, it was not a meaningless series of gestures required as much by civility as by lust and leaving the irritating impression that they were nothing more than simulacra, but love—written without a capital letter and denuded of all the flourishes and other refinements beloved of calligraphers—that (seeking nothing except communication with another person in its most literally naked form) I made with Khadidja.

I was not, as I have said, either in a state or in a mood to accomplish anything analogous to those performances that are featured in the amorous curriculum vitae of certain men and my apparent ardor masked an aptitude in truth so mediocre that long after I was engulfed (suitably stiffened) in the wide open cavern, I had to give up what had finally appeared to me as a dead-end voyage despite the exhilaration I felt at being thus carried along as though on waves and suspended in the imminence, a feeling whose equivalent, almost, I had already felt—on the level of purely metaphysical voluptuousness—one day when I had taken some opium (someone had had me smoke a few pipes): that one is no longer more than a hair away from at last entering into contact with oneself, of contemplating oneself as an object one sees from the outside at the same time as one is interior to it and it is interior to one, to progress constantly in this direction, from landing to landing, but never reach the absolute revelation, to be only at the extreme edge and have in some sense this revelation "on the tip of one's tongue," as one says of a thing forgotten which is there, intensely makes its presence felt but nevertheless slips away; a feeling whose fluctuating force is exerted as though in slow motion and which I had recaptured—in a more mechanical form—by abandoning myself to the swaying of a hammock the day after the day on which I had eaten some opium residue: *The motion of the hammock imitates the motion of a ship, which imitates the motion of death . . . A chain of successive imitations. To go back to the unique Model.* Narcotics such as cocaine and especially heroin procure also a bewildering impression of imminence which I evoke to some degree—though without defining it—if I speak of a sort of abstract tension that feeds on itself independently of all objects, an extreme tension that still dreams of increasing and is nothing other than this very increase dreaming of reaching its height. But even more than with opium, there is nothing there but solitude, emptiness, complete vertigo and not even that quasi encounter with oneself that can be obtained by the use of the substance extracted from the seeds of the opium poppy or of the residue it leaves in the bowls of pipes after the combustion that generates the smoke. How could I, anyway, compare the assuredly vivid but egoistic and chilly pleasures I sometimes derived from these drugs (in experiments, in truth, so rare and so cautious that it would no doubt be better not to refer to them) to the feverish quest for a delirium with which one cannot be rewarded unless one also rewards the living object from which one derives this delirium? Even if they are equally passionate, these attempts do not have the same end in mind and are subject to a distinction more radical than that which English teachers instruct us to make between *to like* and *to love,* the difference being in the present case a real disparity since there is no common measure, even if they must both disappoint us in the end, between a fullness that one only enjoys all alone (or in conjunction with others but without anyone else being the cause of it) and that which one finds in a purely human fusion with another person (who is the means by which I obtain pleasure as in exchange I am the same for her).

It was at about five in the morning—and as though emerging from an intoxication in which visions and somnolence had alternated until the moment of plunging into the shadows—that I resumed, in order to see it all the way through, at last, what I had abandoned late in the night when, to my great detriment, there had been a relaxation of the physical and strictly localized tension that until then had unfailingly expressed the exaltation of my whole being straining toward the moment (too often one-sided) when the erotic climax takes place, the entire body overflowing and being reabsorbed in one decisive fulguration. A short time before the moment when I had realized that there was no use persisting and that I was even losing the means to do so—a renunciation soon transformed into total abdication since yet again I slipped off to sleep—I had, however, discovered that my obstinacy was not pointless, for, secretly, Khadidja revealed to me that she was moved by it: something like the pulsations or slight contractions one could perceive deep in the gallery of a mine if the earth were alive and if the men who work it, lost in its folds, received a response emanating from the most distant part of that great sentient animal; something comparable for me—since I have been interested in books about alchemy for a long time and passionately fond, as an amateur, of old theories about the nature of fire as well as modern hypotheses about the structure of matter—to the proof (administered *ad hominem*) of the real, rather than mythological, existence of a sexuality hidden within metals, and also to the illusion I had that with my own eyes I had seen the ultimate foundation of the world when (during a visit to the Ecole de Physique et Chimie

I had made at the urging of one of the teachers at that institution) I observed the standard experiment designed to show "Brownian motion": the examination of a sol through an ultramicroscope, revealing the disorderly motion of corpuscles less than four microns in diameter suspended in liquid and inducing me—who was amazed by the spectacle of points illuminated by the oblique light that changed them into stars moving about against the dark background—to imagine that I was penetrating the arcanae of molecular life; also something that recalled to me, well after the ephemeral conjunction of my fate with Khadidja's, that ultimate reality which it seemed to me I touched miraculously in a dream or nocturnal revery almost thirty years ago now: having spent the day in the studio of that friend for whom the word *eternal* had such a special force and having seen drawings of his showing nudes in architectural forms, these sketches came into my mind again while I slept and seemed to me, not so much drawings, as prophetic graphics, diagrams, or, even better, *designs for the truth;* through these designs I saw my life (whose larger lines coincided with them) and behind my life a thing, indescribable in form and substance, that I called "resistance." It was almost this heart of the earth, mineral soul, innermost being of fate and of things that I had thought I was touching when I perceived the tangible signs of Khadidja's joy.

"*Titus reginam Berenicen, cui etiam nuptias pollicitus ferebatur, statim ab urbe dimisit invitus invitam;* Titus, who, it was believed, had even promised Queen Berenice he would marry her, sent her away from Rome, despite himself and despite her, in the first days of his rule." It is in these few lines that Racine, quoting Suetonius, presents the argument of *Bérénice* and I still recall, when I was in the eleventh or twelfth grade, one of our professors inviting us —with a greedy air, behind his glasses and his flamboyant beard—to appreciate the beauty of the Latin phrase, whose last two words sum up the whole drama: *invitus invitam,* "against his wishes, against her wishes," the only fragment that has stayed with me from that phrase, along with the verb *dimisit,* which for a long time my memory erroneously placed at the very end of the passage from Suetonius and transformed into *dimissit,* as though the barbarism that consisted in doubling the sibilant consonant had, by introducing

a hesitation or a suspense, accentuated the signification of indefinitely prolonged farewells that this verb lent to the story of the Roman lover and his
Jewish beloved. *Invitus invitam dimissit:* murmured to oneself during some
soliloquy, this group of words—of which the second, coming before the long
rustling sigh, is only the almost unchanged echo of the first—loses all trans-
latable meaning and becomes (well beyond the man who sends her off as
much against his own will as against hers, even beyond the desolation of two
separated lovers) an adage expressing an irreducible impossibility as is insinu-
ated by the first two words with their symmetrical barriers, the whole (suitably churned and stewed) finally resolving into one of those all-purpose for-
mulas which impart to many folklorical songs a burden of melancholy having
nothing to do with the song's content and age: *invitus invitam,* "our good fortune, hey nonny-nonny-no, our good fortu-u-ne."

It was perhaps from Iphigenia, "the pure blood of the god who throws
thunderbolts" and the central figure in the tragedy that moved me the most
when I was studying the classics, that Khadidja derived that bloody signature
that one of her earlobes had left on the pillowcase, elevating to the rank of an
innocent already touched by the knife of the sacrificer a woman who, ripened
by the African sun, had arisen at a bend in my road like a sidewalk Venus revealed by the bewildering arabesques of her behavior and her long goatish
legs (for lack of some infernal mark such as a forked hoof) as a spectral Empusa or a temptress of my middle age. Clearly she never had the elegiac tenderness of Berenice and, in any case, to soften her to the point of tears would
have required someone other than I, who seemed to her (I would like to
think) a good and not overly tiresome customer but was obviously not the
ruffian capable of metamorphosing her into a docile lover. If it hadn't been
for her long white robe and her head turbaned in green the morning the two
of us played the great farewell scene, it would only be out of a ludicrous desire to poeticize that I would refer to Titus and Berenice in speaking of an adventure none of whose strictly verifiable episodes exceeded what was in principle a love affair between an NCO and a soldiers' whore.

During the several days that remained before our departure, first for Oran
(where I revisited the old Spanish fort from which we could see the roads of

Mers el-Kebir sheltering its warships, a place that would, in the not very distant future, become part of history in the space of a single day) and then to
Port-Vendres (after embarking on a requisitioned steamboat, two nurses in
Red Cross caps posted on either side of the gangway to give each of us as we
went by single file two cigarettes and a life belt as viaticum), I was hardly seen
in our barracks outside of duty hours, for I had gotten into the regular habit
of going off to sleep in the *bousbir* once I had eaten dinner with the others in
the dining room of the dilapidated building with the cracked facade that was
the Hôtel du Sahara. At Khadidja's, it was now as though I were staying with
the manager of a boardinghouse, sharing her bed even at hours when her
presence there was only virtual; once or twice it happened that I slept alone
almost the entire night in that great bed while she poured her bottles of beer
for other customers, danced for them (as she did, according to what she al-
leged when she had to leave me, for a European civil servant who had come
with his wife to enjoy himself in this evil place) or quite simply sold herself
(as I must conjecture, for she was delicate enough to refrain from uttering the
least word that would have clearly indicated to me that I was not the only one
with whom she was exercising her principal calling). When I was with her,
and generally also with another girl who lived there (who was slighter,
plumper, and had a gentler physiognomy, and with whom my friend the Legion corporal, whom I was treating that evening after dinner, once spent the
night while I, for my part, was shut up in that bedroom face-to-face with the
taller, thinner, fiercer-looking woman next to whom the other appeared to be
a humble servant rather than a comrade), I imbibed—without wanting to,
but because Khadidja urged me to and I was anxious to seem gracious in entertaining the ladies, to whom the operation was doubly profitable—an excessive number of bottles of her vile beer. Very soon my physical condition
began to suffer the effects of this in a tiresome way and there came a night
when, my bowels tormented by cramps, I disappeared again and again to go
visit the latrines, which I had located in the courtyard; not once did I leave,
my stomach ravaged, without Khadidja joining me in that stinking spot—as
though to make sure I hadn't strayed into a rival bed or to put a stop to whatever I might be conniving with the impure spirits that roamed around the

rubbish—and saying to me in a suspicious tone: "What are you doing there?" Her comrade no doubt knew she was vindictive, jealous, and in addition determined not to yield an inch of her control, for I recall how firmly— and as though, in caressing her lovely chest, I had committed an impropriety —she repulsed my advances one evening when we were alone together, our friend occupied elsewhere with her sordid duties but surely about to surprise us, since she had the power to make a silver cross and gold rings appear out of nowhere as though by an invisible stroke of the wand.

Supreme magician as she might seem to me sometimes—or temptress of my middle age or even Lilith, spectral woman born of Adam's defilement when God hadn't yet provided him with a companion—Khadidja, too, felt the effects of our drinking, and I recall that once we went to the latrines to pee together like two kids without any modesty, I standing, she squatting and releasing into the darkness a thick stream of the liquid she had absorbed in considerable quantity as much because she liked it (I think) as for the sake of good business relations. Rather than a perverse pleasure, I believe I found in this total abandonment of the reserve that obtrudes between a man and a woman, however intimate their bond, the contentment of a momentary return to the state of nature and that same feeling of *touching the depths* that had intoxicated me when I had encountered, in the most secret part of Khadidja, the proof, not so much of our communion, as of the obliteration of the limits of our two bodies under the foam of the most elementary organic fluctuations.

(To say good-bye to her dead body, so youthful despite the disease that had been eating away at her lungs for a long time, my hand placed for a few seconds on the cold forehead of a woman of my period and my region for whom I had felt the deepest friendship, I who—without being a homosexual—regard friendship as a kind of love and am probably—whatever distaste I may have for the sublimity of platonic love—a man more drawn to friendships with women than passion; I discovered later that this final gesture, made to a person who for years had been on such a familiar footing with the angel of death that she seemed to have borrowed from it a little of its marble impenetrability, had actually been the involuntary though tender duplication of an earlier gesture, made at a time when she was still more or less in good health: one evening when a few of us were hanging about in the bars of Montmartre and she had gotten drunk, as often happened when she could no longer sustain the effort she needed to preserve an equilibrium that never held by more than a thread, suspended as she was between ice and fire by her severity and her passion, her distaste and her taste for life, her social messianism and her incapacity to submit to constraint, I had put my hand on her forehead to help her rid herself of her nausea by vomiting, a unique caress that my right palm—pressed down upon by that head which was giving way, as much because of the effect of the alcohol as because of the implacable paradoxes of which she was eternally the victim—has never forgotten. As one can see from certain of the pages she wrote, this friend had chosen to describe herself by the moving name "Laure," a medieval emerald coupling her somewhat feline incandescence with a vaguely parochial sweetness like a stick of angelica.)

"Messieurs, et cric! . . . Et crac!" When I have told how touched I was, at night, to hear Khadidja coughing (a crocodile tenderness, mixed, as though to dignify the pleasure, with remorse at having caused her to catch cold by stripping her, more or less, when she was in a sweat, with remorse at being, even despite my paltry attentions, one of the accomplices with whom she was hastening toward her physical ruin), when I have described our last meeting in the sun on a morning that was already almost torrid despite the coolness of the night, the shadow of Khadidja—stretched to the uncertain limit beyond which a shadow is no longer discernable—will bury itself in a recess of my memory without my ever being able, probably, to grasp it again as I am doing now, endeavoring to reconstruct our story.

The evening before the departure for Oran (the first stage of a journey toward a region where winter had raged while we were settling into the war without foreseeing that it would soon turn to confusion and massacre) I prudently went home with my companions, perhaps because I would not be able to break camp the next day without some preparation impossible to manage in the course of a morning that would necessarily be rushed, perhaps also because I would have committed rather too flagrant a breach of comradeship if I had abandoned the barracks room assigned to us to the extent of not staying there even one more night, perhaps most importantly because I felt it was better not to tempt fate and that another visit to the *bousbir* would risk adding nothing to an adventure that until then had remained—as though by some remarkable piece of luck—unblemished, nothing except perhaps some affront that might spoil everything. In place of the fully living Khadidja by whose side, had I strongly desired it, none of the specific motives I am alleging (my preparation for departure, my fear of going too far in neglecting my comrades) would have had enough weight to stop me from spending this last night, I preferred, in short, Khadidja the relic, the one whose image—with an overly devout caution—I was trying not to compromise and whose memory I was already cultivating, as though she were dead.

An episode that I now have great trouble situating on its proper plane— as I skirt two dangers: that of coloring it, romantically, with the flame of a mad love incubated between the sheets of a prostitute and that of, inversely, debasing it to the filthiest level in a frenzy of puritanism—would seem to have been closed once and for all (and through my own efforts) at the hour when the sun rose once again on Béni-Ounif, reanimating for a few more hours the great, but wretched, dusty setting in which the little town kept body and soul together, flanked by its palms and its Arab village. Accepting an offer made with an urbanity always embellished with a thin smile by one of my comrades—a serious, discreet boy with a certain ironic impassivity to whom I had confessed an uneasiness that had been vague up to then but was now intensified by the idea of our imminent return—I had drunk a chemical compound calculated (according to his assurances) to diminish the risk of my organism's suffering any retribution for a sexual conduct contrary to my circumspect habits. Perhaps my confidence in the power of this product was a shade naive, perhaps it was also enhanced by the joyous atmosphere in which we were packing our bags, chatting and joking all the while; but I was sure that in every respect—most importantly, by nipping in the bud this possibility of putrid consequences—I had put an end to an adventure that thenceforth would appear to me like one of those moving, infinitesimal plant-life discoveries that had so enchanted me when we were obliged to do whatever we could to deny the desolation of our rocky plateau.

Toward the end of the morning—having been called into town by something connected with my duties or some errand, unless it was that once I had settled all my affairs I wanted to stroll around a little more in those streets where nothing kept me any longer—I was passing near the *bousbir*. A street urchin hailed me: "Sergeant! Sergeant!" As he explained to me in a rather uncertain French, "Mlle Khadidja" had sent him to ask if I was not coming to say good-bye to her. I followed him.

Wrapped from head to toe in a vast, immaculate white robe belted at the waist, her forehead crowned with a coil of green muslin, my friend was waiting for me on the doorsill of her workplace like the mistress of some sisterhood adorned for a ceremony and with strict orthodoxy wearing the colors of her patron saint. She was on a chair, surrounded by the madam, standing, and other women. Whether upon leaving the barracks I had already, as I sometimes did, removed my kepi and slipped it between my jacket and my belt, or whether I had taken it off as I stopped in front of this group of women, I was bareheaded and—as usual—displayed a shorn skull. Khadidja in her seat and I standing straight before her looked at each other and it seemed to me I was seeing a completely new person: Khadidja no longer in motion, quick to wiggle her hips, but as fixed as a religious image or a wax museum figure; Khadidja in the grand array of a princess coming to haunt the traveler's dreams at the hour when vertical rays of sun reach down even to the bottom of the well; Khadidja, perhaps, as she would have been in a world that had not been degraded by whatever had made her an avowed prostitute and me a caricature of a soldier. "You're not afraid of the sun . . . ," she observed without moving her torso or her head an inch and as though this sentence had come from very far away, through the medium of her voice, always a little hoarse and too unskilled at handling French sounds for me to be able to tell if the phrase thus articulated was merely a statement or implied a nuance of questioning. Leaning down to put my face on a level with hers, I exchanged with her the simplest of kisses, mouth barely grazing cheek, the sort that might have been given by two people joined by a sentiment in which there wasn't even a hint of depravity.

(At a time when the phony war was stored away in an already distant past and France rid of its army of occupation, as I was traveling along a road on the British Gold Coast to visit some gold mines in Konongo, having left the large commercial center of Kumasi that morning, I was to hear, uttered by a woman I did not know, almost the same phrase as the one I had received as an oracle when it came to me from the lips of Khadidja. A great tree had fallen across the road—a frequent occurrence in the damp forest region because the giants of the plant world are more vulnerable than one would think—and obliged us, my companion and me, to stop our van, which was being followed at a short distance by another vehicle; while some manual laborers roused by our black driver were using axes and machetes to cut up the trunk that was obstructing our passage, we struck up a conversation with a very young and very cheery Anglican nun who was riding in the other van in company with a group of African women, all catechumens she was leading in a change of location that had some edifying motive behind it; this gracious person with the transparent complexion of a Palmolive ad rather than a cloistered nun or a Madonna, and dressed all in white and light gray while the other travelers set off their dark skin with the lively colors of printed cotton fabrics from Manchester, wore a cork sun helmet over her head veil; she talked to me about an uncle of hers, an American sculptor who had settled in a spot in the Gâtinais whose name was part of my childhood treasure trove—Bourron, close to *mourron* [chickweed], which is a kind of honey for little birds—and she asked me to convey a message to that uncle so that he would have the pleasure of receiving news of his niece by someone who had seen her recently; she had to search her mind for a long time to discover what might be the name of the villa where her relative lived, in English "Green Shutters," a locution for which we could only with great difficulty arrive at the French equivalent: *Volets Verts*, which we adopted after having rejected *Verts Volets*, *Persiennes Vertes*, and also *Vertes Persiennes*, which we had chosen first. During the course of the conversation, which lasted for about an hour while we stood in the middle of the road and watched the work, as I had descended from my van bareheaded, she politely urged me to put my hat back on, pointing out to me that it was hardly prudent to expose myself like that to the tropical sun for a period of time that had already been too long. "No horseplay," "Play fair or don't play at all," she might have said to me in that model-child tone of voice. Once I was back in Paris, I made sure to convey her news to her uncle, as promised; he responded by expressing his great pleasure at hearing of the good health of this niece he knew only by hearsay—having never had, in fact, the opportunity of meeting her—and invited me to come have lunch at his home if I should ever be passing through Bourron.)

Whereas because of a zealous attachment to the memory that would remain to me of a brief idyll I had, of my own accord, reduced it by one night —interrupting (in my eternal incapacity to break the circle of myself) a succession of events of which I wanted, instead of recklessly hurling myself into it, to preserve intact the sort of perfection I attributed to it in my greedy jubilation—Khadidja had conducted herself as though she were intending to show me that I was strongly mistaken in believing her capable of degrading what I was hoping to protect. Not only, during this last meeting, had she done nothing that might lead me to feel that her behavior was inopportune or frankly annoying, but she had been the one to set down, like an expert artist, the decisive mark that would cause the whole of the picture, now lit by the most tender sort of light, to assume at last its true form. Chance, too, intervened in what was happening to me that day and when, several minutes before departure time, near the train that was waiting in the station, I noticed the tank truck which during our stay at Base 2 had daily brought to our station, served only by a "dead-end road," the ration of liquid that it was my role to divide up among laboratory, kitchens, and washrooms, it seemed to me that even the things—and not only people—with which I had been involved in this intractable country were coming to me to say good-bye, in keeping with one of the simplest and most cordial of all protocols. Was it to the truck that brought the water, to the person driving it, or to the last ambassador of all those people and those things that I said my good-bye when, wishing him good luck, I tightly clasped the hand of the driver, a large fellow from Martigues, dark skinned and jovial, who generally made his delivery assisted by a man from Oran with a flat, olive-colored face, large dark eyes, and the monkeylike bearing of a picador's boy, with whom we would go and drink an anisette once our distribution was finished, which sometimes meant three anisettes because of the ritual of buying rounds?

(*Formalism*, in accordance with which I would like to see things order themselves as in a ceremonial, and *formulation*, which I impose on what passes into me so that it will cease to be alien. Except for an occasional sudden plunge into the rejection of all forms—a plunge that is, anyway, immediately taken up and treated as though it were necessary to grasp the form of that plunge that negated all forms—it is only when things or my thoughts submit to a certain arrangement in which logic plays no part that I feel myself carried beyond my singularity, in communion with the outside and very close to a state that one could call *total.* By chance, it can happen that a thing reveals its formula of its own accord right away, so that one has only to secure it: in the countryside in Limousin where I went immediately after my demobilization, later returning many times to visit those of my close relatives whom the anti-Semitic furor had forced to take refuge there, I happened to observe, in the course of a number of walks, the humble bird of the poultry yard which is the turkey, actually one of the most beautiful creatures I've ever had the opportunity to see; the motion of the turkey when, the wheel of his tail completely tightened, he pivots lightly on his feet, touching the ground with the tips of his lowered wings and emitting a soft breathing sound, all the while strutting about; it reminds one of certain movements made by the matador when the bull won't charge and the man, in order to provoke him, stamps lightly and shakes his *muleta* a little.)

This public farewell which Khadidja seemed to have been expecting even before she sent the boy to me—for, had she been less certain I would come, would she have dressed that way and then installed herself before her door and among her companions at the risk of the offense that would have been represented by the futile deployment of such a production?—did she value it because of an affinity real enough for her to refuse to let me go without taking leave of her? Concerned about her duties toward a faithful customer and wanting everything to be correct to the very end, did she, rather, see this farewell as a formal obligation which neither she nor I had the right to shirk?

Or, confident of her power, did she take pride in showing her comrades that an NCO would go to some trouble for her or that the least sign from her was enough to take him out of his way? Greedier and less coquettish, did she think that coming to say good-bye to her I would feel obliged to give her a present? I'm inclined to think there was a little of all this in the motive for her conduct and that by going to her without realizing that she might assume I would have something more substantial to give her than my emotional kiss, I sinned at once against the code of proper behavior and against friendship. Nevertheless, if she was vexed, she had enough manners not to let me suspect it, or—who knows? (and in this case my failure of generosity would show a certain tact)—the very absence of a gift might have been quite in line with what she wanted since it enabled her to feel proud that she was being treated like a lady.

"You're not afraid of the sun . . . ," she had said in her harsh voice and I, childishly vain, chose to imagine that she, speaking in the neutral, almost absent tone of a sibyl, had defined my destiny just as an emissary from the beyond would have done, revealing a pact that allied me to the solar element; but, far from admiring my lack of fear of sunstroke, perhaps she intended to give me, the foreigner, a sensible piece of advice or, she being the shameless one who showed herself in broad daylight, sitting in the middle of the street with her face uncovered, she simply felt it was shameful for someone to whom she attributed a certain rank to display himself, in the eyes of everyone, without any protection against the heavenly body and thus to put himself on the same level as men with the crudest sort of skin? By now I have given up sorting out what exact intention could have been hiding behind Khadidja's words, and I have also ceased to believe there was any real intention there: no doubt she resorted to an ordinary remark—the first that occurred to her—to show me discreetly (with that professional consciousness that seemed to preserve her from all falsehood) that she was *attentive* to me. A sort of thorough authenticity which she, the prostitute, had known how to preserve within our relations and which in itself alone would explain why it seemed to me I owed her a kind of fidelity: spending several hours at Saïda when the train that was taking us to Oran stopped there, I went with a comrade to see the whorehouse after stopping in at the Moorish bath; here, there was a girl neither ugly nor pretty but rather fresh and of a touching modesty whom it truly distressed me to turn away because I could see how humiliated she was by it but with whom—all the while heaping her with protestations of affection—I refused to go upstairs, not wanting to play with fire yet again and especially not on my way home, also not wanting another adventure at a brothel to ruin what I had found unique in Khadidja during encounters of which only one, the last, had not been marked by a commercial transaction.

In a pocket of my tunic or my khaki trousers I carried away, leaving North Africa, the silver cross to which I clung as though to an unexpected sign but which, not conforming to this fashion any more than I had adopted the local baggy trousers, I refrained from pinning on my chest as did so many of my comrades with similar jewels that shopowners had sold them and that they were almost as proud to show off as though our stay in the desert, the fact that it was a long and distant exile compensating for its lack of heroism, had earned each of us the honor of a medal hanging from some ribbon. Why, instead of putting an end to the peregrinations of that Southern Cross by keeping it, as one should in the case of a gift (and even more when a specific sentimental meaning is attached to it) did I feel—when I was back in Paris—that the present that had so delighted me when it came to me from that girl, one evening when she had been touched by some mysterious whim I still wonder about, could have no more honest fate than to pass from my hands, which had received it from those other hands, for once not paid, to those of my wife?

My mobilization, followed a few days later by my departure for North Africa, had opened in my life a large parenthesis. Being torn from the flow of the life one has created and having one's persona, as defined by one's affections, one's occupations, one's idiosyncrasies, obliterated—this is what gives the civilian when abruptly transformed into a soldier the illusion of starting from zero again, in a world where, no longer having to hold himself more than half responsible, he feels freed of a part of his ties and, however unsatisfying his new condition may be, suffers less from its weight at the same time that he has available to him, in practical terms, a convenient alibi. The nauseating simplification which in certain cases anonymity and the facile excuse of not having one's hours free give to the person who, in normal times, doesn't dare take it upon himself to do what he wants. Having become, upon my conscription, subject to the crude arithmetic which knows no other measure of things but that given by regimental numbers, my life, profoundly divided for the past several months, had recovered a semblance of unity.

Ceasing to continue without too many serious deviations along the path laid out for me by my monogamous union, I had learned from experience that it is not arbitrary to speak of a left hand and a right hand, this existence (until then progressing along an axis rarely and only for short lapses deflected, whenever a little too much rectitude passed the point after which there is nothing but boredom) having revealed itself to be no more than a shadow or a half an existence because for me the sun had risen whose sensuous beams, turned on an object which is exempted by such light from intellectual or moral justifications, tend to make everything vanish but that object. Beauty: that which discredits, which deprives the rest (for all women will become ugly because of a single woman who is beautiful). Beauty, always "of the Devil's party without knowing it," as it is said of the true poet in *The Marriage of Heaven and Hell.* Uncertain beauty, of which too often we will be surprised, almost, at having been to such an extent enthusiasts or instruments, discovering that it was a mere straw fire, a bloom of youth that consumed itself without a trace or apparition projected illusorily before us by an arrangement of mirrors. Beauty, nevertheless, with incarnations so numerous that it will not cease to shine here or there, as long as we escape final blinding under the veils of our fatigue, growing every year. A morocco-leather trinket having the very form and the color of love, the soldier's knife (offered perhaps mistakenly, since it demonstrated how friendships are severed), the specter of the *muleta* whose corporeal undulation subjugates the bull and that of a high-pitched drumroll summoning to the splendors of a sabbat my accomplice day and night desperately alive have become for me the distant emblems of that incarnation of beauty, an incarnation whose imagined succubus nudity was replaced by a flesh-and-blood nudity because of the upheaval of mobilization, the state of availability which this disruption of acquired habits had created, the species of legitimacy, too, that the gravity of saying good-bye conferred on licentious vaudeville gestures.

Obedient to the hateful mechanism that often leads one to proceed from one act to the next as though an earlier act over which our good conscience suffers could later be associated with another act in order to change its meaning or make it a fair counterbalance, I had discovered in a new and twofold betrayal—in which Khadidja had been my partner—the means of minimizing the betrayal for which my lifelong companion had a right to refuse to forgive me: it was as though the sudden impulse resulting from my solitude in the Sahara proved that there was also only a sudden impulse involved in the illicit relationship to which I had been so quick to prove unfaithful; to hand over as an acquittal for the first betrayal the jewel I had received was (without any doubt) to acknowledge that over me it had a kind of dominion and over the other betrayal a preeminence of a sort to make me feel, in the end, almost cleared of guilt in the very moment in which I was exhibiting the token of my repeat offense. Beyond any opportunistic cunning, it also seemed to me that by presenting as a gift this jewel that had its own history, I was making a more valid gesture than if I had simply given the traditional gift of a travel souvenir: the object that had come to me without my buying it represented my own property and in some sense a portion of myself which I was giving up; though less attentive than my companions (one of whose main concerns, once the time approached when we would be returning, had been to acquire this sort of souvenir to bring back to their families), didn't I have an advantage over them since, far from returning home empty-handed, I was bringing back this miniature star, a silver cross enriched by a significance much weightier than that of any other curio I could have procured by normal means?

(*Everything, as it falls, takes with it its little CUM*. Of this fake statement by Paracelsus, a vestige from a treatise on falling bodies I had imagined in a dream—or rather dreamed that I was imagining—and that, except for this vestige, disappeared when I woke up, I had been determined, some thirty years ago, when I wanted to make everything fit into the framework of an esoteric doctrine, to establish a mnemonic figuration using a bronze coin, such as still existed at that time, and the five dice of a game of poker-dice—also called *poker-d'as*—of which two, joined and forming a horizontal block, had been placed in a carefully perpendicular position on a table or some other piece of furniture with an adequate surface at the top and to the left of the figure, two others, separated, in an oblique position and on a line descending toward the right at a forty-five-degree angle—the second of these dice positioned on the thick penny—and the fifth, also isolated and vertical like the first two, halfway up toward them and the bronze disc, as though halfway up the slope of a line that, also pointing toward the right, would be the ascending response to the other line; the surfaces presented respectively by the five dice of which this figure was composed were a king, an ace, a ten, a nine, and a jack, the last acting as substitute for the joker who is reminiscent of the Mountebank of the tarots and whom I, stammering metaphysician, saw as, relatively, the demon without which there would be nothingness, so that the figure could be read by anyone who shared my views as a thorough hermeticist: king, *every;* ace of hearts, the *thing* as pulp or heart of the world; slanting ten, *as it falls,* this number appearing to me through my uncertain knowledge of arithmosophy as that of Man and consequently of the Fall; ten-centime piece, *takes with it,* its form being that of a wheel; slanting nine—positioned perpendicular to the ten to express the meaningful rise of hope—*its little,* because the nine is the weakest value in the game of poker-dice; jack—in other words assistant, necessary crutch—*CUM,* that entity about which I write in a gloss contemporary with the figure: "The *CUM*—Latin for 'with' —is the adjuvant, the cluster of relations, that is, of accidents, that a body drags with it when it moves from its place. It is also a fraction of the substance of neighboring bodies, every relationship between two bodies being necessarily a physical thing, partaking of the substance of both bodies at once. A body is therefore at once itself and all other bodies since one can connect it to all of them and conceive of them all as existing only in relation to it. Thus, the visual universe is identified with myself, since I have knowledge of it only through *my* perspective, which I displace along with myself. In the same way, as men fall into death, they take with them a baggage of perceptible links, filaments of fleshly survival they have obtained from the world during their passage there." Once back from these utopias, I still continued to assign a symbolic value to my five dice—concretions of fate that one holds in one's hand, not on the level of a sacristy or fortune-teller's parlor redolent of incense paper, but on that of a low-life bar in which *passe anglaise* and other illegal games are played—and it was, probably, as one does with a talisman or a viaticum that I deposited them, when she was dead, in the coffin of that friend whom I had helped to vomit one evening of heavy drinking in Montmartre and who, as she was dying, had caused me to feel, beyond all pity and all sorrow, the true holy terror: a great cold that ran up my spine and that the close companion of the dying woman, as he assured me shortly afterward, had observed in the form of a bluish fulguration emanating from my head, when we saw the woman who seemed to exist no longer except at a fabulous distance attempt a half sign of the cross, backwards—the gesture of touching herself on one shoulder, then the other, and that was all—with an expression of intense joy and irony, like a little girl who wanted to play a naughty joke on us; to attempt but not to achieve it, as though she had wanted to go to the very edge, in order to scare us by raising before us, her friends and atheists like her, the specter of a possible conversion, though clearly a heterodox one. Did I hope that, placed in the safest hands, the cross that Khadidja had given me would one day be deposited in a similar way in a corner of my coffin impervious to any hope of survival several seconds or minutes before the cover was closed?)

The object that, for Khadidja, perhaps represented the price of the obscenities she had performed, either while taking her own pleasure in them or with the same cynical indifference as that other girl from the *bousbir* who, for the sum of forty sous, publicly put a bottle of beer in her vagina (a spectacle at which I refrained from being present, despite being invited, and which Khadidja also, along with most of her companions, seemed to view as an extreme of which they would leave the monopoly to their colleague, the most inexorably ugly and withered of them all); the object that had passed from those impure hands, then from mine, which were hardly more worthy, into others absolutely faithful and clean did not stay very long in the possession of the woman who, in full knowledge and in full rectitude of heart, had accepted it as deposit. In that Limousin countryside where my wife's brother-in-law had settled at the time of the 1940 exodus—forced like so many others to seek shelter from the Hitlerites' outburst of racism—we were looted by Gestapo cops one night in 1943: a sham search motivated by a hunt for a supposed arms depot; in fact, a burglary, one man with a machine gun posted in the garden and all of us who happened to be in the house kept under watch while awaiting, the cops said, the arrival of the car that would take us to Limoges for the interrogation (especially worrying for the one among us who was not "Aryan" and whom in one way or another the occupying force would certainly arrange to hold there, whence an inexpressible anguish that oddly enough had its ebbs and flows, without any direct connection with the course of our thoughts and like a physical nausea subject to its own rhythm so that it sometimes attained its height at the moment when one was formulating to oneself some reassuring thought); then, the cops having slipped away under the pretext of going to see if the tardy vehicle had not broken down or stopped for some reason in the vicinity of the house, our cautious exit from the living room in which we had been confined under the threat of revolvers and, very quickly, the discovery of the truth, when we had visible confirmation of what—without at first daring to believe we would be let off so cheaply—we had for a certain time reckoned, namely that the operation had no other end but to steal all there was in the way of jewels and other easily transportable valuables. For my part, I left in the hands of the looters the pen that I had already used to write a good part of *Biffures,* the only fountain pen that has been really satisfactory (a Parker replaced today, though it is nowhere near its equivalent, by a 51 model with hooded nib); in addition, I was robbed of all my cigarettes, a rare commodity whose theft I resented as a gratuitous piece of malice, our police certainly numbering among the last to be anxious about procuring tobacco for themselves. As for my wife, she lost, along with her rings and various jewels she prized highly because they had belonged to her family, that silver cross, which she had become accustomed to wearing on her wrist attached to a bracelet hung with many other trinkets. Thus, in accordance (one might have believed) with a scenario for a charade illustrating the proverb Easy come easy go, the object brought back from the brothel van-

ished almost directly to the Gestapo as though prostitution and police maintained an obligatory collusion in the as yet undestroyed world of which they
are cornerstones. When, long after the Liberation, I learned from the newspapers (where I recognized him from the mention of his name and reference
to his past as chemist employed in the perfume industry) that one of my
messmates in the Hôtel du Sahara had, during the Occupation, joined the
SPAC, or Anticommunist Police Service, and was now being hunted down as
a member of a team of torturers, it was with a mixture of repugnance and
shame that I thought of this boy. In truth, I had never had much liking for
him—because of his overly self-satisfied air, his ambitions as a rowdy, and the
dullness of mind evident in his approval of the most vulgar slogans of the day
—but I put it down to his credit that he happened to be, militarily, one of
the few in our group to have taken the bull by the horns by applying for assignment to a fighting unit (one of the few and not the only one, since a similar request had been formulated by the manager of our mess at Base 2, a vis-
cous character whose lack of bone structure disgusted almost all of us and
whom, playing rather histrionically the braggadocio, I had been one of the
very first to bully, going so far, one evening of drinking, as to slap him in public because he had once said, with the little laugh of a salacious sacristan, that
he liked to get whores to "tell him their life stories," without blushing at taking pleasure in extracting confessions that were sometimes accompanied by
tears from these women who were of course prepared to do a great deal—
theatrical or real—to satisfy the knowing or innocent cruelty of such a large
part of their clientele). After everything had been called into question again
by the war, that *hour of truth,* I could not forget that, either out of nonchalance or motivated by a conceited desire for popularity among those whose
behavior seemed to prove that they "had what it took," I had treated a potential persecutor as an individual with whom, without losing prestige, one
could maintain an excellent friendship. In the light of such a revelation about
the ignominious bent that could be followed by someone with whom I had
consented to be on familiar terms without entertaining the least illusion
about his mediocrity, which was at once too complacent and too anxious to
impress not to be alarming, it appeared to me that during my period in the

Sahara I had, all in all, seriously degraded myself and that in believing I was disengaging myself from a certain bourgeois conformity I had fallen into something even worse. Would that corporal of the Legion who had one day spoken to me—without being more precise—about the time when he was "in politics" and of the exaltation he felt then speaking at public meetings, have limited himself to this vague allusion if he had been anything else but a paid agitator, working for some mafia or other? Wasn't Khadidja, though I am tempted to hail her as my tutelary angel or demon, in some sense the equivalent (since being compliant toward a master was part of her profession) of those atrocious whores who, between one torture session and the next, caroused with the members of the Gestapo or the militiamen? As for me, who, after our banquet, had offered her to my companions the mercenaries (for fear, perhaps, that she would do this herself), hadn't I, by treating her like a prize that one passes from one soldier to the next, embraced a good deal of the degradation that she shared with all those, men or women, who in some way or other use themselves for commercial transactions? But if I justly accused myself of having often been—however scornful toward certain people —too indulgent in my choice of male companions, wasn't it because of an old Manicheism originating in my childhood (when everything, despite the compromise of Purgatory, was either theological virtue or capital sin, treasure of the good or arsenal of the wicked) that after having endowed this girl with an almost sidereal brilliance I was prepared to suspect her of having harbored in her flesh the most abject potentialities?

The cross, then, which for a certain time I had kept in my pocket like a coin attesting to a vanished era or like the entry token to a paradise of my own invention, was lost to me in the same way that so often, emerging from my dreams, the object was lost that had proved to me that at least once this marvel had existed. Even before I had been irremediably deprived of this small treasure whose existence was reassuring since I am always seeking some sort of philosopher's stone (the absolute held in one's hand or encompassed with a single look, like the perceptible mass of the fledgling fallen from the nest; the object with a special aura whose discovery would fill the hole of solitude; the event immediately presenting itself in the solemn arrangement of a

crucial experience; the thing with any sort of rigor which the magic of formulation endows with a fascinating power), even before this proof of my former, but quite real, embroilment with Khadidja was filched, the war had
ceased to be a distant background against which my actions appeared in profile without there being any precise relationship between them and it; recalling me to the brutal truth of certain primary imperatives at the very moment
when I was neglecting them in favor of the comedy I was enacting for myself,
this war, having become intensely present, stripped me of my great primary
role and seemed destined to reduce my employment to that of a mute character without any other contribution than the dumb show of his eyes, now
unsealed and opened wide by horror. In the Landes, where I was sent in a
military capacity (having been assigned to the munitions depot of the Sen,
near Labrit) and where the exodus, driving my wife from Paris, had led her
quite naturally to join me since she was my wife, we watched, by the side of
a road where this encounter had immobilized us, as a heavy convoy of trucks
and armored cars filled with German soldiers went by. Not entirely released
from my obligations by the armistice, which had just been signed, that same
day I had to go to another camp in the region, to which I had withdrawn because it was situated on the other side of the demarcation line in that area
which the occupying forces were willing to spare temporarily. As we watched
these troops, which had been almost imaginary up to then and, reading this
page of history with our living eyes, as we found ourselves together like two
children on their way to school staring hand in hand and mouths wide open
as a regiment files by, this as we were on the point of saying good-bye to each
other, I understood, as an obvious truth, produced in a cartoon strip image,
that our fates were inseparable since now and henceforth we recognized
(without saying a word) that they were bound together for the difficult times
inaugurated by this scene and it was therefore improbable that a bond whose
firmness had been thus tested would later loosen. Not long after that, the in-
famy of these times was to be harshly revealed in a scene of the dimensions of
eternity even though its real duration, in fact, hardly exceeded a few seconds:
my wife and I, back from Limousin, where she had joined her family and
where I too had gone as soon as I was demobilized, were returning to Paris by

train, uneasy about the responsibilities that the new course of things had imposed on us, even if only on the very prosaic level of our family interests, whose defense we were now the only ones capable of trying to safeguard; the Germans assigned to check those crossing the line did not even examine our papers but ejected a Jew traveling in the compartment next to ours: *"Jude! Jude!"* they said furiously in that tone of hateful superiority that will only be assumed by the most appalling idiots, without wanting to listen to the protests of the unfortunate man, who was explaining how he was on his way up to the capital to find his family again, lost from sight since the exodus. Measured against this, the queens of Sheba and other concubine queens issuing from the harsh reflections of the sterile expanses or from the thin radiance that, every year, again gilds the houses in which our old Paris spleen settles no longer had more than the diaphanous and almost substanceless grace of stucco figurines in a rococo decoration. As for the jewel that would soon be reduced to even less than those enchanted coins which turn to dry leaves the day after the payment, though I had endowed it with the magic of a slipper given by an attendant of Isis or some other mother goddess to one she has initiated into orgiastic mysteries, this complacency did not last: very soon, I was surrounded by realities too harsh for me not to regard any yielding to such reveries as vain and—all poetry having been absorbed—the rigorously worldly conviction gradually took shape that I had behaved toward my benefactor not as one of the elect but as a nonentity, for the more I mulled it over the more obvious it was that since one gift in all humanity demanded another, I should have responded to this one with something more tangible than a dreamily romantic thought.

Before the blossoming of the June of Liberation, the four years of Occupation were a long winter whose rigors, cruel even to those whose lives fell short of being real hell, were nevertheless tempered by the solid counterpart of the sympathy among people of the same opinions and all the joys that could be extracted from the trifling things that in the old days one hadn't prized at their true value. If I had required many months in the desert to learn all that an expanse of grass could signify in the way of promise of happiness and also what intoxication could be derived from a sudden warmth emanating from the marble that is, by definition, a whore, I required the Occupation to be able, for example, to recognize the value of a few simple days of tranquil freedom in a countryside where one is welcomed in an honest and cordial manner, the suffocation of the city finding its antidote—then more than ever—in the salubrious air of those less populous regions settled, in growing numbers as the oppression became heavier, by what were called the maquis, as though the group of outlaws—as a group of partisans would be regarded by the police—had merged with its scrubland surroundings through an osmosis comparable to that whose image is proposed to us by fauns, centaurs, and other creatures still involved up to the waist in pure nature. This slice of life less peasant than pagan—in the most complete etymological sense of the word—I happened to witness during one of the visits I made to Saint-Léonard-de-Noblat, before the search (or rather the burglary) carried out by the Gestapo had driven to another refuge those whom I periodically went to see there, has not ceased to move me, just as much because I associate the memory of it with the memory of a Khadidja now remote enough to have one foot in mythology as because of the guise of a *lull* assumed in my eyes by each of these visits to the country. One morning full of birds singing, apple trees in bloom, and rhododendrons whose fragrance recalled that of sevillan jasmine, I saw, on the outskirts of a farm managed by some Poles, a ewe being shorn: tied down to a table, the animal was bleating and attempting to get free, while two men busied themselves passing the shears over her; little by little relieved of her thick wool, she presented herself as though unclothed, and the sight of her pink udders was disturbing, feminine breasts which jutted up between her two back legs (and not, as one would have expected, between her front legs or arms); thus lying down and, it seemed, prepared to be put to death in all placidity of spirit on the occasion of some spring sacrifice, it was of the famous *Battle of the Minotaur* series executed by Picasso that, despite its solar brilliance, I was immediately reminded by this almost human ewe on her back on the wood of a table like—in the etching in which the only source of light is a candle held by a little girl who is also carrying a large bouquet—the woman in torero's costume, chest bared, who has collapsed tragically over the back of a lame horse; but, as in the *toros,* what predominated in this recall to the bitterest realities of life, which necessarily imply the reality of death, was the gladness of a *fiesta* in immemorial harmony with the progress of the seasons. As I thought about it later, the exposure in full sun of this animal who seemed about to have its throat cut and who, being only by allusion a woman, seemed more naked than any other, and more present at the same time as extraordinarily alien, appeared in its ambiguity to be closely related to the Algerian woman with the striding walk of a goat girl who bled so suddenly from one of her ears at the moment of the festivity for which our bodies were preparing, not unlike a clock with incomprehensible works.

"Gentlemen, and *cric!* . . . and *crac!*"

Whereas her still-enduring image needed no feature I might have added to it to affirm its contours, I had chosen to see Khadidja as an equivocal fleshly disguise assumed by the angel of death in order to insinuate itself close to me and cause me to absorb, without rebelling against what is just as natural as beauty, the supremely poisonous idea of the fall that lay ahead. Could it be that the feeling I had, that with her I had touched the depths, and that she had led me, as though by chance, to penetrate the secrets of the deepest level of organic life, in itself persuaded me to regard the woman who had been my companion for several days as more than just a faun who had amiably welcomed me into her miry lair? Could it have been her gravity as guardian of the threshold, and that species of white simar (after the ear suddenly wounded to the point of bleeding, the song of one possessed, and the jewel she seemed to have caused mysteriously to spring up from the ground) that elevated her—when a sentence in which the word *sun* caught fire allowed her to fill the emptiness that yawned between us—to a rank to which she certainly made no claim and at which she probably would have laughed had she learned that I had bestowed it on her? Did it come from the shadow that floated over her because of the Colomb-Béchar incident, a simple fight between women with at most some clawing, or a true brawl after which she would have had no other solution but to take off? Or was it immediately founded on the deadly character she derived from her North African beauty and from everything that her face, so curiously inlaid (the blade of a dagger or scimitar), conveyed that was brilliant, suspect, and dangerous, like the name of the Algerian town I read about when I was a child in a story by Alphonse Daudet, "Milianah," which lays out before me a sunny street scene filled with the smell of leather, with striped rags, beggars, cripples, and perhaps knife thrusts, a dusty luminosity the impression of which I rediscovered in part when, as an adult, I was taking some air on the balcony of the pension in Cairo where I was staying and saw a poor young wretch without any legs dragging himself down the middle of the street in his pitiful box on wheels by holding—either clutching it directly with his hands or by means of some extension—the axle of the back wheels of a hackney carriage? Wasn't it true, though, more than anything else, that Khadidja the nocturnal, Khadidja the solar, coughing in her large iron bed and probably infected with syphilis, harbored enough death in her so that she would have been the last one to let me forget, when I caressed her, that unless one drifts lazily with the flow of habit or abandons oneself body and soul to animal innocence, one can't embrace any creature in shared pleasures without a whisper of the gloomy angel being mixed in with the obscure discourse one wrests from it, since it is difficult for us not to view the loved object—confounded as we are to see it lost in the tenuousness of the instant (that very instant in which we possessed it)—as the evil messenger who, behind its seductive guise, recalls to us what is precarious about what we have? But for all of this to crystallize around her form, it was still necessary for Khadidja to exchange her tawdry carnivalesque finery (her fiery red blouse, her oriental pants or the poor faded undershirt she would pull off with both hands when stripping completely) for the robe which, falling to her feet and hiding her long, agile legs under its fullness, endowed her with a surprising majesty: abruptly seeing her clothed in garments at once chaste and royal, this deplorable courtesan in whom I had tasted (as in the suddenly innervated arms of a sea nymph from a Roman mosaic) a unique combination of hardness and softness, how could I have helped, once the thick curtain of lands and sea had fallen behind me, but orient her memory to the point of changing this portrait doomed to become too quickly confused into the effigy of the creature who, toward midnight, appears within your door frame to notify you—implacably though in the most caressing tones—that the final expiration is close at hand? The older I get—proceeding on a course parallel to this dizzying succession: the "phony war" that had collapsed in the exodus; the Occupation, at first partial and then, abruptly, total; the uprising, heralding the Liberation; followed by the various phases of the peace and the disquieting hybrid known as the "cold war"—the more I tend well and truly to see Khadidja, loved so unthinkingly and so fleetingly, as the first woman with whom, where love for love's sake is concerned, I began to experience a decline that has continued ever since (as though we met at a zenith that was thenceforth passed) and therefore the one who appeared —like a statue animated by the imminence of some plague or assassination of Caesar—at the exact point where my path began to bend in the direction in which one wishes, in vain, not to see it bend.

"*Cric,* gentlemen!" ("And *cric!*" repeats the chorus.) "And *crac!*" (The chorus repeats "And *crac!*")

My life, which does not need to think in order to continue, goes more quickly than I advance through the twists and turns of what I am writing about it. For months now (and if I were to count them, I would only augment the anguish caused me by a daily increasing lag) I have been pursuing this tale, though it is simply an outline—quickly skimmed by anyone who will want to read it—of what will have been, even including its sequence of repercussions and the end of them, an episode that I would describe as a "Don Juan adventure" if I hadn't played in it the modest role of a client to whom this same cross was perhaps awarded as, for advertising purposes, a shopkeeper awards a premium. Whatever I may do to improve my text, nothing will render its reality obvious for all that and I have no power over the dubious idol now armed with her phantasmal spur by the trace left in my brain by the asperity of pinkish flesh that lay above the humid ravine opening in the brown of her thighs. After what will soon be fifteen years of prospecting in all directions—in a series of marches and countermarches that I began when Béni-Ounif was still very close and that have ended in this sort of memorial wake during which I have tried to put into somewhat intelligible form an adventure that, in its time, had charmed me because at each moment it seemed to take form quite independently of me—I am still only reaching the end of the second stage I had set for myself: these *Fourbis,* which are supposed to be followed by hazardous *Fibrilles,* then by difficult *Fibules* or buckles by means of which the whole thing will have to be adjusted. I am so slow that the practical pursuit I began with (the search for a set of rules, which I would have ample time to apply after they were discovered) has been replaced, in fact, by the drafting of a sort of testament. New signs are being added to those that, for so long now, have obliged me to acknowledge my decline. I see them in my external appearance—wrinkles evident enough so that my facial expression is easily a grimacing one, a more pronounced baldness (whence the need to resume the hairstyle of an ascetic or young convict), a frequent swelling underneath and around the eyes (the right eye, especially, sometimes indiscreet to the point of nearly watering), a belly whose muscles are relaxing despite the happy absence of obesity, a greater vulnerability to sleeping too little as well as to eating too much—and the bitterness that I feel about it interferes with all the rest: whether because of the mood (I like to think) or inclination of a mind beclouded by the accumulated diversity of its literary and other works, or the unremitting disgust (I'm afraid) that one inevitably conceives for his own body, or (which would be the worst) pure and simply decay, one is no longer seized except rarely—and almost always without the beautiful spontaneity of youth—by priapic enthusiasm; as though all sensuous images were dissolving in the perception of this humiliating inertia, one remains almost insensitive to the presence of the other and has only, at the very most, an infantile desire for effusion (to embrace, to be embraced), unless the evil spell is finally broken by the good luck of some caress; since there is nothing magical now about lying undressed next to someone in bed, one loses the pleasure once found in vestimentary elegance; one shuts oneself up in a narcissism that is no longer superficial (that of someone acting as though he were in front of a mirror) but that of Narcissus himself drowning in the depths of his viscera (worried about the functioning of his internal organs and hardly having eyes, any longer, for what is outside); beyond this almost physiological tendency to withdraw, one feels even more alone and as though in fact deprived of a respondent because a friend died with whom, there being implicit harmony, one could choose to say nothing at all or (without boredom) talk in order to say nothing to each other; except for a few fortuitous escapes, one walls oneself up, gets stuck in the mud, is no longer able, even, to explain oneself. *Not making love, one loses that minimum of contact with life* and (a play on words disguised as a word of conclusion) *loses touch with everyone else.* Twenty years ago already, I noted this one evening before going to sleep, and, if I had nothing to add as to the reasons one can have for feeling separate from others, I would now be on the verge of an irreparable exile, since I abandon myself less and less often to the pleasure that allows one to know one is virile and since in this way, at the same time that a primary means of responding to the need to act upon another person—even if only on one single person who is alive and acknowledged to be so—is growing more remote, the great source of wonders proves to be nearing exhaustion.

During these past few months, in my daydreams—sinister ones, if I have drunk a little the night before or the night before that, and am not in good condition—I have been chewing over the old theme of suicide like a refrain coming back to me from very far away: the urgent need to have in the house something that ought to help one to live!—certainly not a revolver (because it is too frightening) but the exact dose of sleeping medicine that would allow one gently to do away with oneself some day; the progress in civilization that would be represented by the existence of brothels where one would go to have oneself killed by beautiful, expert, and compassionate women, this progress in addition to the improvement in household arrangements consisting of installing in each apartment a body chute just as there are garbage chutes in quite a few modern buildings (this being the logical way to process the deceased, since we lack the belief that in Egypt justified depositing them in a sarcophagus between two representations, carved or even in relief, of nude female figures: on the verso of the cover, Nut, the celestial goddess, her arms raised and her nocturnal charms floating like a ceiling over the dead person; on the inner surface of the bottom, and with her arms lowered, the infernal goddess Amentit lying beneath the form of the deceased).

To my city dwelling of 53 *bis* quai des Grands Augustins, where I moved right in the midst of the Occupation, a country house situated in the Etampes region was added about eighteen months ago. A large house with a number of granaries, outhouses or other dependencies, and even a Roman chapel in ruins, this is what I—who used to dream I was some sort of foster brother to the "outlaws"—now co-own, in practical terms. My wife, myself, and the relatives with whom we live spend almost every weekend there. Built on the site of a priory that had its own ossuary (as was discovered during some digging which resulted in the unexpected exhumation of a number of skulls and pieces of skeleton belonging, evidently, to the old nuns) this house has been occupied, since it has belonged to us, by a family from Guadeloupe whose adult members are friends of ours almost as much as they are caretakers; the wife, a mulatto, serves as housekeeper and the husband, a black, takes care of the garden, a little Negress (who is, I think, seventeen) looking after the housework and the cooking. Along with some poultry, a few rabbits, a cat, and two pairs of birds (turtledoves and rock pigeons) there is a bitch who is called *Dine,* as in the song of the Valois, but was almost named *Diane, Didon,* or *Dina,* the initial *D* being required of us by the custom according to which pedigreed dogs born in the same year are all given names beginning with the same letter.

These people, whom I knew in their own homeland—when I sweated (always too much, in my opinion) under the island sun; this animal who always wants to play or take a walk and gives everyone a lavish welcome; a house nearly a century and a half old; a pretty view, trees, space, a fairly isolated spot: in short, a good many of the things that allow one to be happy. Is it on this estate that I would like to be buried? I had that idea for a short time, but I quickly rejected it, not wanting to play the part of a squire bent on resting in his own lands anymore than I want to be the falsely modest fellow who insists upon the potter's field—an elegant way of disowning one's family in the apparently egalitarian wish to mingle with everyone—and also regarding it as absurd for a non-Christian like me (or even for a Christian) to attach any sort of importance to the fate of his remains. Similarly, I rejected the plan, formed on another day of macabre daydreaming, of having myself buried dressed in the smoking jacket of a slightly too blue tropical fabric that I wore (not without uneasiness, because it was more garish than I had expected) both times I went to Venice for the opera performances which, during the music festival, take place at the Fenice (or, in French, *le Phénix*) Theater. Worthy of a more serious examination than these egoistic confessions (those of a bachelor having the only say in his final disposal, to the exclusion of a partner who might be justified in considering that she shared the responsibility) is the plan of making the eyeballs of my future corpse available to surgeons for blind people: here, one would be accomplishing something useful and not simply rectifying what was perhaps a failure of taste in assigning a mortuary role to a showy suit of clothes which one hesitated to wear while still alive; to suppress the little chill in the back engendered by the prospect of a posthumous butchery ought not, certainly, to cost me much, for one certainly has no need to be very courageous to display some valor beyond the tomb.

If it appears untenable to express on our own account—as though preparing an entrance to a masked ball for the absent one which we will be—any sort of desire having to do with our own funeral arrangements, is it similarly senseless to wish that our life, instead of stopping short like a serial story that has been suddenly interrupted, should be extended, even if only a little, in what a few other people might derive from it? After my separation from Khadidja, followed by an enormous jostle of events, had caused her to become, for me, almost the equivalent of a dead woman (whom I would have liked to see reappear in a pool of shadow or light when, in Algiers, I visited the Casbah), that jewel which disappeared in the end played—without the faraway woman knowing anything about it—the role of another of her incarnations, whose story was linked as a new phase to the brief episode of our encounter. Is it stupid of me to wish that once I am dead, a legacy concerning my inward parts (my two eyes if I make up my mind to it and, in any case, a written work resembling me, though the usefulness of that particular legacy may be terribly debatable) may allow me, as was the case with the cross given by Khadidja, to open the chapter—whose unfolding, to my very great annoyance, is unforeseeable—in which my story will come to an end?

But, in recounting the blackest thoughts one by one like this, as though I enjoyed improvising a depressing recitative on some out-of-tune instrument,

I am probably just as ridiculous as those comrades of mine in the army who could see nothing else in the spot to which we had been led by a *dead-end road* but a backwater where they would perish of immobility and desolation.

Rebecca, the servant Agar, Naomi, Rachel (who also appears in the card game, along with Judith, Pallas Athena, and the unknown Argina, whom one never worried about): beauties with insidious names which, in Hebrew legend, confront a comic Potiphar and—like the young girl as thin as "the E string of a mandolin"—correspond to a moving capacity for invention, whose sparkling productions are also signs of gratitude. Khadidja the promiscuous, crowned with a piece of green muslin like a sharif's turban to speak to me about the sun and more naked perhaps than in our past embraces when my mouth rested against her cheek for a good-bye kiss simply exchanged from one person to another; that friend, on whose pale forehead my hand pressed twice and who died so radiant after a sign almost as confusing as the sight of a watch suddenly beginning to move backwards, denying the order of things as well as the passage of time: truthful images which, I will dare to say, are for me, even though imbued with melancholy, rather comforting, their magic causing me to forget, in the case of the first, the pitiful life led by the woman herself and, in the case of the second, the fact that it is nothing more than the trace left at the bottom of several memories by a person as unshakable in her demand for high ideals, as those close to her knew, as she was violent in her rebellion against the norms to which most people subscribed. However demoralizing our condition may be and however frankly detestable our institutions make it for a great number—which increases my discomfort at adding to it a bad conscience—can I despair completely and give up trying to discover a program other than an abandonment to the undulation of personal desires and repulsions or a morose utilitarianism, as long as this world appears to me as the place where a quantity, even if infinitesimal, of acts and words came into being in which a human accord was formulated in a pure state, so to speak, and which (even if only in the lightning flash of a fortunate throw of the dice) organized themselves into crystals of a design so perfect they made me cry out in admiration?

Vedi? . . . di morte l'angelo
Radiante a noi si appressa . . .

sweetly sing Radamès and Aïda, almost happy, though half dead of asphyxia-
tion in their funeral cave; as though, within the darkness in which they are illuminated by love, these two lovers—of a kind, however, never thus far encountered outside novels and operas—imagined in the dazzling guise of a
single archangel the burn that Aïda was, at least, for Radamès and Radamès
for Aïda.

1948–1955

About the Author

Michel Leiris was born in 1901. While "vaguely" pursuing studies in chemistry, he associated with the nightowls of postwar Paris and became friends with Max Jacob and the painter André Masson. Passionate about poetry, he joined the surrealist group in 1924. From this initiation into the arcana of dream and language were born the poems in *Simulacre* (1925), later the games in *Glossaire, j'y serre mes gloses* (1939), and the novel *Aurora*, which was not to appear until 1946. Anguished by writing, by his marriage in 1926, by his break from the Surrealists, Leiris went into psychoanalysis in 1930. Out of a subsequent desire to measure himself against reality, he accompanied the 1931–33 "Mission Dakar-Djibouti," an ethnographic expedition of which he published a "personal chronicle," *L'Afrique fantôme*, in 1934. He worked as an ethnologist at the Musée de l'Homme until 1971 and, parallel to this study of other peoples, conducted an extensive study of himself. His first autobiographical essay, *L'Age d'homme* (1939), only revealed to him new games involving masks, the rules of which he proposed to discover in the four works that constituted *La règle du jeu* (*Biffures*, 1948; *Fourbis*, 1955; *Fibrilles*, 1966; and *Frêle bruit*, 1976). *Le ruban au cou d'Olympia* (1981), a collection of essays, similarly belongs in the vein of autobiographical texts dominated, although without complacency or vanity, by a concern to know himself—which necessarily brings with it, according to Leiris, knowledge of the other, knowledge of the world. Leiris died in 1990.